CONCORDE

By the same author

Harrier
Giants of Steam
Spitfire: The Biography
Nagaland: A Journey to India's Forgotten Frontier
Tornado: 21st Century Steam
The Story of Architecture
London: Bread and Circuses

CONCORDE

The Rise and Fall of the Supersonic Airliner

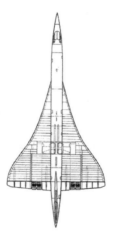

JONATHAN GLANCEY

Atlantic Books

London

First published in hardback in Great Britain in 2015 by Atlantic Books, an imprint of Atlantic Books Ltd.

1 2 3 4 5 6 7 8 9

A CIP catalogue record for this book is available from the British Library.

Hardback ISBN: 978-1-78239-107-4
E-book ISBN: 978-1-78239-108-1
Paperback ISBN: 978-1-78239-109-8

Printed and bound by CPI Group (UK) Ltd, Croydon, CR0 4YY

ENDPAPER IMAGE: Concorde's final voyage, 24 October 2003
(*Bruno Vincent/Getty Images*)

Atlantic Books
An Imprint of Atlantic Books Ltd
Ormond House
26–27 Boswell Street
London
WC1N 3JZ

www.atlantic-books.co.uk

CONTENTS

LIST OF ILLUSTRATIONS   vii

INTRODUCTION   1

1   HATCHING A SPEEDBIRD   7

2   THE SOUND BARRIER   29

3   CHASING THE DREAM   51

4   THE RIVALS   95

5   CLEARED FOR TAKE-OFF   115

6   THE SERVICE RECORD   139

7   UNPREMEDITATED ART   169

8   PHOENIX RISING   193

9   SUPERFAST FUTURES   233

10 AN END TO ADVENTURE   263

    EPILOGUE   291

    ACKNOWLEDGEMENTS   297

    SELECT BIBLIOGRAPHY   298

    INDEX   299

ILLUSTRATIONS

Section One

Miles M.52 (*Courtesy of Philip Jarrett*)
Papier mâché and sticky tape models (*SSPL/Getty Images*)
Handley Page design (*Courtesy of Philip Jarrett*)
HP.115 (*Courtesy of Philip Jarrett*)
BAC 221 (*Courtesy of Philip Jarrett*)
Concorde 001 at the Paris Air Show, 1967 (*Courtesy of Philip Jarrett*)
Concorde 001 on its first flight, 2 March 1969 (*Courtesy of Philip Jarrett*)
Concorde 002 lands after its maiden flight, 9 April 1969 (*SSPL/Getty Images*)
Andre Turcat and Brian Trubshaw (*Courtesy of Philip Jarrett*)
Air France Concorde cockpit (*Jean-Claude Deutsch/Paris Match via Getty Images*)
Concorde assembly at Aerospatiale, Toulouse (*Courtesy of Philip Jarrett*)
Concorde with a Citroën DS (*magiccarpics.com*)
Tu-144 prototype (*Courtesy of Philip Jarrett*)
Boeing 2707-300 mock-up (*Courtesy of Philip Jarrett*)
Concorde over Trafalgar Square (*Central Press/Getty Images*)

Section Two

Portrait of Sir Morien Morgan by John Ward (1976) (*Courtesy of The Master, Fellows and Scholars of Downing College in the University of Cambridge*)
Concorde wind tunnel models (*SSPL/Getty Images*)
Vortex pattern (*Photo12/UIG via Getty Images*)
Concorde afterburners (© *Reuters/Corbis*)
Concorde flying overhead (*Allan Burney/Barcroft Media/Getty Images*)
Concorde G-BOAG salutes QE2 with Red Arrow Hawks (*Adrian Meredith Photography*)

Concorde aircraft in formation (*Adrian Meredith Photography*)
Concorde G-BOAA with Mk IIa Spitfire P7350 (*Adrian Meredith Photography*)
Concorde's mach-meter (*Martyn Hayhow/AFP/Getty Images*)
Concorde G-BOAF flies over Clifton Suspension Bridge (*Adrian Meredith Photography*)
Virgin Galactic's White Knight Two (*Frederic J. Brown/AFP/Getty Images*)
X-43A (*Tom Tschida/Nasa Photo via Getty Images*)
Snow Goose (*Delmas Lehman/Shutterstock*)
Concorde's final flight (*Adrian Dennis/AFP/Getty Images*)

'What man-made machine will ever achieve the
complete perfection of even the goose's wing?'
Abbas Ibn Firnas, 852 AD

'It's a lovely shape – one feels that if God wanted aircraft
to fly he would have meant them to be this shape.'
Sir Morien Morgan, 1964

'A very friendly boom, like a pair of gleeful handclaps.'
Sir James Lighthill, 1971

'I am pretty satisfied that the airlines do not want it
and that the people of the world do not want it.'
Jeremiah Dempsey, Aer Lingus, 1964

INTRODUCTION

ON a looming day of low cloud and swept snow in February 1969, test pilot Jack Waddell lifted a massive Boeing 747 into the air above Everett, Washington. The maiden flight of the Jumbo Jet lasted eighty-five minutes. The aircraft was, Waddell told waiting journalists on landing, 'ridiculously easy to fly, a pilot's dream . . .'

The following month, on a dull and damp day in southern France, Concorde 001 reached for the clouds brooding over Toulouse. André Turcat had the dream job of piloting this pencil-thin machine, a supersonic rapier to Boeing's subsonic broadsword. Keeping Concorde's drooping nose-cone and stork-like undercarriage down throughout the twenty-seven-minute rite of passage, Turcat returned to tell a packed press conference, 'Finally the big bird flies, and I can say . . . it flies pretty well.'

These two first flights a few weeks apart were to change the way we fly and see the world forever. Boeing executives, who had staked their company's future on the Jumbo Jet, had kept a weather eye on the development of the exquisite Anglo-French Concorde. At that moment, just months before NASA rocketed Neil Armstrong and Buzz Aldrin to the surface of the Moon and safely back to Earth, it looked as if supersonic was the way to go, with commercial space travel not so very far into the future. Only the year before, in 1968, cinema audiences had watched the luminous image of a remarkably convincing Pan American Space

Clipper waltzing towards an orbiting space station, complete with a Hilton Hotel, in Stanley Kubrick's *2001: A Space Odyssey*. Concorde was a small, if significant, step for civil aviation; soon enough, we would all be hurtling around the world, immaculately dressed and impeccably served, in luxurious aircraft even faster than Turcat's 'big bird'.

Boeing imagined it could sell 400 747s as airliners before the market was saturated. It would then focus on production of freighter versions of the new jet. And, when the world's leading airlines had bought fully into Concorde and the passenger Jumbo was made redundant, those first 400 747s could also be converted into freighters. In the event, some 1,500 747s had been built by mid-2014, with more to come. Air China took delivery of its first 747-8 Intercontinental in September 2014; this stretched version of the successful 747-400 can seat 467 passengers in a three-class configuration and fly 8,000 miles without stopping to refuel. In fact, in 2015 hundreds of 747s were in regular service and, given that an average Jumbo has a life of forty years – it can last for very many more – the latest versions could still be in service until the mid-2050s. Although no-one can predict with certainty just how long the Jumbo will ride the world's airwaves – reports of its demise were rife in 2015 – it might just fly on until its centenary in 2065.

Designed, built and tested at a spanking pace, the mighty aircraft made its first fare-paying flight, with Pan Am, from New York's JFK to London's Heathrow Airport on 22 January 1970. While the flight was delayed in and out of London by technical glitches, the Jumbo, with its spacious cabins, stable ride and all the positive associations the Boeing name brought, was adopted wholeheartedly by airlines and passengers alike. Within a year of its launch, seventeen airlines were operating 747s and seven million people had flown on a Jumbo. Pan Am's 1966 order alone, for twenty-five 747s, had been bigger than those for all Concorde aircraft.

Concorde's gestation had been slightly longer than that of the 747, which had been built on the shoulders of Boeing's first jetliner, the elegant and supremely successful 707, first flown in 1958 and for many, then as now, an emblem of the Jet Age. Concorde was something altogether new. Its genesis can be dated officially to November 1956, when the Supersonic Transport Aircraft Committee (STAC) first met in London. Eight years later, Julian Amery, the British minister of aviation, and Geoffroy de Courcel, the French ambassador to the Court of St James's, signed an Anglo-French treaty to develop and produce a 'civil supersonic transport aircraft'. The first metal was cut in 1965, although it was to be another ten years before Air France took delivery of its first Concorde in December 1975, followed by British Airways in January 1976.

By this time, however, Pan Am and TWA had decided not to take up options to buy Concorde, and other airlines that had seemed so keen on the supersonic airliner were also beginning to waver as the Oil Crisis hit business confidence, especially in the transport industries. Air France responded in 1974 with a headline-stealing transatlantic demonstration flight. On 17 June, the fourth Concorde built and the second pre-production aircraft took off from Boston's Logan Airport for Paris Orly at the same time as the airline's scheduled 0822 (Eastern Standard Time) 747 flight from Orly to Boston. Then sporting Air France livery on one side and British Airways on the other, F-WTSA passed high over the Boeing across the Atlantic. It spent sixty-eight minutes on the ground at Orly before heading back west to Boston, where it arrived eleven minutes ahead of the regular 747 flight.

Politics and environmental concerns – some genuine, others spoilers – held Concorde flights to and from London and Paris and New York at bay until November 1977. This was the route Concorde was destined to fly, and it was essential for it to do so to pay its way – the aircraft's limited range meant that, unlike the Jumbo, it was unable to fly non-stop across the Pacific. As it was, the 747 was still very much in production when scheduled Concorde flights came to an end on 24 October 2003. The last of three flights into Heathrow at 4 p.m. that day, BA002 from JFK, was flown by G-BOAG, one of the last of a grand total of twenty Concorde aircraft, of which just fourteen entered service, seven each with Air France and British Airways.

Before that final flight left New York, pilot Mike Bannister gave passengers a crisp and moving pep talk. He told us that Concorde 'could do things no other aircraft can do', and that 'We're going to take you to the edge of space, where the sky gets darker, where you can see the curvature of the Earth. We're going to travel across the Atlantic at twice the speed of sound, faster than a rifle bullet, twenty-three miles every minute. We're going to travel so fast, we're moving faster than the Earth rotates, and the world will be watching us.' He also reminded his passengers that Concorde was the world's only supersonic airliner.

And therein lay the tragic nature of an otherwise sublime and magisterial aircraft: Concorde was one of a kind. For all the talk in those heady Space Age days of sensationally fast transglobal and even interplanetary flight, the Boeing 747 paved the earthly skyways for low-cost, mass-passenger flight. Just two months before Air France and British Airways began regular transatlantic Concorde flights, Laker Airways launched its budget Skytrain service from London Gatwick to New York with a clutch of wide-bodied McDonnell Douglas DC-10s. Fares were very low indeed. They helped to open up a new market of young and eager travellers for whom a champagne-and-caviar flight aboard a 100-seat skyrocket flying twice as fast and twice as high above them would be out of the question for many years and, possibly, for their entire lives. And at much the same time, it was easy enough to fly short-haul trips – London to Rome, for example – on legs of long-distance flights operated by Boeing 747s for precious little money. What fun it was as a student to fly Japan Air Lines on this very route when there were plenty of seats to fill on a 747 and to be treated like a young emperor and served delicious food in the company of polite and well-dressed passengers.

In 2003, when 99 per cent of commercial flights were made in subsonic aircraft, a return trip across the Atlantic by Concorde cost a staggering £8,000. A first-class flight by 747 cost at least half of this. And, because there were just fourteen Concorde aircraft, they needed special attention, parts, labour and crews. The managements of both British Airways and Air France had increasingly, and unsurprisingly, come to see aircraft as coaches with wings, and built either by Boeing or the new interloper Airbus, and they had less and less time for an aircraft that was too individual by half. Indeed, the singularity of Concorde was underlined by the way in which people would point up from

London streets as one of the supersonic jets, with the voice of Jove, descended over the city towards Heathrow and say, 'Look, there's Concorde,' as if there was just one of these commanding aircraft, a lone eagle among gaggles of budget-airline geese. (Which is perhaps why, according to one of its most experienced pilots, the plural should never be 'Concordes' but always 'Concorde aircraft'.)

And yet, even if the odds had been stacked against Concorde – and there had been naysayers from the 1960s onwards – the aircraft itself was a soul-stirring achievement and a glorious design. The product of intense research and development, it was a mechanical and scientific marvel. It was also, quite simply, very beautiful indeed. The engineers who created Concorde gave us a machine that caught the imagination of artists, architects, writers, photographers and filmmakers worldwide and across several generations.

It really was something to have shaped a machine that could fly so high and so fast for so long without it spilling a drop of passengers' drinks. Concorde flew largely above turbulence while setting and smashing records. It treated runways like a fashion model parading aloofly along catwalks. It could outfly a jet fighter, cruising serenely at Mach 2 for oceanic spells. From 1976 to 2003, Concorde was civil aviation's most compelling wonder. It has yet to be replaced.

ONE

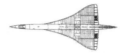

HATCHING
A SPEEDBIRD

WHEN was Concorde conceived? The idea of supersonic airliners had been brewing for at least a decade in Britain, France, Germany, the United States and the Soviet Union before decisive action was taken in London on Monday, 1 October 1956. On that momentous day, Sir Cyril Musgrave, permanent secretary of the Ministry of Supply, chaired a meeting in Shell-Mex House, the imposing Art Deco building fronting the Strand and overlooking Westminster and the Thames. It was the most notable work of Ernest Joseph, a founding member of the Liberal Jewish Synagogue, an architect who had done much to find homes for Jewish refugees from Nazi Germany in the lead-up to the Second World War.

It was the fight against Hitler that had seen the Ministry of Supply and the Ministry of Aviation move into this gloriously optimistic building in the 1940s. It was the fight against Hitler that had also, of course, all but bankrupted Britain, although not in terms of new ideas, new science, technology and highly advanced aircraft. Britain's initial lead in the development and operation of jet airliners, however, had been scuppered following a sequence of disastrous accidents with the de Havilland Comet, the world's first jet airliner. Flown as early as 1949, the Comet took the world of civil or commercial aviation by storm. It could fly considerably faster than the very best contemporary piston-engine airliners and turboprops, and it could fly much higher, above turbulence, and therefore far more smoothly than its rivals. It also *looked* like the future of long-distance passenger flight.

Sadly, the Comet suffered three fatal crashes, due to structural fatigue, within two years of entering service with BOAC in May 1952. The Comet was grounded, not to fly again until 1958, when it worked the first scheduled transatlantic jetliner service with BOAC. But this was also the year Boeing's highly successful, and indeed epoch-making, 707 jetliner made its debut with Pan Am. The Comet's transatlantic triumph was short-lived. The rival Douglas DC-8 entered service with United and Delta airlines the following year. Boeing was to build no fewer than 1,010 707s, and Douglas 556 DC-8s. The total number of Comets built, including prototypes, was just 114. As Sir Cyril Musgrave recalled, 'All the major airlines were buying the 707 or the DC-8 and there was no point in developing another subsonic plane. We felt we had to go above the speed of sound, or leave it.'

This was the gist of that October meeting in Shell-Mex House. It was attended by representatives of Britain's leading aircraft manufacturers, its two state-owned airlines, BOAC and BEA, high-ranking civil servants from the Ministries of Transport and Civil Aviation and, crucially, by Morien Morgan, a deputy director of the Royal Aircraft Establishment (RAE), Farnborough. Engineers and aerodynamicists at the RAE had been holding more or less formal meetings concerning commercial supersonic flight over the previous two years. In fact, the October meeting had been prompted by their concerns. Britain, a pioneer – *the* pioneer – of civil jet aviation, was being left behind by the Americans. In terms of economics, the future of its aircraft industry, the financial welfare of its airlines, and not least of national prestige, Britain needed to do something, and quickly. And the best thing it could do was to leap ahead of other nations by designing and building a new generation of Mach-2 airliners.

This was thrilling stuff and, as far as Musgrave's historic meeting in Shell-Mex House was concerned, entirely the right stuff. The meeting itself concluded with a decision to set up a Supersonic Transport Aircraft Committee (STAC) with Morien Morgan as chairman. Matters supersonic moved apace. The first meeting of STAC was held in the Ministry of Supply's offices at St Giles Court, close to the junction of Oxford Street and Charing Cross Road, just over a month later, on Monday, 5 November 1956. This was Guy Fawkes or Fireworks Day, an appropriate moment perhaps to light the blue touch paper that would send the world's first and, to date, only supersonic airliner rocketing into high and sustained Mach-2 flight. There was, though, much to do before that. Politicians of both main parties, along with aircraft manufacturers and airlines, had to work together. The aircraft that was to become Concorde would always require considerable direction and finance from the state. Private industry alone could never have brought the project, and the adventure, to fruition.

At that 5 November meeting, Morgan needed to bring everyone who might be involved in the project together. At the time, Britain was still home to a large number of competing aircraft and aero-engine manufacturers. Sitting around the table and looking into the glum, lavatory-tiled courtyards of the glum St Giles Court building – an early 1950s scheme since demolished and replaced by bright new offices, cafés and bars by the Genoese architect Renzo Piano in the colours of a packet of Refreshers – were representatives of A. V. Roe, Armstrong Whitworth, Bristol, de Havilland, Handley Page, Short Brothers and Vickers Armstrong, along with four engine manufacturers including Rolls-Royce.

A technical committee and seven sub-committees were set up with the manufacturers agreeing to co-operate fully in this flag-waving national enterprise. If only that meeting had been filmed. How utterly fascinating it would be to see men who had lived through both World Wars, dressed in hefty three-piece suits and ties, puffing on pipes and cigarettes and working their way through cups of tea and perhaps a plate of biscuits – food rationing had only finally been abolished in 1954 – in an office where the sound of rattling, pinging typewriters mingled with the 'ring-ring' of sturdy desk-top GPO telephones, and observe them creating a world of aviation that, for the public at least, was the stuff of science fiction.

As they plotted the course of what was to become Concorde that day, the London outside the windows of St Giles Court – whether down at ground level or up in the air above the smog and, later on, the pungent smoke from bonfires and fireworks – could hardly have seemed more different from the realm of gleaming white airliners cruising at Mach 2 in the mind's eyes of Morgan and the members of his new committee and sub-committees.

As they framed the future, *The Bristolian* was scurrying up to Paddington from Bristol Temple Meads. With a four-cylinder Great Western King or Castle class 4-6-0 at the head of the seven coaches, the flyer, which left Bristol at 4.30 p.m., would average 67 mph over the 118-mile trip, sometimes reaching speeds of up to or just over 100 mph. This was Britain's fastest train, relying on a form of traction developed by the Stephensons and harking back to Trevithick, Watt and Newcomen. The empty stock of *The Bristolian* might well have been taken away for cleaning at Old Oak Common by engine number 3409, the last of a class of 210 Great Western pannier tanks, built – well after the nationalization of the railways – at the Yorkshire Engine Company, Sheffield, a month before the inaugural meeting of STAC. Main-line steam locomotives to standard British Railways specifications were to be in production for another four years. The government might have published its £1.2bn Modernization Plan for BR in January 1955, but Britain's railways, and especially its fastest and most prestigious long-distance trains, were decidedly – and happily for enthusiasts – the preserve of reciprocating steam traction.

Railways were often the quickest and most attractive way to travel in a pre-motorway era and long before bypasses allowed motorists to escape the appalling congestion encountered in the narrow streets of old towns straddling arterial roads. Pre-Beeching and the slashing cuts made to Britain's railway network in the following decade, rail travel could be either frustratingly or charmingly slow. While Morgan and his nascent team were bringing together the know-how, materials and science to make sustained supersonic flight a reality, the journey by train from London to, for example, Lyme Regis on Dorset's appropriately named Jurassic Coast was completed with a change of trains from the mile-a-minute *Atlantic Coast Express* at Axminster, Devon, followed by a delightful crawl, at an average speed of a little under 20 mph, up and down a ruling gradient of 1 in 40 and around improbably tight curves in a pair of veteran carriages, all cart-spring suspension and horsehair-stuffed seats, tugged along by one of three surviving former London & South Western Railway Atlantic tank locomotives built in the early 1880s, some twenty years before Orville and Wilbur Wright made the first successful powered flight. Meanwhile, with the exception of a clutch of hard-to-come-by Aston Martins, Bentleys, Jaguars and highly taxed exotica such as Ferraris and Maseratis, most new British cars were hard-pressed to cruise much above 55 mph. When the first section of the London-to-Leeds M1 motorway opened in 1959, breakdowns and complete engine meltdowns came thick and fast as drivers floored the throttles of cars that were never intended to travel at speed over long distances.

Looking down from windows facing the street from St Giles Court, members of Morgan's committee might have spotted some of the first of London's new Routemaster buses, an up-to-date design despite its elegantly conservative appearance, making use of lightweight aluminium construction and knowledge gained by London Transport engineers from the wartime aero industry. If they walked back through Soho on their way home, they might have heard some of the latest sounds seeping out from the new 2i's coffee bar on Old Compton Street. This is where, among many others, Tommy Steele and Cliff Richard made their names. Elvis Presley had yet to get to the Number One slot in the British charts, but rock 'n' roll was on the up and up.

Even if mid-1950s Britain was still a world of gas lamps, coal dust, Ascot heaters, weekly baths with three inches of tepid water, few fridges, even less in the way of central heating, ice on the inside of bedroom windows in winter, whistling milkmen, cloth caps, musty overcoats, trolleybuses and tungsten lamps, *Children's Favourites* with Uncle Mac and *Mrs Dale's Diary* on the Home Service and sterling films such as *Reach for the Sky* and *Battle of the River Plate*, the winds of change were blowing ever harder above and below the surface of a superficially old-fashioned country that, by the skin of its teeth, had pulled through the Second World War.

This, 1956, was the year that the first delta-wing Avro Vulcan strategic bombers arrived at RAF Waddington and that the Royal Air Force retired its last Lancaster heavy bomber. In France, the prototype Dassault Mirage III, a superb and long-lived tailless, delta-wing supersonic interceptor, made its maiden flight. And on 10 March, as if to blow the piston engine era away for good, Peter Twiss took the exquisite Fairey Delta 2, a supersonic research aircraft first flown in 1954, past 1,000 mph – the first aircraft to reach this speed – and on to a record-breaking 1,132 mph, or Mach 1.7. Flying westwards over the West Sussex coast, Twiss noted that the sun appeared to be moving backwards in the sky: he was, he liked to say, flying faster than the sun. The mercurial Fairey Delta 2 was later modified to play an important role in the development of Concorde. (See Chapter Three.) Morien Morgan and his fellow scientists and engineers at Farnborough would, however, have been all too aware that the Ministry of Aviation had reported thirty claims for damages in the old-fashioned and deeply Conservative Worthing area immediately after Twiss had shot through the sound barrier. His flight encouraged a future ban on supersonic flight over Britain.

Conservation was becoming an important issue. The Clean Air Act, the designation of the Gower Peninsula as Britain's first official Area of Outstanding Natural Beauty, and increasing concerns over the ruthless demolition of historic buildings and even entire city centres, along with sonic booms, all highlighted the fact that the Modern World came at a price. The aerospace industry, however, guzzled fuel unrepentantly as it stretched the design and performance of a new generation of jets and rocket planes, some of which were morphing into spaceships, to remarkable heights. On 7 September, the USAF's Captain Iven C. Kincheloe, a Korean War ace, became the first pilot to climb above 100,000 ft at the controls of the Bell X-2 rocket plane. Kincheloe was to die in a crash two years later piloting a new supersonic Lockheed F-104A Starfighter. But despite a mounting number of fatalities, a wide public was clearly excited by the feats of rocket planes, by the burgeoning American and Russian space programmes and by a spate of science-fiction books, films and comics that encouraged even that most railway-minded publisher, Ian Allan, to produce an ABC book of *Rockets and Space Travel*, price 3/-.

Closer to the ground, civil aviation was on the cusp of change. With the Comet temporarily out of action, the Atlantic was crossed slowly, if in some style, by piston-engine airliners, notably the Boeing Stratocruiser with its lower-deck cocktail bar,

Lockheed's Super Constellation and the Douglas DC-7. Flight times from New York to London were around the fourteen-hour mark, although transatlantic crossings could either be a little faster or quite a bit slower than this depending on wind direction and speed. From 1958, jets were able to more than halve this time. Concorde, of course, was to be twice as fast again.

From 25 September 1956, there was an even quicker way of crossing the Atlantic, albeit in a different medium, that of pure communication. This was the day TAT-1, the transatlantic telephone cable between Britain and the United States, was inaugurated. In the first twenty-four hours, 588 calls were made from London to the United States. The virtual world was on its way, even if computers were still the stuff of tall, whirring and bleeping cabinets molly-coddled in special, air-conditioned rooms. Although Concorde was to be in part a product of the computer era, it also belonged very much to an analogue age where the slide-rule ruled.

This, however, really was an era of radical change in Britain, let alone the United States and the rest of Europe, with the age of steam, slide-rules, analogue instruments, cinemas, open windows and men in hats rapidly moving into that of nuclear power, computers, jets, television, air-conditioning, informal manners and, for a dizzy spell between Queen Elizabeth II's Coronation in 1953 and the Oil Crisis twenty years later, what might justifiably be called a barely mitigated neophilia. The exploits of supersonic jets in the air were mirrored on the ground by new forms of radical architecture, furniture, fashion, materials and art. In the summer of 1956, London's Whitechapel Gallery played host to 'This is Tomorrow', a collaborative show by young artists and architects heralding Pop Art. And more importantly, perhaps, to everyday households and to Britain's future as a nation of shoppers rather than makers, and even while the Queen opened the world's first large-scale nuclear power station at Calder Hall on the Cumberland coast and the Cuban revolutionaries embarked from Mexico on board the motor boat *Granma* to overthrow the vicious and criminal US-backed dictatorship of Fulgencio Batista, Tesco opened its first self-service store in a converted cinema in Maldon, Essex.

Meanwhile, new forms of music and noise, from rock 'n' roll and avant-garde orchestral works to the breaking of the sound barrier itself, were changing the soundtrack of Britain, Europe and the United States, if not the Soviet Union. In 1956, both Karlheinz Stockhausen and Iannis Xenakis made their names with challenging electronic music that broke far from the norms of orchestral scores and sounds. Even composers like Ralph Vaughan Williams, who had made his name before the First World War with music based on the melodies of age-old English folk songs, experimented boldly; his 1956 *A Vision of Aeroplanes* for organ and choir is a powerful, unexpected piece, which, along with excerpts from Olivier Messiaen's contemporary *Oiseaux Exotiques*, might form a suitable score for some future documentary film on the life and times of Concorde.

As it was, a very different form of music was on offer in central London on 5 November 1956. Among those billed to star in the Royal Variety Performance at the London Palladium that evening were Gracie Fields and Liberace, the showman American pianist who was reaching the peak of his wildly ostentatious, star-spangled career. The grand finale would have seen the entire cast, including Laurence Olivier, Vivien Leigh, John Mills and the Crazy Gang, dressed in Liberace suits. But the Queen cancelled. This was the very day British and French paratroopers had landed in Egypt and were fighting their way to Port Said in response to President Gamel Abdel Nasser's nationalization of the Suez Canal. This was indeed a crisis, with Moscow threatening to take retaliatory military action and Washington refusing to support the Anglo-French venture.

The then British prime minister, Anthony Eden, had wanted to secure the vital trade route of the Suez Canal, to guarantee supplies of oil, to get rid of Nasser, and to restrict Soviet influence in the Middle East. He was to fail on all four counts. As Eden's biographer D. R. Thorpe has pointed out, 'It was a truly tragic end to his premiership, and one that came to assume a disproportionate importance in any assessment of his career.' It was certainly a blow for Liberace in London. He broke down in tears while rehearsing when he learned the show had been cancelled, but Gracie Fields made everyone a nice cup of tea and the crisis on stage blew over.

The Suez Crisis, however, was a fiasco. The British and French backed off and, in January the following year, Anthony Eden resigned. His place was taken by the arch-modernizer Harold Macmillan. Three months later, Macmillan's minister of defence, Duncan Sandys, published his infamous White Paper, *Defence: Outline of Future Policy*, which aimed to trim £100m from Britain's defence budget. Among its proposals was an effective end to new jet fighters for the RAF; these were to be replaced by Bloodhound ground-to-air missiles. Along with cuts that led to the cancellation of a number of promising military aircraft and ultimately to the loss of 70,000 skilled jobs, the White Paper also promoted far-reaching mergers within the British aviation industry. From the very beginning then, in this era of rapid change, Morien Morgan and his gifted team must have known that an expensive, long-term project for a radical new type of airliner to be funded by the British government would be liable at any time to social fads and follies as well as to the self-aggrandizing dreams and unreliable whims of politicians.

Morien Bedford Morgan – 'Morgan the Supersonic' and the 'Father of Concorde' – was born in Bridgend, South Wales in 1912. The son of a local draper and grandson of John Bedford, a Birmingham-born ironmaster, he progressed from a local primary school to St Catherine's College, Cambridge. In 1935, after an apprenticeship with the engineering firm Mather and Platt in Manchester, Morgan joined the Aerodynamics Department of the RAE at Farnborough, where he developed an expertise in aircraft control, handling and stability. Many wartime aircraft, including the Spitfire, benefited from his research work, as did pilots, of course, to whose suggestions he listened carefully and respectfully. Indeed, to understand their concerns fully as well as to experience aircraft behaviour in flight, in 1944 Morgan gained a pilot's licence.

Noted for his charm, eloquence and love of music, he had the ability to get on with just about anyone – politicians, engineers, civil servants, mechanics, trade unionists, academics, the media, the English and the French – a virtue that helped immeasurably in the development of Concorde. He was, Professor John 'Shon' Ffowcs Williams, who worked on the aero-acoustics of Concorde, told the BBC in 2012, 'an ebullient sort of a chap who would talk the hind legs off a donkey'.

'He just loved aeroplanes,' according to his daughter, Deryn Watson, Professor of Information Technology and Education at King's College, London. 'We would go on holiday and I'd end up wondering why we were sitting in a field having a picnic in some obscure part of Switzerland – it was because he wanted to watch some particular airplanes flying. He was very direct and straightforward. He had no side to him at all. He always had a twinkle in his eye and smoked a pipe non-stop.'

Morgan would get through many tins of tobacco over the next two and a half years as his committee and sub-committees got to work proving that a civil supersonic transport was technically possible and commercially viable. Brian Trubshaw, Concorde's chief test pilot, summed up those long months of work by recalling that they 'covered every aspect of aerodynamics including handling qualities, structures, systems, propulsion, economic and social impact (sonic boom and noise), the effect of kinetic heating, flight controls . . . vibrations and flutter, and operational flexibility.'

Altogether some 400 papers were submitted to STAC, all-day symposia were held at RAE Farnborough and each idea put forward was scrutinized through the lens of safety as well as practicality and desirability. A number of key questions arose, notably those concerning the shape of the various aircraft and especially that of their wings. What type of wing could balance the need for a supersonic airliner to scythe smoothly through the air at high speed and the low-speed flight that would allow it to operate safely from conventional airports? This, after all, was not some kind of rocket plane, but a civilized and commercially successful airliner. It would, for example, have to take its place in queues of aircraft landing at busy airports, so it would need to fly slowly at low altitudes as well as streaking across the Atlantic at up to 60,000 ft.

Meanwhile, an outline of a research programme for two lines of development was agreed, one for a 100-seat, Mach-1.2 (800-mph) machine for distances of up to 1,500 miles for service, presumably, with BEA and other short- to mid-haul airlines, the other a 150-seat, Mach-1.8 (1,200-mph) aircraft with a range of 3,500 miles for intercontinental airlines including BOAC. A third version with a cruising speed of Mach 3 was ruled out for the time being as too complex and expensive. Because of the tremendous heat build-up at this great speed, the aircraft's fuselage would need to be made from titanium rather than proven and much less expensive aluminium. But by 1960, STAC, which funded research into supersonic design by British aircraft manufacturers, had chosen Bristol's 223 proposal as the basis for what would eventually become Concorde.

From then on, the actual design and construction of Concorde was not too lengthy a process given the novelty and complexity of the aircraft's design and the sheer challenge it presented all those concerned with its development. What held it back from earning its living in airline service was the need to test the airliner exhaustively, and politics, of both lobby groups and national governments. Politics were so important a part of the Concorde story from its inception because it was clear that no one country – or certainly no single European country – was able to fund such a radical aircraft from its own coffers.

After Duncan Sandys had toured Europe looking for partners to divvy up the cost of a supersonic airliner, Britain turned to

France. In terms of research and development into supersonic flight, France had been making great strides. There was also shared technology. Sud Aviation flew its first Caravelle, an eighty-seat short-to-medium-range jet with engines mounted aft of the passenger cabin, in May 1955. These engines were Rolls-Royce Avons, powerful and reliable jet equivalents of the British company's famous Merlin piston engine, while the French aircraft had also adopted its nose section and cockpit from the de Havilland Comet. It was clear to STAC that a partnership with the French was on the cards.

There also had been discussions led by Peter Thorneycroft, Sandys's successor at the Ministry of Aviation, regarding collaboration with the Americans, yet Washington was keen to go its own way and had its own Mach-3 agenda, one pursued from 1955 with the development of what was to be the thrilling North American XB-70 Valkyrie long-range bomber. The B-70 project itself was cancelled in 1961 – the newly developed ICBM (Intercontinental Ballistic Missile) was a cheaper and probably more effective long-range weapon – but the XB-70 would nonetheless prove the technology necessary to build a very fast American airliner. Two examples were built, and the first made its debut flight in 1964. One was destroyed in a mid-air collision in 1966, and the other retired shortly before Concorde first flew. It can be seen today in the National Museum of the US Air Force, six miles from Dayton, Ohio, birthplace of Orville Wright, the first pilot of a successful powered aircraft.

For Morien Morgan, partnership with the French proved just the ticket. In later years he said, 'In aeronautical design and research a combination of Gallic fervour and British phlegm produces pretty impressive results by any standards.' This, though, is jumping the gun. By the time STAC produced its report for the Ministry of Supply in March 1959, Britain and France were still going their separate ways, the French keen on the idea of a mid-range supersonic airliner – a Super Caravelle that would glide in debonair style across continental Europe – while the British were set, as the Americans were to be, on a transatlantic aircraft, believing – correctly – that it was on longer routes that a Mach-2 airliner's speed would pay off in terms of profitability.

The STAC report was an enormous thing; attached to it were some 500 study documents. And despite what must have been many misgivings, it recommended the go-ahead for both a medium-range Mach-1.2 and a long-range Mach-1.8 airliner. Bristol was awarded the contract for the former, Hawker Siddeley that for the latter. Nor were all members of STAC perfectly happy with the report. Airline representatives serving Morgan's committee were concerned with the uncertainty of the market for such aircraft, and, although their fears were to be justified, it was hard to take issue with their chairman's stated belief that the proposed supersonic aircraft would be 'of immense value to this country as an indication of our technical skill'. Morgan's point was prescient. From 1945, Britain and Europe's future as internationally competitive manufacturing bases depended increasingly on the technological sophistication as well as the quality of new products. Although his view was not stated in the STAC report, and nor did cost-benefit analyses feature, a supersonic airliner might be a good investment for Britain as a whole, even if it lost money.

There was, though, at least one major and highly controversial problem Morgan tended to gloss over, or believed would be solved soon enough. This was noise, and it led to a battle of wills over Concorde's engines between Rolls-Royce and an Anglo-French alliance engineered by Sir Arnold Hall, the managing director of Bristol-Siddeley, between his company and Snecma (Société nationale d'études et de construction de moteurs d'aviation). A state-owned company from 1945, at the end of the war Snecma had co-opted 120 German BMW engineers who went on to develop the successful jet engine that powered the Dassault Mirage IIIA fighter and enabled it in 1958 to become the first European combat aircraft to exceed Mach 2 in level flight. From 1951, Snecma had been building Bristol Hercules engines under licence, so Hall had a head start when it came to discussing a joint engine design for what was to become Concorde with the French company.

The engine chosen, though, was a reworking – a considerable re-working, it is true – of the Bristol-Siddeley Olympus, an effective yet noisy and smoky twin-spool axial-flow turbojet first run in May 1950. Intended for the subsonic delta-wing Avro Vulcan V-bomber, it was tested on an English Electric Canberra long-range bomber and reconnaissance aircraft from August 1952. Was it the right engine for a supersonic airliner? Naturally, Rolls-Royce thought not. The company produced a hefty report for STAC, stressing the point that not only had the Port Authority of New York and New Jersey introduced a maximum noise level of 112 Perceived Noise Decibels (PNdb) at Idlewild Airport – from 1963, John F Kennedy, or JFK for short – but also that London's Heathrow was likely to follow suit. 'The next generation of subsonics,' the report stated, 'is being designed to be appreciably quieter – of the order of 100 PNdb – and this is the order to which the supersonic should be designed throughout.'

But the Olympus already existed and could be modified. Rolls-Royce would have to start more or less from scratch if it was to produce a rival engine, while Sir Arnold Hall had pulled off a diplomatic coup. It was, in fact, the twists and turns of Anglo-French relations that were to determine the fate of Concorde. While manufacturers were first off in this particular great game, national politicians were soon in on the act, as they had to be if the supersonic airliner was to have a chance of lifting off from drawing boards and the pages of reports.

Although the British prime minister, Harold Macmillan, and the French president, General Charles de Gaulle, duly met in June 1962 to discuss matters European, the technical groundwork was prepared very effectively by talented British and French engineers, who were directed to do so from Whitehall. In October 1962, the technical directors and chief engineers of BAC Filton (Bristol had been merged with English Electric, Vickers-Armstrong and Hunting Aircraft into this new company in 1960) and Sud Aviation met in Paris to establish a design acceptable to all parties. These were Sir Archibald Russell and Dr William 'Bill' Strang from Filton and Pierre Satre and Lucien Servanty from Toulouse, where Sud Aviation was based. The one big compromise was an agreement to pursue both the short- and long-range version of the supersonic airliner, a decision – necessary at the time to keep all parties happy – that was to waste a lot of time and effort and fray tempers over the next few years.

It was the following month that the Rt Hon Julian Amery, the British minister of aviation, and His Excellency Geoffroy de Courcel, French ambassador, were to sit down together at a desk in Lancaster House, London – a grandiloquent late-flowering Neo-Classical design by Robert Smirke and Benjamin Dean Wyatt completed in 1840 by Charles Barry – and toy with a large model of the as yet unnamed supersonic airliner before signing an agreement between the British and French governments to fund its development and manufacture. A model of concision, the document was to lock both Paris and Westminster into what was to prove to be a very expensive enterprise indeed.

For the British, at this point anyway, the price was also expected to include the entry fee to the European Common Market. For the French, the financial contribution from Britain would help raise France's technologically driven post-war profile and enable it to compete head-on with the Americans. As it turned out, the cost of the project rose quickly, doubling by the time Harold Wilson's Labour government was elected to office in October 1964. Meanwhile, General de Gaulle had said 'non' to British membership of the European Common Market, while, to add fuel to the French president's suspicion of Anglo-American relations, BOAC, a company that had been, at best, dubious about the idea of the Anglo-French project, placed options on six embryonic US supersonic airliners, believing even the 100-seat British design to be too small for the transatlantic market. How could the French trust the perfidious *rosbifs*?

For British politicians leading the case for the supersonic airliner – first referred to as Concorde in a speech given by de Gaulle on 13 January 1963 – it was a matter of all or bust. As

Peter Gillman, the *Observer* journalist, wrote in *Atlantic Monthly* in 1977:

> Julian Amery, the man who finally signed the Anglo-French treaty . . . was ambitious, politically adroit, and a gambler: three characteristics which were to see the project through. Soon after becoming minister, Amery sent his new parliamentary secretary at the ministry, Basil de Ferranti – whose family made electronic aviation equipment – to Farnborough to assess the project. Ferranti remembers being impressed by the argument that the plane would sell 'either none at all or a hell of a lot'. The attitude he and Amery took was: 'It is a gamble. But if we can do it with the French, it will halve the ante. So, let's have a go.'

The Treasury in Whitehall was certainly dubious, and yet as Amery told the House of Commons in late November 1962, 'This aircraft has every chance of securing a substantial part of the world market for supersonic airliners. This is a chance that will not return.' And, just three weeks before the signing of the Anglo-French agreement, the deputy prime minister, Richard 'Rab' Butler, had signed off a report by the Cabinet Committee on Civil and Scientific Research and Development, which he chaired. Butler wrote:

> We have not reached any final conclusion. This proposal may well constitute a natural and inevitable step in technological advance, offering the benefits

of such advance and a moment of opportunity to enhance British and French prestige, but we may find in later years that United States industry ousts it with something better, and we are left with too small a market for our pains. And some of us believe that the right lines of technological advance for this country to exploit cannot be selected without regard to commercial prospects. On the other hand to decide not to venture in this field while America and perhaps Russia and France go ahead could well mean contracting out of the large passenger aircraft business.

Morgan and his committee had estimated the market as being somewhere between 150 and 500 aircraft, and that the project would be profitable if just thirty were sold. Amery, however, was to be proved right on both counts. The world market for supersonic airliners was fourteen, all of them Anglo-French Concorde aircraft. By 2015, the chance to build or buy a supersonic airliner had not returned. In 1962, however, work was finally to start on the world's first such aircraft. And, for much of the British and no doubt the French public, too, there was pride in the fact that their countries were leading the way into this exciting new era when, soon enough, they would all have the opportunity to break the sound barrier.

TWO

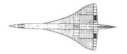

THE SOUND BARRIER

THERE was no doubt about it. It might have been a popular misconception, yet as far as much of the British public was concerned, a British aircraft flown by a British pilot was the first to break the fabled sound barrier, a wall of air that somehow confronted aircraft as they approached Mach 1, the ratio of a moving object to that of the speed of sound, first observed and documented by the Austrian physicist Ernst Mach in the mid-1870s. Shock waves building up around an aircraft as it closed in on the seemingly malevolent barrier could, it was commonly thought, do all sorts of disturbing things to it. It might even break up.

The concept of the speed of sound itself was a matter of confusion. How fast was it? That depended, and still does, of course, on how low or how high an aircraft was above sea level. Sound travels at different speeds at different temperatures and, as every schoolchild should have known in the early 1950s, temperature drops with altitude. So, at sea level the speed of sound is approximately 760 mph, while at 20,000 ft it is 660 mph. Whatever the speed, this was very fast indeed in a Britain where few express trains averaged as much as 60 mph, with the occasional downhill burst of up to 100 mph, and when children sitting beside their father or mother at the wheel of upright cars would have been thrilled to see that same figure – 60 mph! – indicated on the speedometer.

In any case, the sound barrier had seemed insurmountable, even in very recent years. Writing in the October 1944 edition of *Popular Science*, the magazine's aviation editor C. B. Colby did his best to answer the headline question: 'Can we ever fly faster than the Speed of Sound?' 'Let's take a plane weighing 10 tons with an engine of 5,000 hp flying at a speed of nearly 500 mph. At this speed, the air going over and around parts of the plane has already reached the speed of sound. Waves of compressibility appear in many places on its surface. These waves prevent the plane from going faster, for they need more power to drag them along through the air. We cannot just add another 1,000 hp and reach 600 mph. We will have to add 37,000 hp to get that additional 100 mph. This is obviously an impossibility . . .'

In a world of radial engines, of Wright Cyclones and Pratt & Whitney Double Wasps, and propellers this might have been true. But jet and rocket engines developed during and immediately after the Second World War gave the levels of thrust – quite different from horsepower, a measure of work done inside an engine – needed to go fast enough to break the sound barrier. Power, though, was not the only requirement. What was missing when Colby was writing in 1944, and even ten years later, was a full and practical understanding of the aerodynamic characteristics and qualities of a successful supersonic aircraft.

What gave British cinema audiences in the summer of 1952 the confidence that one of their aircraft was first to record Mach 1 and even beyond, however, was not the necessary understanding of science but *The Sound Barrier*, a tale of pluck, emotional reserve and derring-do directed by David Lean, of *Brief Encounter* and, later, *Lawrence of Arabia* fame, written by Terence Rattigan and starring Ralph Richardson, Ann Todd and Nigel Patrick, who played the role of an inevitably lantern-jawed test pilot killed in the attempt to break the sound barrier. In real life, Patrick had served in action in the Middle East, North Africa and Italy with the King's Royal Rifle Corps, rising to the rank of lieutenant colonel.

Fellow actor John Justin, another Dan Dare lookalike who in real life had learned to fly at the age of twelve in Argentina and served as a test pilot and flying instructor with the RAF in the Second World War, was seen later in the film diving triumphantly through the shocking turmoil of the sound barrier at the reversed controls of *Prometheus*, which was in fact a less than successful and accident-prone, subsonic Supermarine Swift single-seat jet fighter.

Captain Charles 'Chuck' Yeager of the USAF, a Second World War fighter ace, had, in fact, been the first through the sound barrier on 14 October 1947. His bright-orange, 3.5-ton Bell X-1 rocket plane *Glamorous Glennis* was dropped from the bomb bay of a modified B-29 Superfortress before shooting across a clear blue Californian sky in sustained level flight above the Mojave Desert at 45,000 ft and recording Mach 1.06 (700 mph). The experience had proved to be rather less dramatic than John Justin's in *The Sound Barrier*. 'I thought I was seeing things,' said the laconic West Virginian some years later. 'We were flying supersonic and it was as smooth as a baby's bottom. Grandma could be sitting up there sipping lemonade.' In years to come, Concorde passengers sipping champagne would be wholly unaware they had passed through the sound barrier unless the captain told them, which he always did, or else they looked up from their books or papers to the digital mach-meter at the front of the cabin.

And yet those British cinema audiences not in the know in 1952 – Washington took a defensive and secretive stance over the exploits of its record planes – were not wholly wrong in their belief that Britain was capable of supersonic flight and had finally managed as much, in tragic circumstances, the best part of a year after Chuck Yeager. In fact, the Bell Aircraft Corporation design team had visited Britain as early as 1944 to discuss details of supersonic flight with their counterparts at Miles Aircraft at Woodley, Berkshire. The year before, Miles had been commissioned by the Ministry of Aircraft Production to develop, build and fly a supersonic jet within just nine months. The aim was to beat the Germans in the battle for aerial supremacy at a time when jet and rocket-powered aircraft were now no longer the stuff of science fiction.

The Miles contract called for an 'aeroplane capable of flying over 1,000 mph in level flight, over twice the existing speed record, and to climb to 36,000 ft in 1.5 minutes'. It is widely believed that the figure for the top speed should have read '1,000 kmh', or 620 mph, the top speed of the Me 163 Komet, the futuristic German rocket fighter then known to the British first and foremost through reconnaissance photographs. Designed by Alexander Lippisch, a gifted aerodynamicist who had watched Orville Wright fly over Tempelhof Field in Berlin in 1909, some 370 Komets were built, and from summer 1944 they flew sorties against Allied bombers. On 28 July of that year USAAF B-17 Flying Fortresses were set upon by an Me 163 over Germany, the first ever attack – unsuccessful in this case – by a rocket-powered aircraft. But, although the Me 163 was very fast, its range was just twenty-five miles. Allied fighter pilots would learn to bide their time before taking on fuel-spent Komets.

Heini Dittmar, a brilliant pre-war glider pilot, had taken an early Me 163A to a shade over 1,000 kmh on 2 October 1941. Dittmar went on to beat this new world record on 6 July 1944, reaching 1,130 kmh (702 mph) with an Me 163B. The Allies certainly had something to fear, and they possessed little precise knowledge of how quickly the Germans were developing aircraft such as the Komet. Lippisch himself was packed off to the United States in 1946 as part of Operation Paperclip, through which some 1,800 German scientists and engineers were resettled across the Atlantic with the aim of developing highly sophisticated military technology, snubbing the Soviet Union and keeping ahead of leading-edge British research and development. As it was, two dozen Komets were shipped to Britain at the end of the war for evaluation at the RAE and elsewhere.

Meanwhile, whatever the top speed involved in the contract with Miles, the British military and politicians were right to have been concerned with new threats from Nazi Germany. At any time soon, the Luftwaffe, which was already testing the fast albeit subsonic Me 262 jet fighter, might be on the attack with aircraft capable of flying at speeds in excess of Mach 1. The Germans, in fact, had already broken the sound barrier with a different type of pilotless flying machine, and one that threatened terrible destruction. Working with a team of brilliant fellow scientists, engineers and technicians, Werner von Braun, the most celebrated of the German scientists dispatched to the United States through Operation Paperclip, had developed what was effectively a rocket that could fly faster and higher than anyone might have believed possible at the outbreak of the Second World War.

This, of course, was the V-2, the world's first ballistic missile. Launched successfully in October 1942, the V-2 'Retribution Weapon' went into action in September 1944. More than 6,000 were built, of which 3,225 rained down on European cities. Antwerp was hardest hit, with London second. Duncan Sandys, the future British minister of defence, recalled hearing a double bang – a sonic boom – over London before a V-2 exploded somewhere in the city. The maximum speed of a V-2 was an unprecedented 3,580 mph, or above Mach 4. The Allies had nothing like this to hurl back at the enemy, although, in the 1930s, the young Werner von Braun had been in contact with Robert H. Goddard, the American pioneer of liquid-fuelled rockets. Goddard had successfully launched the very first of these in March 1926, when the world's fastest aircraft could just about reach 250 mph.

German ingenuity had certainly been remarkable. It was fortunate that some of the ideas proposed for new types and forms of military aircraft never got off the ground. As the Avro Lancaster made its debut with the RAF, Eugen Sanger, an

Austrian engineer, and Irene Brandt, his wife, a mathematician, had been busy at work on the design of a suborbital transatlantic rocket bomber. The Silbervogel, or Silver Bird, was a proposal for a winged rocket capable of 5,000 kmh (3,100 mph) and carrying a 4,000-kg bomb to be dropped on New York or Washington DC. Although the project was cancelled in favour of more easily produced conventional bombers, Sanger, a pioneer of ramjets – jet engines that use an aircraft's forward motion to compress air without the use of a rotary compressor as with Whittle's gas turbine – was sent to work in Prague with fellow Austrian engineer Otto Kauba on the design of the 1,000-kmh Skoda-Kauba Sk P.14 ramjet. This was only one of many top-secret emergency designs for Nazi Germany's last-ditch defence as Allied armies closed in on Berlin from East and West after D-Day and as thousands of decidedly subsonic piston-engine bombers, escorted by thousands of 450-mph piston-engine fighters, rained hell on the cities and factories of the Third Reich.

Many of these same concepts – including swept-wing jet fighters, flying wings and jet bombers with engines hung from wing pods – went on to influence thinking in the design and development of British, American, French and Russian supersonic aircraft from the mid-1940s until remarkably recently. Meanwhile, in the spirit of wartime co-operation, and pressured by both Westminster and Whitehall, the Miles design team was asked to hand over the drawings of the M.52 to Bell. When it appeared in late 1945, the X-1 looked remarkably similar to the Miles M.52, including its bullet-shaped fuselage and small, thin wings. The Miles team had, in fact, investigated the flight of bullets as these were the only man-made artefacts that flew faster than the speed of sound and had done so since the eighteenth century. The latest bullets were also stable in supersonic flight. Bell engineers even described the X-1 as a 'bullet with wings', its shape resembling, they said, a Browning .50-calibre machine-gun bullet.

What was galling for the small, innovative British aircraft maker is that not only did the Americans take away their designs and expertise to help shape the X-1, but also out of the blue the M.52 was cancelled in 1946 when the first of what were to be three aircraft was more than 80 per cent complete. Drastic post-war government budget cuts are held to be one reason the M.52 was cancelled, although Sir Ben Lockspeiser, the government's director of scientific research and a former RAE chemist who went on to become the first president of CERN, the Geneva-based European Organization for Nuclear Research famous for its researches into the Big Bang and instrumental in the birth of the World Wide Web, believed that lessons should be learned from Nazi German high-speed aircraft design. It was, Lockspeiser thought, the swept wing – not the straight wing of the M.52 and X-1 – that appeared to be the way forward to the speed of sound and beyond.

Whatever the reasons for the cancellation, Miles Aircraft was put into receivership soon afterwards, while Britain's role in supersonic design and technology was delayed for several years. It was all a great shame, especially as the Americans admitted the design lead the British designers had over them; they also wondered, while cracking on with the X-1, why the British were allowing them the first shot at breaking the sound barrier that had a realistic chance of success.

What was more disappointing in many ways is that the M.52 would have been jet-propelled whereas the X-1 was not – at the time the US lagged behind in turbojet technology. So, although its rocket engine gave the X-1 the sheer oomph needed to accelerate quickly up to Mach 1, its range and endurance were limited. The M.52, however, was to have been powered by one of Frank Whittle's turbojets, which would provide sufficient thrust to push the aircraft through the sound barrier in a shallow dive. Furthermore, Miles were in discussion with Whittle regarding a reheat jet pipe, or afterburner, that would allow the aircraft to maintain 1,000 mph in level flight.

The M.52 also quietly boasted several key aerodynamic features that went on to affect not just the X-1 but supersonic aircraft for years to come. These included a conical nose and sharp leading edges to apparently razor-thin, or Gillette, biconvex section wings. This wing shape was adopted from the pre-war researches of Jakob Ackeret, a brilliant Swiss aeronautical engineer whose students at Zurich's ETH technical and scientific university included Werner von Braun. Most importantly of all, and certainly from a pilot's point of view, the M.52 was to be fitted with a power-operated stabilator, or all-moving flying tail. This would enable pilots to counteract forces caused by shockwaves in steep descents that had prompted deeply unsettling, and possibly downright terrifying, control reversal in conventional aircraft when they were dived as closely as possible to the speed of sound.

In autumn 1944, the RAE fitted a stabilator to a Supermarine Spitfire. Test pilot Captain Eric 'Winkle' Brown made several steep, high-speed dives with the modified fighter in October and

November, attaining Mach 0.86 while maintaining control. In fact, the RAE – with Morien Morgan playing a prominent role – had been experimenting with high-speed flight since late 1943. A part of the intention was to see how close current RAF fighters could get to the speed of sound and, in the process, to understand their handling characteristics as they approached Mach 1. In the event, the Spitfire PR Mk XI was selected. Four of the six test pilots appointed to the RAE's wartime High Speed Flight Unit were killed. Eric Brown, a survivor of the unit, went on to become the only British pilot to fly the Me 163 under power soon after the German surrender in May 1945.

During these trials with the PR Mk XI Squadron Leader J. R. Tobin, flying Spitfire EN409, reached Mach 0.891 or 606 mph in a 45-degree dive. And, in April 1944, Squadron Leader Anthony Martindale dived to Mach 0.92, although, at this great speed and pressure, the propeller broke off. The Spitfire climbed back to 40,000 ft, and Martindale had blacked out as it did so. When he regained consciousness, he noted that the aircraft's wings had been slightly swept back. He was able to glide to a safe landing. Although a propeller-driven aircraft was never going to break the sound barrier, or at least not in one piece because the drag caused by the airscrew itself holds the plane back, it was astonishing for RAE staff to witness just how close a Spitfire came to doing so. Mitchell and Shenstone's thin, elliptical wing was the secret. And it was the understanding of the ideal supersonic wing that was to test aerodynamicists and aircraft designers in the years separating Squadron Leader Martindale's near-fatal headlong dive and Concorde's successful maiden flight a quarter of a century later.

It is just possible that a late-model Spitfire PR Mk XIX flown by Flight Lieutenant Ted Powles from RAF Kai Tak, Hong Kong in February 1952 got even closer to the speed of sound. Climbing to 51,550 ft, an outstanding feat in its own right, Powles was forced to descend quickly as cabin pressure fell dangerously low. Plunging into a very steep dive, he was only able to regain control of the shuddering aircraft below 3,000 ft. Powles landed safely. During his precipitous dive, it seemed at first as if he had reached Mach 0.96, but this was later put down to instrument error. Even so, the piston-engine Spitfire, a design of the mid-1930s, had got remarkably close to the sound barrier. As Jeffrey Quill, the highly experienced Spitfire test pilot, put it, 'That any operational aircraft off the production line . . . could readily be controlled at this speed when the early jet aircraft such as Meteors, Vampires, [Lockheed] P-80s etc could not, was certainly extraordinary.'

Stage by stage, knowledge of how to design an aircraft that would break the sound barrier was accumulating. But, although early post-war jets fitted with swept wings soon proved able to reach Mach 1 in dives, the goal of sustained and level supersonic flight by regular military jets was still some way off. Yeager's X-1 was, after all, an experimental rocket plane. And while discussions at the RAE and elsewhere gradually turned to the idea of supersonic airliners, the sound barrier, or 'sonic wall', remained a challenge into the 1950s.

The British finally broke the sound barrier, or so it seems, in September 1948 when test pilot John Derry, a wartime Typhoon pilot and commanding officer of 182 Squadron, put one of the three ill-fated de Havilland DH.108 Swallows into a shallow dive and flew at just over Mach 1. Geoffrey de Havilland Jr, the company's chief test pilot, had been killed two years earlier when the second DH.108 broke up over the Thames Estuary during a high-speed test. (His last flight formed the basis of Terence Rattigan's script for *The Sound Barrier*.) The first DH.108 crashed in May 1950, soon after the third in February of the same year. John Derry himself was killed along with twenty-nine other people when the prototype de Havilland DH.110 Sea Vixen, a twin-boom, twin-engine Royal Navy fighter he was demonstrating, broke up after breaking the sound barrier at the 1952 Farnborough Air Show.

Pathé News caught the moment on film. Immediately after this harrowing accident, Neville Duke, the Spitfire ace with twenty-seven enemy kills to his credit, put on a supersonic display with a new Hawker Hunter jet fighter in tribute to Derry and all those who had died, and as a clear signal that Britain's supersonic future should not be in doubt. 'My dear Duke,' wrote the prime minister – himself a pilot – the next day. 'It was characteristic of you to go up yesterday after the shocking accident. Accept my salute. Yours, in grief, Winston Churchill.'

The French went supersonic without the help of an afterburner and in level flight, on 3 August 1954, with the new delta-wing Nord Gerfault 1A experimental research plane designed by the brilliant engineer Jean Galtier. A more refined Gerfault II was flown successfully in 1956 by Major André Turcat, a former wartime pilot who flew with the Free French Air Force along with Pierre Mendes France, the future French prime minister. Turcat left the military to join Sud Aviation. He was to become Concorde's chief test pilot, commanding the aircraft's maiden flight from Toulouse in 1969 and taking it through the sound barrier for the first time that autumn.

Turcat's co-pilot on Concorde 001's maiden flight was Jacques Guignard, yet another veteran of the Free French Air Force. He flew 370 missions with Spitfires. Guignard was also the lead test pilot of the prototype SO.9000 Trident, a scimitar-like interceptor designed and built by SNCASO – or Sud-Ouest, later merged with Sud Aviation – between 1948 and 1957, when the project was cancelled after only twelve Tridents had been built. Guignard flew the first Trident I on 2 March 1953. Equipped with more powerful engines in March 1955, the Trident went supersonic in shallow dives. During an eighteen-month test programme, Guignard raised the pointy aircraft's speed to Mach 1.8. In January 1956, having run out of fuel on an approach to the Istres military air base, he ejected safely from a Trident II, an aircraft powered by a combination of turbojets and a twin-chamber rocket engine.

Sud-Ouest had built France's first jet aircraft, the SO.6000 Triton, during the Second World War. This was done clandestinely, the design work led by Lucien Servanty. A svelte and even chic machine looking more like an early executive jet than a potential fighter, the Triton remained engineless until the end of the war. It was then fitted with a Junkers Jumo 004.B.2 engine and first flown by Daniel Rastel on Armistice Day 1946. It proved capable of 955 kmh (593 mph), faster than an Me 262. Servanty, whose design work began with piston-engine fighter prototypes in the mid-1930s, was to become one of the principal engineers behind Concorde.

Turcat, meanwhile, was also test pilot for the extraordinary Nord 1500 Griffon, a bulbous flying ramjet from which an exquisite, long-nosed jet fighter appeared to be emerging, like some mythical dragon from its egg. If the Griffon looked like two aircraft in one, in a sense it was, being a turbojet fighter boosted by the mighty ramjet it rode. Two prototypes were built. The first, put through its paces by Turcat from September 1955 without the ramjet installed, proved capable of Mach 1.7. In 1958, Turcat took up the Griffon II, complete with ramjet, and accelerated to a blistering Mach 2.19 (1,450 mph) – blistering because the metal skin of the aircraft was raised to temperatures that would have been unacceptable in a production aircraft. Today, the Griffon II can be admired in the hallowed hangars of the French Aerospace Museum at Le Bourget. Close by the Mach-2 Nord aircraft are a Triton, a Trident and a pair of Concorde aircraft, F-WTSS, or 001, with 812 flying hours and the first aircraft to fly, and F-BTSD, which was delivered to Air France in 1978. One of the very last Concorde aircraft built, F-BTSD holds the around-the-world air speed record in both directions. She flew westwards in October 1992 in thirty-two hours, forty-nine minutes and three seconds and eastwards in thirty-one hours, twenty-seven minutes and forty-nine seconds in August 1995.

The Dassault Mirage III is not yet a museum piece: in 2015 some sixty of these supersonic fighters, up to forty-five years old, remained in service with the Pakistan Air Force. The Mirage III first flew in November 1956. It exceeded Mach 1.5 on its tenth flight. By the end of 1958, the pre-production Mirage IIIA had become the first European aircraft to fly at Mach 2 in level flight, peaking at Mach 2.2. It proved that a conventional jet could outperform ram jet-hybrids at lower overall cost and without the complexity of its supra-hi-tech rivals.

Significantly for the future of Concorde, the Mirage III was the product of collaboration between France and Britain, just like the Sud Aviation Caravelle jet airliner. This highly competent Mach 2 jet was at heart, and certainly in the way it looked, a military production version of Britain's record-breaking Fairey Delta 2, an aircraft that had been tested at Toulouse as well as from Farnborough, with the result that its design, specification and performance were well known to the French team working on the Mirage. And just as one of the two Fairey Deltas was transformed into what emerged in 1961 as the BAC 221 as part of the Concorde development programme, so the Mirage IIIB was used for the same purpose.

As it was, in 1957, and sadly for Fairey, Harold Macmillan's Conservative government cancelled the production version of the Delta 2 for the RAF. The lead designer of the FD 2 was Robert Lickley, a Scottish engineer who had worked on the Hawker Hurricane, rising to become chief project director of the same company's Typhoon, Tempest and Fury. If it had been put into production, the FD 2 might well have been his most successful aircraft in terms of performance, endurance and sales. The saga of this fine aircraft had been a little too much like that of the Miles M.52 for comfort. Dassault, meanwhile, went on to manufacture no fewer than 1,422 Mirage IIIs, and the aircraft has served with the air forces of twenty countries.

A significant impetus for this international and increasingly co-operative drive to fly so very fast both militarily and then commercially was to keep ahead of the Russians. The Cold War really was a time when Western governments and other liberal democracies around the world expected a communist invasion and even a Third World War at any moment. Air superiority was deemed crucial. So, although the quest to break the sound barrier and to fly on to Mach 2 and beyond was partly driven by the simple desire to do so – just as, say, ambitious mountaineers in the years following the Second World War were determined to be first to conquer Mount Everest – the more pressing factors were a need to keep at least one step ahead of the Soviets and, wrapped up with this, to maintain a sense of national self-worth.

The Russians, too, were nosing their way towards the sound barrier. After the fall of Berlin in May 1945 and the defeat of Hitler's Reich, German scientists, engineers and technicians as well as skilled pilots were taken to Russia, along with prototypes and parts of those highly advanced secret jet and rocket aircraft Nazi Germany had developed in the later stages of the war. Yet, while these assets, both human and technological, undoubtedly assisted the Soviet effort, Russian rocket scientists and aircraft engineers had been pursuing new approaches to high-speed flight from the early 1930s.

Sergey Korolev, the father of Sputnik and Vostock, of Yuri Gagarin's 1961 space flight and the Soviet lunar programme, had begun his momentous life in aerospace designing gliders. In 1932, he began work on a rocket-powered glider. This finally flew in February 1940, although by then Korolev had been arrested on trumped-up charges during Stalin's 1938 purges, tortured and packed off to a Siberian gulag. Even when he was re-tried and brought back to Moscow to work, he was forced to toil in a slave labour camp. These cruel absurdities were to hold back the development of Soviet rocketry and Russia's nascent space programme by several years, a delay that was, of course, helpful to Western powers.

Two young Soviet engineers, Alexander Bereznyak and Alesksei Isaev, working at the experimental design bureau OKB-293 on the edge of Moscow built rapidly on Korolev's pioneering work. After they had submitted a report to the Kremlin on 1 August 1941, they were ordered to complete the aircraft they had outlined in just thirty-five days. By then, Hitler had launched Operation Barbarossa – the invasion of the Soviet Union – and OKB-293 had been relocated to Koltsovo Airport, Yekaterinburg, east of the Urals. The largely plywood-and-canvas BI – *Blizhnii Istrebitel* (close-range fighter) – was built with the help of local furniture workers. It first flew under power on 15 May 1942, but was damaged beyond repair on landing. The following March, a second BI went into a 45-degree dive, killing its test pilot, fighter ace Captain Grigori Backchivandzhi. It was widely believed that the aircraft had been flying at 990 kmh (615 mph) before it crashed. It was certainly moving very quickly, yet whatever his speed Backchivandzhi appears to have lost control as he headed towards the sound barrier, experiencing what the Russian engineers described as a transonic 'shock stall'. Although a further seven BIs were constructed back in Moscow between 1943 and 1945, none could be considered to have been a success.

In 1945, Bereznyak was teamed up with the German engineer Hans Rossing to develop the captured DFS 346, a swept-wing rocket plane designed by Felix Kracht, a young German aero-engineer who was to end his long career in Toulouse as the first production director of the A300 Airbus programme. Powered by Walther liquid-propellant rocket engines, the DFS 346 was to have been a reconnaissance aircraft capable of Mach 2.6 and gliding safely home after it had burnt up its limited fuel supply. Work was progressing on the all-metal aircraft, with the aid of slave labour, at the Siebel Flugzeugwerke in Halle an der Saale, Saxony, when the town was occupied by the Americans, who seem not to have come across Kracht's rocket plane and a month later withdrew, allowing the Red Army to seize Halle and the embryonic DFS 346.

Renamed *Sazmolyot* (aircraft) 346, Kracht's plane was eventually completed, although it was a third 346, jettisoned from the belly of a captured USAAF B-29 and with a German pilot, Wolfgang Zeise, lying prone at the controls in its glazed nose-cone, that made what seems to have been an attempt at supersonic flight on 13 August 1951. As with so many other aircraft of the period, whether piston-, jet- or rocket-powered, it began to go out of control as speed built up to 900 kmh (560 mph). Zeise was ordered to bail out as the machine plunged to the ground.

While tests continued with these exotic experimental aircraft, two Russian test pilots had already broken the sound barrier flying the La-176 swept-wing jet fighter prototype. Captains Ivan Fyodorov and Oleg Sokolov both achieved Mach 1 in several flights made from Saki in the Crimea in December 1948. Sokolov's later flights were made to confirm Fyodorov's, as the Lavochkin test team had been concerned with the accuracy of their instruments. The La-176 was powered by a Soviet version of the Rolls-Royce Nene turbojet. Russian spies and their English chums had not secreted blueprints from Derby: the designs, together with forty engines, had been handed over freely, and rather naively, to surprised Soviet officials by Clement Attlee's

Labour government in the spirit of international co-operation and to the tune of 'The Red Flag'. Stafford Cripps, the steely chancellor of the exchequer, had urged caution, yet Rolls-Royce was keen to win new business as its busy production lines slowed down at the end of the war and had lobbied the government to sell designs for the Nene to foreign governments.

The La-176 was a modified version of the La-168, which was a rival design to the Mikoyan MiG-15. Despite the achievements of December 1948, the La-168 lost out to the highly successful MiG, which went supersonic at the end of the following year. Captain Sokolov died soon afterwards in an La-176 test flight, and the project was abandoned. 'From a great height,' one of the two pilots had said in an official press release, 'the pilot accelerates the La-176. You can hear a monotonous low whistle that increases with speed. The plane is hurtling towards the ground. The plane begins to shake as if it has caught a fever. And then – silence! This is what it is when breaking the sound barrier.'

By the beginning of the 1950s, supersonic flight had become a reality, but it was a rarity and often dangerous. And while by late 1953 both the US and Soviet air forces boasted jets capable of exceeding Mach 1 in level flight – the first were the F-100 Super Sabre and the MiG-19 – neither they nor anyone else possessed an aircraft that could maintain supersonic flight, or supercruise. It was, in fact, the British who got there first, beginning in 1954 with the remarkable English Electric P.1 Lightning. Along with the Fairey Delta 2, the P.1 was one of the aircraft that emerged from Morien Morgan's Advanced Fighter Project Group formed at RAE Farnborough in 1948, a team that had been able to assess the very best in advanced German aerodynamics. Its mission was to develop fighters capable of intercepting a new generation of high-speed, high-altitude Russian nuclear bombers.

Designed under the direction of Freddie Page, who had trained under Sidney Camm at Hawker during the Second World War, the production model Lightning featured wings swept back at 60 degrees, a minimal front area, a pair of vertically stacked Rolls-Royce Avons fitted with afterburners and, crucially for the most efficient supersonic flight, variable exhaust nozzles that allowed pilots to squeeze the best from the aircraft's variable thrust reheat system. It was this system that was later adapted and applied to Concorde's Olympus engines, allowing them to run at optimum power with or without reheat.

While the Mach-2 Lightning was very fast, highly aerobatic and could climb, vertically if called for, at a phenomenal rate up to a maximum recorded 88,000 ft, even this military sky-rocket found Concorde a challenge. During trials conducted with British Airways in April 1985, a number of NATO fighters, among them the F-15 Eagle, F-16 Fighting Falcon, F-14 Tomcat, Mirages and F-104 Starfighters, were invited to intercept a Concorde over the North Sea. Only a Lightning flown by Flight Lieutenant Mike Hale was able to overtake the supersonic airliner. Hale was flying at Mach 2.2 at 57,000 ft. Meanwhile, Freddie Page, who was to work on the design of military jets from the Canberra through the TSR2 to the Typhoon Eurofighter, rose to become chairman of the aircraft division of British Aerospace. In 1977, he made the official handover of the last Concorde to be built to British Airways.

Thus, a sequence of jet and rocket prototypes and fighters from the 1940s and through the 1950s led not only to the breaking of the sound barrier, but also to the reality of sustained long-distance supersonic flight. Rocket planes flew ever faster. Weeks before the first meeting of STAC chaired by Morien Morgan, Captain Milburn Apt broke the Mach 3 barrier in the Bell X-2, although he lost control of the aircraft in a turn and was killed. Mach 4 came up in 1961, a year before the Anglo-French Concorde agreement was signed, with Captain Roger White and the North American X-15, and Mach 5 and 6 that same year, again with White and the X-15. The following year, White – who flew in combat in the Second World War, over Korea and in Vietnam – took the X-15 up to over 314,000 ft and the pilot of a winged, supersonic aircraft had become an astronaut.

Crossing the Atlantic supersonically in 1961 was almost as much of an adventure. In fact, only one aircraft managed the feat. This was a Convair B-58 Hustler, a rakish delta-wing USAF bomber with a long, pointed nose, four huge General Electric turbojets mounted on pods under the wings and an even bigger fuel and weapons pod suspended from the belly of the fuselage. The three-man crew were shoehorned into three separate cockpits along the spine of the fuselage. The pilot could look out through a windscreen and side windows, but the views of the bombardier navigator and defensive systems operator behind him were extremely restricted.

Brian Trubshaw, the British Concorde chief test pilot, flew a B-58 for ten hours from Edwards Air Force Base, California. 'The ten hours,' he recalled, 'took nearly one month, as it was necessary to change one of the engines after each flight due to unforeseen circumstances.' But the Hustler could certainly go. On 26 May 1961, a B-58 commanded by Major William Payne flew non-stop from Carswell Air Force Base, Fort Worth, Texas to Le Bourget Airport, Paris, travelling 3,626 miles in three hours, nineteen minutes and forty-four seconds at an average speed of 1,089 mph. It had slowed from cruising at Mach 2 only to refuel from a Boeing KC-135 tanker, a development, like the 707, of the company's 367-80 prototype of 1954.

The B-58 crew had to concentrate at all times throughout the flight. No napping, no drinks trolley, no flight attendants, no lavatory and, when the aircraft came down to land, no view of the runway as the nose came up. Piece of cake, really, although there was no cake or any other pudding, much less the fine wines and gourmet meals served on board Concorde. A week later, the Hustler went out of control and crashed during a flight display at Le Bourget. All three crew members were killed. Five days after that, a team from the British Aircraft Corporation arrived in Paris to discuss plans for working together on the development of a supersonic airliner with their counterparts at Sud Aviation. It was less than a decade since *The Sound Barrier* had premiered in London, and just twenty years since glider pilot Heini Dittmar had rocketed up to over 1,000 kmh (620 mph), more or less in control of an Me 163 Komet.

THREE

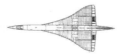

CHASING
THE DREAM

'BY the end of the 1950s,' wrote Brian Trubshaw, 'the problems of supersonic flight from a technical standpoint were well-known and flight at M = 2.0 could be regarded as routine.' Routine perhaps for skilled and highly experienced test pilots like Trubshaw, who had joined the RAF in 1942 aged just eighteen and had flown Stearman biplanes in the United States, Stirling and Lancaster four-engine heavy bombers back in Blighty and, after the war, had put the Vickers Valiant V-bomber and the Vickers VC-10 airliner through their pre-production paces and of course had even clocked up ten hours with the B-58 Hustler. From Tiger Moths and Boeing B-52 Superfortresses and on to Concorde, Trubshaw was to pilot more than a hundred types of aircraft in a career of 11,000 flying hours.

Flying at twice the speed of sound was one thing in a rocket-like military prototype, but commanding a supersonic airliner in daily service would be a very different matter. Aside from actually achieving this speed and sustaining it safely and smoothly over thousands of miles, such an aircraft would have to negotiate busy airports. It would need to be able to take off laden with passengers, luggage, cargo and the accoutrements of commercial flight. It would need to land calmly. At low altitudes and around airports it would have to mix with subsonic aircraft. In short, it would need to fly slowly and be able to maintain low speeds without juddering, much less stalling. It would need to behave like any other airliner until, soaring into its very own high flight path and away from land, it could let rip and be its own true Mach-2 self.

Unlike almost any other supersonic aircraft, the purity of Concorde as an exquisite Mach-2 dart would have to be compromised. The very wings that would optimize such an aircraft's flight at supersonic speeds would offer precious little lift at low speeds and especially when taking off or coming in to land. If the wings were to be cluttered with flaps and their control mechanisms, there would be a penalty to pay both in terms of weight, and thus fuel consumption, and in a loss of streamlining: Concorde's wing would need to be as thin and smooth as possible. And yet without some way of allowing the aircraft to fly slowly, airport runways would have to be extended to unacceptable lengths or the aircraft would have to be small and light and carry few passengers, which would make it a wholly uneconomic proposition.

When, in fact, Morien Morgan produced the RAE's first tentative report on the feasibility of a transatlantic airliner in 1954, it suggested that a fifteen-seater might just be a possibility. This would take the form of a pencil-thin, rocket-like design with thin, unswept wings, but every drawing made suggested an aircraft that, even if it flew successfully from a technical point of view, promised to be a commercial disaster. As Morgan put it, 'Some horribly large aeroplanes resulted for quite small passenger loads, even when one cheated a little by skimming down on fuel reserves and using quite a lot of reheat for take-off. In fact, only silly aeroplanes emerged if one attempted the full non-stop London–New York range; one could get in fifteen passengers for an all-up weight of about 300,000 lbs at take-off, giving a direct operating cost five or more times that of the then subsonic long-range machines.'

At 336,000 lbs, the take-off weight of a transatlantic Boeing 707-320 capable of 570 mph was not much higher than RAE's first stab at a supersonic transport or SST; it could carry more than 200 passengers in a manner that would have been impossible on board the putative British fifteen-seater. And, perhaps even more importantly in terms of Concorde's future, the prototype 707 – the Boeing 367-800 – had taken to the air in July 1954. It was no surprise, then, that, although the makings of an Anglo-French SST were very much on the cards as collaboration between the aircraft manufacturers of the two countries grew in the late 1950s, Morgan, STAC and industrialists talked to other parties. The Germans said no early on, while the Americans remained heaven-bent on a Mach-3 SST that would have raised costs further than the British on their own or even an Anglo-French consortium could bear.

The 1959 STAC report had included a number of conceptual designs for supersonic airliners for both medium-range and long-distance flight. Produced by Armstrong Whitworth, Handley Page, Hawker Siddeley and Bristol, these were developed over the next three years before the Anglo-French agreement effectively settled the matter. While some form of delta wing had clearly taken the lead early on – Bristol was clearly on to something with drawings for what became the six-engine BS.198 design that looked rather like Concorde itself – other configurations were explored. Hawker Siddeley worked up the idea of an airliner with an integrated fuselage and wing, while Armstrong Whitworth proposed an M-wing medium-range Mach-1.2 airliner in the form of the AWP.13, an extraordinary-looking thing with a lance- or spear-like nose leading a wasp-waisted fuselage and engines mounted in thin wings swept back in the form of a giant letter M. A stunning wind-tunnel model proved its aerodynamic qualities, but the medium-range option was dropped in 1962 and, anyway, the AWP.13 seemed ungainly; it really did look too much like a 1950s alien spaceship for the comfort of transatlantic earthlings. Indeed, the aircraft might have made a perfect means of transport for the Mekon – space pilot Dan Dare's Venusian nemesis in the pages of *The Eagle* comic – to tour the Earth should he ever have managed to conquer it.

Slightly previous to its radical AWP.13, Armstrong Whitworth had produced designs for an even more remarkable, if rather beautiful, supersonic jet, a VTOL flying wing. This was the AWP.171. It was so slim that the pilot would have to lie on his stomach to fly it. With ten Rolls-Royce RB.108 engines blasting away, the aircraft would take off vertically before employing a pair of wingtip-mounted Bristol Orpheus jets to propel it up to Mach 2 in horizontal flight. At the time, concepts such as the AWP.171 appeared to offer a quantum leap into the future. Imagine this proposal for a single-seater transformed into a transatlantic airliner. With its ability to take off vertically, it would circumvent the problem of slow flight altogether, its tiny, or low-aspect ratio, wingspan no hindrance at all and, in fact, an advantage at very high speeds. In 1969, an RAF Hawker Siddeley Harrier jump jet with Squadron Leader Tom Lecky-Thompson in the hot seat gave a very convincing demonstration of what this might have meant in practice, flying from London to New York in just six hours and eleven minutes and so winning the *Daily Mail* Trans-Atlantic Air Race.

Such an aircraft would, however, have been expensive to build, costly to fly and unwanted by airlines. A VTOL Concorde carrying 100 passengers? The idea was at least toyed with. Imagine, though, the sheer number and power of the engines needed to get it airborne, the fuel consumption and the maintenance involved. In any case, work on the AWP.171 was cancelled in 1957, along with that on so many British military designs, when the government decided the ground-to-air missile was the way forward and that high-speed jet interceptors were both too costly and outmoded. The English Electric Lightning slipped through the official net nonetheless. It could accelerate to Mach 2 very quickly indeed and, if not VTOL, it could climb vertically at an initial rate of 50,000 ft a minute. And even if a prototype had been built, the Armstrong Whitworth delta-wing jet would have been left trailing in the conventional interceptor's wake.

Between the STAC report and the signing of the Anglo-French Concorde treaty, Handley Page proposed what looks to have been a perversely strange slew-wing Mach-2 airliner. The aircraft, known as the Sycamore, was essentially a single sycamore or boomerang-shaped wing with a crew nacelle at one tip counterbalanced by a tall fin at the other. Passengers would be carried, along with baggage and fuel, inside the wing. In supersonic flight, the wing would be slewed back up to an angle of 72 degrees, with the crew nacelle now leading the passenger accommodation and with the fin behind. Wind-tunnel tests on models had demonstrated that the slew design would be stable and efficient in supersonic flight, while, when in a more or less horizontal position, as it would be when taking off or landing, the aircraft would generate sufficient lift at low speed.

The engineer in charge of this remarkable proposal was Godfrey Lee, who had co-designed the efficient and distinctive crescent wing of the successful Handley Page Victor V-bomber, another striking design of the 1950s. Lee's colleague was Gustav Lachmann, a German engineer who had joined Handley Page in 1929. Responsible for the HP Hampden twin-engine bomber, which took part on the first RAF raid on Berlin, he was interned as an enemy alien in Canada and then the Isle of Man during the Second World War and, when allowed back, resumed employment with Handley Page from Lingfield Prison.

The United States' National Aeronautics and Space Administration (NASA) pursued the idea of a slew-wing airliner in the 1970s, and again at the beginning of the twenty-first century. The idea stemmed from Richard Vogt, who had worked for Zeppelin and Dornier in Germany and Kawasaki in Japan, where he was head of aircraft design, before joining Blohm & Voss as chief engineer of the shipyard's aircraft division. As part of the emergency fighter design programme of 1944, Vogt proposed a twin-engine slew-wing jet fighter. It was never built, but the ideas were carried forward through Lachmann and Lee at Handley Page and again by Robert Jones for NASA. Vogt, meanwhile, was sent to the United States through Operation Paperclip, and it is to him that we owe the winglets on the wingtips of the latest airliners that improve aerodynamic efficiency by lowering fuel consumption.

The complexity of the control required for a practical slew-wing airliner, however, was effectively beyond the capabilities of aerospace technology in the early 1960s. The level of computer assistance needed to make the operation reliable and efficient was unavailable at the time. It remains, though, fascinating to see how Concorde might have adopted a different form and the extent to which the work of German aerodynamicists and aircraft engineers working for the destruction of the free world in the 1930s and 1940s played so influential a role in the development of Concorde.

The key to Concorde's success, indeed its very existence, was the design of its wing. This proved to be perhaps the greatest compromise in its design, a brilliant trade-off between low-speed lift and high-speed flight that took several years to finesse. But ultimately, Concorde's Anglo-French design turned almost each and every necessary compromise into an opportunity to shape a supersonic airliner that performed exceptionally well in almost all circumstances. Indeed, it was the painstaking work undertaken over many years, and especially on the form and performance of its wings, that made Concorde not just one of the best-looking aircraft of all time but one of the most beautiful machines and, perhaps, artefacts yet created by the human mind and hand.

A supreme example of highly resolved engineering design, Concorde was to be, de facto, a work of art. Getting Concorde to behave like an everyday airliner while outperforming military jets over long distances, however, proved to be a very demanding task, and this had to be achieved on paper and in wind tunnels in Britain, France and the Netherlands before computers arrived, late in the day, to help crunch some of the numbers. Concorde was essentially a pre-digital aircraft. Meanwhile, the other method of testing ideas that were to be either incorporated into the design of Concorde, or, of course, rejected, was to design and construct, or procure and modify, much smaller and far less complex prototype aircraft that would serve as flying guinea pigs for a very civil Mach-2 bird of prey. These aircraft would ensure that Concorde could be a Pegasus called on to do a milk round when necessary or the equivalent, perhaps, of a Formula One car driven down to the shops in traffic to pick up a pint of milk, the newspaper and a packet of fags. First, though, the wing had to be thought through and worked on, and, as events proved, tirelessly so.

In 2007, a box of papier-mâché aircraft held together by sticky tape and tucked away and all but forgotten for several decades in a warehouse became a treasured part of the London Science Museum's Concorde collection. These particular models were made by W. E. Gray, a former Royal Navy pilot turned aerodynamicist who worked at RAE Farnborough. Tested for their aerodynamic qualities in the RAE's mighty wind tunnels in Surrey and Bedfordshire, and following experiments undertaken from the tops of ladders and roofs, even from a helicopter, the most successful were remodelled in wood, resin and metal, and retested. The Science Museum has a collection of these later models, too. They are very special things, even if it might at first appear that they have more to do with school playground adventures or the kind of ancient artefacts found – and all too often described as being to do with fertility rites in far-off and long-forgotten parts of the world – in the drawers of Victorian cabinets in Oxford's Pitt-Rivers Museum.

And yet, as anyone who enjoys making planes from paper or any suitable material to hand knows, such simple models can be made to fly in any number of ways. They teach and demonstrate the laws and possibilities of wing design in a straightforward but truly exciting way. As Peter Turvey, a curator of the Science Museum, said at the time of their discovery, 'The models themselves were probably made by fairly skilled craftsmen who would have tested all sorts of shapes – including things that looked nothing like the final Concorde. This was real boffin stuff. It was a case of shouting, "I have an idea" and then giving it a go. Some of Gray's team even tried out their paper planes in the open air, throwing them by hand.'

Alan Perry, a member of the Concorde team who started work at Bristol Aircraft in 1959, recalled, 'There's no better way to test an idea than to take it outside and see if it flies. Sometimes we'd even use our punch cards. We'd fold them up, take them outside at lunchtime if the weather was nice and see who could fly them furthest from the hangar. It may seem strange by today's standards, but those simple trials were a great help at the time. Bigger and more complex models were used throughout the design process.'

Looking at these models, however, really does help to make sense of the ways in which Concorde's remarkable and elegant wing was developed: through mathematics, fluid dynamics, aerodynamics, imagination and, of course, trial and error. The wing itself proved to be a subtle and complex ogival delta, significantly different from the comparatively strait-laced deltas of earlier military jets and of, too, the proposals for two supersonic airliners, one by Sud Aviation, the other by Bristol, that pointed the way to the aircraft that finally flew in 1969 at much the same time as the NASA space programme, in large thanks to Werner von Braun and his Operation Paperclip colleagues, took Neil Armstrong, Buzz Aldrin and Michael Collins safely to the Moon and back.

Although the research carried out at Farnborough for STAC and on into the Concorde project proper from 1962 was very much a collaboration between all parties involved, certain figures alongside Morien Morgan stand out, in particular Dietrich Küchemann, the quiet German cellist and aerodynamicist. Küchemann was born in 1911 in Gottingen, where the university had established itself as perhaps the most advanced centre for research into aerodynamics. The young Dietrich had planned to study pure physics under his father's friend, Max Born, to whom we owe the subject of quantum mechanics. However, along with several Jewish colleagues, Born was expelled from Gottingen when the Nazis were voted into power in 1933. Küchemann instead chose to study fluid and aerodynamics in the university department headed by Ludwig Prandtl, who brought mathematics and the theory and practice of flight together. As a result of his researches into high-speed flight, he advanced the idea of the thin wing. As his research took him further into the realm of supersonic flight, he teamed up with his Gottingen colleague, Alfred Busemann, on the development of supersonic wind tunnels, the first of which were built in Germany shortly before the outbreak of the

Second World War. Busemann himself proposed swept wings for supersonic aircraft as early as 1935 and presented a paper on the subject in Italy that year. He was, to say the least, slightly ahead of his time, although the following year he published a paper recommending swept wings for fast subsonic aircraft, too. These ideas were applied to designs for last-ditch German jet fighters in 1944–45 and, ultimately, to jet fighters and airliners worldwide.

Busemann, who went to work in 1946 with NACA Langley, the US National Advisory Committee for Aeronautics facility at Hampton, Virginia, designed a conceptual supersonic aircraft that would break the sound barrier silently. Busemann's Biplane has not yet been built, but it remains a remarkable exercise in the applications of maths and ingenuity to aerodynamics. The problem yet to be solved is that this intriguing machine would certainly do what Busemann claimed – a model was tested in a supersonic wind tunnel – but it would generate no lift: it could fly, but it would be unable to take off, whereas Concorde was to take off in spectacular fashion, and could fly up to Mach 2 with consummate ease. Concorde was also pretty noisy, especially in prototype and pre-production form, and noise caused by sonic booms was to be one of the key reasons the aircraft almost never flew at all into, let alone over, the United States. The shock waves that build up in front of an aircraft as it approaches the speed of sound do so in the form of a cone that, just as the wake of a ship, spreads out behind it. This cone spreads down to the ground covering an area of about twenty-five miles, within which each and everyone are subject to sonic booms. No city dweller or countryman would tolerate this kind and level of noise on a regular basis.

Back in 1936, having completed his doctoral thesis that year, Busemann volunteered for military service. He worked in signals and saw no action in the war, although he was able to continue research into swept wings and high-speed flight. In 1946, he came to England, where he joined the RAE at Farnborough, playing cello for the local symphony orchestra and writing his still topical book *Aerodynamics of Propulsion* based on his wartime work in Germany. It was published in 1953. Max Born had recently retired as Tait Professor of Natural Philosophy at Edinburgh and, squaring a circle, returned to live in Gottingen. The following year he was awarded a Nobel Prize for his research in quantum mechanics. In his address, he underlined the importance of the idea of uncertainty in maths as in physics and, as Küchemann understood, in aerodynamics, too.

'I believe,' Born said, 'that ideas such as absolute certitude, absolute exactness, final truth etc are figments of the imagination which should not be admissible in any field of science. On the other hand, any assertion of probability is either right or wrong from the standpoint of the theory on which it is based. This loosening of thinking seems to me to be the greatest blessing which modern science has given to us. For the belief in a single truth and in being the possessor thereof is the root cause of all evil in the world.'

The design of Concorde's wing was like no other. It even appeared to break the laws of the aerodynamic certainties that had served subsonic aircraft fairly well for half a century. In particular, the flow of air over the leading edge and along the wings behaved in quite a different way from conventional wings. In a regular aircraft wing, the flow of air over the top and underside of the wing does not – in fact, it must not – separate from the wing. As an aircraft accelerates, the airflow over the convex upper surface of the wing has to speed up to catch up with the flow beneath the wing. As it does, its pressure lowers in relation to that of the air below. Quite naturally, although greatly aided by the power of engines, this drop in pressure causes the wing to lift. And this was the way aircraft had flown since the Wright brothers. If this airflow is upset, by turbulence for example, the wing will stall.

What Küchemann observed, among others including French aerodynamicists at ONERA from the early 1950s, was that small vortices of air, with lifting properties, are generated at the tips of a conventional wing as higher air pressure from below mingles with lower air pressure above. What if much bigger, more powerful vortices could be induced by deliberately separating the airflow over and under the entire span of an aircraft's wings? If there was a way of doing this safely, these vortices would induce tremendous and stable lift. This is just what Küchemann proposed and achieved in the intensely subtle shaping of Concorde's wings. As a result, these ran almost the length of the aircraft and were swept back to an exceptional degree. And yet to generate these uplifting vortices, Concorde would need to fly at a steeper angle at low speed than subsonic airliners. And because it would have to land at a steep angle for the same reason, it was fitted with very long-legged landing gear to enable it to touch down safely.

The vortices were highly visible as the aircraft took off at its characteristic steep angle in wet or misty weather and even more so on landing. They made a mesmerizing sight, Concorde looking, for all the world, like some great seabird raising itself powerfully up from the water's surface. Not only was this a stirring sight, but it also allowed the spectator to watch Küchemann's theories in practice: you could see for yourself how the forced separation of air flowing over and under the wings generated swirling, inverted tornado-like forces that seemed to suck the 400,000-lb machine up into the clouds and the burning blue beyond.

In a paper he presented in 1971, Morien Morgan made clear just how audacious this idea was in the early stages of Concorde's development:

> To someone like myself brought up years ago in the respectable atmosphere of flight research, 'separation' was – and still is – an emotive and ugly word. It denoted a stall, a breakaway of the airflow over the wings or elsewhere, sometimes widespread, sometimes local. It was almost invariably a nuisance, giving sharply increased drag, sharply decreased lift, buffeting and vibration. Sudden separation of flow a long way from the centre of gravity could readily throw an aeroplane completely out of control – for instance, a tip stall on a highly tapered wing could smartly land the pilot in a flick half-roll and an inverted spin. Even worse, our theoretical fluid-dynamics team and our wind-tunnel colleagues – while extremely helpful when dealing with an aeroplane flying straight and level, with the air flowing around it in an ordered and well-behaved way – seemed much more helpless, and less able to predict flight behaviour, as soon as separation reared its ugly head.

Standing on the shoulders of his predecessors and colleagues at Gottingen, Küchemann had dared to think differently. Although his contribution to the design of Concorde's wings and aerodynamic qualities was enormous and of critical importance, he wanted to push the concept further with the design of a supersonic airliner in which the wing and the fuselage were fused into one and the same thing. While his RAE colleagues believed this approach to be too radical, it was one Küchemann continued to stand up for, notably in his book *The Aerodynamic Design of Aircraft*, first published in 1978 at the tail end of the Concorde production programme.

Küchemann's researches, however, were far from the stuff of perversity, or even serendipity: they were rooted, and square-rooted, very firmly in mathematics. At Farnborough, and working with the aerodynamicist Eric Gaskell, he relied on Johanna Weber, a brilliant German mathematician who, from 1939, had taught at the Aerodynamic Research Institute, Gottingen. Here she had met Küchemann. In 1947, he persuaded her to join him at the RAE, where she did the maths that helped make Concorde possible. She also co-authored Küchemann's books, but shied away from any form of publicity.

Even then, Küchemann needed to be sure his conceptual wing would work at low speed. Jacob Bronowski, the scientist and broadcaster, who was born in Poland but moved to England with his family from Germany in 1920 when he was twelve years old, made a fine BBC2 series commissioned by David Attenborough in the early 1970s on the history of science and its effects on society. In the final episode of *The Ascent of Man*, Bronowski, filmed at Auschwitz, looked into the unfeeling eye of the camera and said: 'Science is a very human form of knowledge. We are always at the brink of the known; we always feel forward for what is to be hoped. Every judgement in science stands on the edge of error and is personal. Science is a tribute to what we can know, although we are fallible. In the end, the words were said by Oliver Cromwell: "I beseech you in the bowels of Christ: Think it possible you may be mistaken."'

The Concorde team were great optimists and, equally, great doubters. There could be no mistake. For the sake of Anglo-French entente, the reputation of the aero industry, of the RAE and ONERA, and of science itself, Concorde needed to be a technological success. And even when tests were more or less complete, Küchemann himself believed the Concorde project – commercially as well as scientifically – to be, in his own words, 'just possible'. The payload of the production aircraft would be just 6 per cent of the aircraft's overall weight compared to the 12 per cent of a Boeing 707, 20 per cent of a Boeing 747 or about 24 per cent for the latest Boeings and Airbuses. And, for all its dynamic qualities, reliability and undimmed popularity, even the 707 made very little money for Boeing.

Yet, as Archibald Russell, then managing director of BAC Bristol, was to tell the eighth Anglo-American Aeronautical Conference in London in September 1961: 'While the estimation of development expenditure is more an art than a science, it is still vastly more accurate than a prediction of the number of aircraft [Concorde aircraft] that will eventually be sold. Acceptance of a particular development is, therefore, an act of faith in pursuance of a line of policy.'

Meanwhile, there had been alternatives to Küchemann's slender ogival delta wing. There was, for example, the swing-wing, championed by Sir Barnes Wallis, of bouncing bomb and Dambusters fame. From the end of the Second World War, Wallis was head of research and development for Vickers Armstrong. From an office in the former Edwardian clubhouse of the Brooklands motor racing circuit in Surrey, Wallis developed a number of intriguing designs that culminated in a study for an all-wing hypersonic airliner capable of taking off and landing, theoretically at least, at conventional airports and devoid of all moving wing parts: pure wing, pure flight.

At the time of Concorde's early development, Wallis put forward the idea of a swing-wing supersonic airliner. Outstretched, the wings would give lift; tucked in, they would allow the airliner to scythe through the upper reaches of the air smoothly and with very little drag. To keep the arrowhead form of the aircraft as true as possible, the cockpit would be lowered into the fuselage at speed. Control of the aircraft was to be through the engines alone. Hung on pods from the wing tips, they would swivel through three axes and replace rudder, ailerons and elevators. It was certainly a beautiful machine and there was some official interest in the Swallow, as the project was known, although this was more for a possible nuclear bomber version than a costly civil airliner.

Wallis flew a model of the Swallow successfully at Predannock, Cornwall, in November 1955; it took off and landed by itself and was stable in the air. A second, smaller model was subject to wind-tunnel tests at speeds of up to Mach 2.5. Swing wings, though, added complexity and weight, and, at a time when there were no sophisticated on-board computers, the idea of the wing-tip engines controlling the aircraft in all flight attitudes must have seemed disturbing to those without Wallis's ingenuity and self-confidence. Supersonic swing-wing technology was, however, to find favour with the military, first with the Mach-2.5 General Dynamics F-111, first flown in 1964 and of which 563 were built and flown by the US and Australian air forces, and then the Mach-2.2 Panavia Tornado, which made its maiden flight in 1974 and of which 992 were assembled in Britain, Italy and Germany between 1979 and 1998. Wallis had also been at work on a swept-wing fighter for the Royal Navy – the Mach-3 Vickers 581 – that was briefly taken up as an idea for the RAF, too, although both concepts were rejected after several years of further research and development.

In fact, Wallis had shared his ideas with American colleagues on a trip to the States and later felt the F-111 to be an unwarranted US adaptation of his 581, even considering suing General Dynamics. This is not true, as swing-wing design was simply in the air at the time. It was even to have been incorporated into the Boeing 2707, the proposed US rival to Concorde. (See Chapter Four.) While there is little doubt as to the supersonic performance of swing-wing jets, the solution they offered to the problem of lift at low speed seemed complex and expensive compared to the RAE's subtly shaped delta wing for Concorde.

To test the thin delta-wing concept beyond doubt at slow speeds, a test aircraft was needed. After toying with the idea of a glider towed by a Canberra jet bomber, the RAE issued a specification for a research aircraft through the Ministry of Supply. Handley Page won the contract with its HP.115. This proved to be the most minimal of machines, a jet damsel fly, with the slenderest possible fuselage, a long, thin delta wing swept back at 75 degrees, a streamlined cockpit resembling an insect's head and a very tall fixed undercarriage. Never meant to fly at much above 200 mph – Brian Trubshaw described it as 'a glider with a small engine' – the HP.115 was powered by a single Bristol Siddeley Viper turbojet. First flown at RAE Bedford in August 1961 by Squadron Leader Jack Henderson, the HP.115 was a great success from the words 'Chocks away', flying at extremely low speeds without stalling and providing a stream of useful airflow data for the Concorde project and beyond.

The HP.115's controls were said to be light and responsive. At the 1962 Farnborough Air Show, and elsewhere, it could be seen waltzing above the crowd, its pilot performing a neat, if involuntary, Dutch roll, rocking left and right while wagging the aircraft's tail. This curious term derived, the Reverend J. G. Wood had written in his book *Skating and Sliding* (1872), 'from the motion being used in Holland by the travelling and trading classes in their common avocation'. The HP.115 was anything but common, and performed everything asked of it efficiently and gracefully. Those who flew and enjoyed it at Bedford included Concorde test pilots and, in June 1971, Neil Armstrong, one of the greatest pilots of all, whether in air or outer space. Armstrong, who had flown the North American X-15 to sensational speeds, enjoyed both the 200-mph HP.115 that day, and a ride as a passenger in the Shuttleworth Collection's 90-mph 1918 Avro 504K, a machine that had gone on to serve in the Second World War and, later, to play a role in the 1956 film *Reach for the Sky* starring Kenneth More as Douglas Bader. Armstrong, Bader, Jack Henderson and the Concorde team would surely have agreed with the rather superior Reverend Wood when he made recommendations for the best way to take up skating: 'Throw fear to the dogs', 'Put on your skates securely' and 'Keep your balance'. He might indeed have been lecturing to test pilots.

After 500 or so hours of test flying, the curiously lovable HP.115 was packed off to the Fleet Air Arm Museum, Yeovilton. Here, the silver aircraft rests alongside the bright-blue BAC 221, which began life as one of the two Fairey Delta 2s and would be converted for the next stage of research into Concorde's high- and low-speed flying characteristics. Progress on this project, which had begun in 1958, was slowed to a sparrow's pace when in 1960 Westland Aircraft bought Fairey and the work was handed over to Hunting Aircraft of Luton, which was then merged into the new British Aircraft Corporation, which in turn moved the programme to the former Bristol team.

Once the corporate dust settled, things moved ahead at Mach speed. Conversion work on the FD.2 began in April 1961 and was completed in early July. This involved fitting an ogee delta wing, a greatly lengthened undercarriage and a 'droop snoot' nose, together with a pivoting cockpit, allowing pilots a decent view of runways as they came in to land at the steep angle necessary to keep the aircraft flying at low speed. This design feature, comprising nose and visor, was carried over to Concorde. It was to give the supersonic airliner the look of a magnificent mechanical stork, or some other long-legged bird, as it took off or came in to land. At take-off and in the climb, the visor would be lowered and the nose drooped at an angle of 5 degrees. In subsonic flight the nose would be raised and in the transition to supersonic the visor would be raised, too, although in production versions of the aircraft this still afforded a good view from the captain and first officer's seats. On the approach to runways below 250 knots (280 mph) the visor was lowered by 5 degrees, and then on landing and taxying it would be lowered further and the nose drooped by 12.5 degrees, giving the pilots a better view than their colleagues in other airliners. Concorde's droop snoot was much loved by cartoonists; it gave the airliner real character.

The RAE conducted flight simulation tests over nine months before it gave its blessing to the BAC 221, an aircraft designed to land at 170 knots, or 195 mph. The beautiful blue aircraft made its maiden flight – the first of 273, mostly from Toulouse and around the Bordeaux region, before its retirement in 1973 – on 1 May 1964 with Bristol's chief test pilot, Godfrey Auty, a wartime Mosquito pilot, doing the honours. Auty was assisted by the aircraft's power-operated controls and an auto-stabilization device that checked unwanted roll and yaw, or side-to-side movement. Together, the HP.115 and BAC 221 proved that Concorde would be able to land and take off and fly slowly both effectively and safely without being encumbered by the weighty, complex and drag-inducing devices that had been and are necessary with conventional wings. And the ogival wing would indeed be a boon in supersonic flight. The final wing configuration, with its lovely visual play of tapers, cambers, droops and twists, was to be more complex than those of these research aircraft, but much had been learned in a long, fascinating and painstaking process that had begun in Germany well before the Second World War.

But what should a supersonic airliner be made of? When flying at such great speeds, might existing materials be unable to cope with the heat generated by friction at Mach 2 and beyond? Might Concorde need to be forged from more costly and heavier stainless steel rather than aluminium? As early as 1954, the British government had called for submissions for the design of a long-distance Mach-3 reconnaissance aircraft and bomber. It would need to cruise at Mach 2.5 at 60,000 ft. Avro won the commission with its 730, a rocket-like machine featuring a small tapered wing carrying no fewer than eight Armstrong Siddeley turbojets in a pair of tip-mounted pods. A research aircraft was commissioned. This was the Bristol 188, a striking-looking machine made of welded stainless steel. This process was difficult enough and it might have been better if the aircraft had been fashioned from titanium. This, though, was very expensive and much of the world's production was in Russia, the very country the Avro 730 was intended to reconnoitre and, if necessary, bomb while flying over it at between Mach 2.5 and 3.

In the event, Duncan Sandys cancelled the project in 1957 long before the 188 flew. When the first of two operational aircraft did fly on 14 April 1962, complete with a quartz windscreen and canopy and a cockpit refrigeration system, and Godfrey Auty in charge, its Gyron Junior jets, the first British gas-turbines designed for supersonic operation, could thrust it to a top speed of just Mach 1.88. Unfortunately, so great was these engines' fuel consumption that the 'Flaming Pencil' was only able to fly for a maximum of about forty-five minutes – and just twenty-five minutes at very high speed – which meant too little time as well as too little speed to gather meaningful data.

Once, one of the aircraft ran out of fuel even earlier than Auty had expected. The anti-spin parachute fitted at the back of the 188, designed to straighten it out in flight in the event of a spin, then opened of its own accord. Forced to apply ever more power to counteract the drag of the 'chute, Auty looked for somewhere to land – he was too far from his Bristol base at Filton – before the tank emptied. Spotting the newly extended runway at RAF Fairford, from where Concorde 002 would make its maiden flight in 1969, Auty came down to land. The 188 needed a long runway. Auty slightly misjudged his approach and had to slam on the brakes, causing a sudden heat build-up in the wheels that burst the tyres. The aircraft was down safely, but Auty very quickly discovered that the runway was about to be invaded by a flock of mighty USAF B-52s descending on Fairford from the States as part of a NATO war game. A US airman turned up in next to no time with a bulldozer in pursuit. 'I have been instructed to clear this runway, sir,' he told Auty. Luckily, a request for a length of rope was met and truly at the last minute the model-slim supersonic research jet was pulled away as the B-52s roared in.

This story is told by Ted Talbot, a Bristol engineer who played a key role in the development of Concorde's engines, in his entertaining and illuminating book, *Concorde, a designer's life: the Journey to Mach 2*. Nevertheless, the ill-fated 188 did help Concorde's design team to decide in favour of aluminium rather than stainless steel: given the maximum speed Concorde would fly at – Mach 2 – aluminium was a safe choice. However, thousands of aluminium samples were tested before a copper-based aluminium alloy, originally developed for use by Rolls-Royce in gas turbine blades, was selected for the superstructure. There were, of course, other materials in the many thousands of components that constituted Concorde, including nickel-chromium-based alloys, titanium, plastics, paints, adhesives, fabrics and, yes, stainless steel.

To test these, two complete airframes were built, one at RAE Farnborough, the other at CEAT (Centre Essais Aéronautiques de Toulouse). At Toulouse, among other tests, the frame was to be heated by 35,000 infrared lamps and then suddenly cooled by 70,000 litres of liquid oxygen, time and again. At Farnborough the exercise was carried out with hot and cold air. Both test centres used hydraulic jacks to impose loads on the airframes. These were the most rigorous tests yet made of airframes. Concorde pilots liked to explain, and show, how the fuselage of their aircraft expanded by between two and eight inches in supersonic flight. This was because the temperature of the aircraft's skin at Mach 2 would rise to 127° C at the tip of the nose and 90° C at its tail, even though at 56,000 ft the air temperature is around 57° C. Sliding connections between parts of the aircraft would allow for such expansion as the aluminium alloy soaked up the intense heat.

As for the problems the 188 faced with airflow into its engines at high speed leading to pulsing, flame-outs and other undesirable characteristics, these were to be turned into opportunities for Concorde by Ted Talbot and his colleagues. The French had no engine of their own that might have powered the supersonic airliner, so the power plant selected was the Rolls-Royce/Snecma Olympus 593, an Anglo-French development of the Bristol Siddeley Olympus 22R produced for the short-lived BAC TSR-2 supersonic tactical strike and reconnaissance aircraft. Although a promising machine, the TSR-2, which first flew in September 1964 a month before that year's general election, was the victim of both military and civil politics; it was cancelled by Harold Wilson's new Labour government the following April.

Wilson and the majority of his ministers and MPs would have liked to cancel Concorde too, if only they could have got away with it. Yet the strict conditions of the Anglo-French treaty and the government's desire to join the EEC – the European Union, as was – made this all but impossible. Cancellation of the TSR-2, however, only added to the cost of Concorde, as from now on the supersonic airliner would have to carry the entire cost of the Olympus 593 programme rather than sharing this with the military jet. Just as every extra pound in weight Concorde put on as it headed towards service increased costs, so did, or so it seemed, each and every political interference – although, of course, Concorde could only have existed with the backing of national governments.

As regards weight, as Sir Peter Baldwin, a distinguished civil servant who was key to breaking the secret Japanese military code during the Second World War and in later years permanent secretary at the Department of Transport, was to recall:

> What happened is that it [Concorde] had to be redesigned twice, perhaps two and a half times, completely because of weight growth, and in the course of redesigning it, more expensive methods of construction had to be adopted and more expensive materials, and the result was that the production cost turned out to be about four times as high as had been anticipated. The economics of it went completely. They had never been very good, but it became obvious from the mid-1960s to anybody that this was economically disastrous, even while there were doubts about whether it was technically possible which still had to be resolved.

As it was, the Olympus 22R engine was a highly uprated and well-resolved version of the original Bristol Olympus of 1950 that powered the Avro Vulcan bomber. (Bristol Aero Engines was merged with Armstrong Siddeley in 1959 and in 1966 Bristol Siddeley became a part of Rolls-Royce.) With its twin low- and high-pressure spools, the Bristol Olympus, and later versions of the engine, was capable of great power. It was also versatile, serving as the power plant for military ships, beginning with *Turunmaa*, a 700-ton Finnish corvette in 1968 and the Royal Navy frigate *HMS Exmouth* later that year, as well as for numerous power stations worldwide. Many remained in service as the gas turbine reached its sixty-fifth birthday in 2015.

Aside from its longevity, reliability and power, the overall thermal efficiency of the Olympus 593 in Concorde's cruise was 43 per cent, a very high figure, and way above that, for example, of most cars; petrol engines have a thermal efficiency of about 25 per cent, although Toyota's four-cylinder, 1.2-litre Atkinson-cycle engine unveiled in 2014 achieves 38 per cent. Thermal efficiency, however, was only one measure of the efficiency of the Olympus. Another was the ingenious ways in which it was able to produce consistent power outputs under a range of conditions from take-off to supersonic flight. As no jet engines can operate with air forced into them at supersonic speed, when Concorde was flying at Mach 2 the intake of air to the engines had to be slowed down by 1,000 mph, and this in just 14 ft of air duct.

This impressive feat was achieved with the use of judiciously positioned electro-mechanically operated ramps and an air door within the air ducts. These could be activated to maintain the flow of air into the compressors at exactly the right speed. Combined with variable-geometry nozzles at the rear of the engines, and airflow around and past the engine, this configuration was so ingenious that, according to former Concorde engineer Ricky Bastin, at the Mach-2 cruise the Olympus itself produced just 8 per cent of net thrust, while the intake assembly produced no less than 63 per cent. (Much of the key research on the air-intake geometry had been conducted at ONERA by the French aerodynamicist Jacky Leynaert, whose book *Transport Aircraft Intake Design* was published in 1988.) Exhaust nozzles generated the remaining 29 per cent. This is why Concorde could cruise at Mach 2 unlike any aircraft before or since without afterburners engaged and why its fuel consumption was lower the faster it flew. Afterburners, which added 20 per cent thrust, were only employed on take-off and then a second time in a regular flight to push Concorde quickly beyond the sound barrier and on to its Mach-2 cruising speed, at which point they could be switched off.

The complete Concorde power plant was first tested in flight in 1966. The Avro Vulcan bomber chosen for the purpose was able to fly perfectly well with just the single Olympus 593 mounted under its fuselage. This engine produced a maximum thrust of 35,190 lbs without reheat, an impressive figure given that the first Bristol Olympus was rated at just under 10,000 lbs. Work on the engine by British and French engineers had begun in 1961, even before the Concorde treaty was signed – although Britain and France were working on the design of separate supersonic airliners until 1962, they had agreed on a common engine. Sud Aviation had displayed a model of its proposed seventy-seat, medium-range Mach-2 Super Caravelle at the Paris Air Show in

June 1961. At much the same time, BAC had unveiled a design for a long-range, 100-seat Mach-2 airliner, code-named Type 223. This had emerged from a number of proposals for STAC beginning with Type 198, a transatlantic airliner designed to carry 150 passengers. Although neither at the time had the full benefit of Küchemann's continuing researches into the ideal, or most satisfyingly compromised, wing, the Super Caravelle and the Type 223 were, scale aside, remarkably similar aircraft. As Archibald Russell of BAC said at the time, 'When we met on a common design, they hadn't any different ideas from ours. It was rather extraordinary, we thought, that two independent sets of feasibility studies and research programmes should have come out so similar to each other.'

You can see the two together in a chart that has been reproduced many times over the years showing Concorde leading a wing of its precursors. On the French side, the Super Caravelle follows with the Mirage, Griffon, Durandal and Trident supersonic jets in its elegant wake, and on the British side, Concorde is pursued by the BAC 223 (originally the Bristol 223, this was a four-engine, 100-seat Concorde template and the last all-British configuration for the airliner), TSR-2, HP.115, BAC 221, Avro Vulcan, Bristol 188 and English Electric Lightning. The chart is rather like those drawings showing primitive humanoids learning to walk erect in several stages and, shedding hair and jutting jaws, metamorphosing into *Homo sapiens*. Indeed, papers released years later by the Public Records Office confirmed suspicions that the 1959 STAC report had been handed over on the quiet to the French as an expression of the British government's desire to become a part of the EEC.

Ted Talbot, who went on to become chief design engineer for the pan-European Airbus, told funny and revealing stories about the ways the initial collaboration on a common engine for the Type 223 and Super Caravelle had begun. The first formal meeting of some twenty engineers scheduled to work on the power plant after an agreement between Bristol Siddeley and Snecma had been signed in November 1961 was held in the Hotel Le Grand, an opulent 800-room affair by Place de l'Opéra that had been designed in the approved Baron Haussmann style of the 1860s by Alfred Armand for the railway magnates Emile and Isaac Péreire and inaugurated by the Empress Eugénie in 1862. It was all rather different from the city centre of Bristol, which still at the beginning of the 1960s bore raw scars from the Blitz, and not least because, aside from Pierre Young, the Olympus 593 chief engineer, none of the British team could string together a coherent sentence in French. But then, few of the French team could speak English. What could they do? Pull out notebooks and communicate with one another in maths and drawings. And eat, drink and party together.

For the British team, there was the excitement of French food, wine and, to an extent, wild women. Off they trooped with their French hosts on their first night in Paris to Les Halles, the city's glorious central food market demolished in 1971, for *langouste et coq au vin* washed down with generous quantities of kir, wine and plum brandy at Aux Crus de Bourgogne in Rue Bachaumont, an archetypal old-school brasserie – it is still very much there – where the new entente cordiale between the French and *les rosbifs* across the Channel was toasted. And toasted again. Now fuelled and oiled, the party moved on to a show at Crazy Horse, the legendary and artistically erotic nightclub, then in its tenth year, on Avenue George V, a street named in honour of the British monarch.

It was a wonderful time to be in Paris, a city undamaged – physically – by the Second World War, and the Bristol team fell for it hook, line and sinker. The next morning, and slightly pie-eyed, they attended a key meeting to decide the shape and arrangement of the air intakes to the Olympus 593 engines. Clearly, working with the French would be hard work, but great fun, too.

The language barrier was to persist throughout the Concorde project, although the French were able to break through it first because, as the commercial aspects of Concorde became ever more important, so the language skills of Sud Aviation's international sales and engineering teams came to the fore. Between them, they had travelled the world selling the Caravelle airliner, and in doing so they had learned to speak excellent English. There were cultural barriers, too, the French working in a more formal, hierarchical manner and, to the British, seemingly all too worked up about *la patrie, la gloire, La France*. To the French, the British seemed informal, ironical and, incomprehensibly, self-deprecating. And yet while British politicians toyed with Concorde – we might cancel it, we might not – French dedication was to see the project through.

As Archibald Russell was to recall years later in his archetypically English way: 'Every bloody thing the French put forward, we'd do our best to knock it down, and everything we put forward they'd do their best to knock it down. So you couldn't get by with a loose proposition. And I think I must put part of the credit of the eventual technical success to the fact that there was no possibility of a loose decision getting through.'

Another potential barrier at this early stage, however, was measurement. The British worked with imperial measures, the French in metric. Remarkably, both Bristol and Sud Aviation, and BAC and Aerospatiale, the companies into which they were merged, continued to use their different systems. Drawings were therefore always dimensioned in both scales.

What, though, made all these ideas – theoretical and practical – fuse together was not so much the Anglo-French agreement of November 1962 but meetings held at first in Bristol in April 1960 and again in Paris in October 1962 between a small team led by Archibald Russell and William Strang from BAC Bristol and by Lucien Servanty and Pierre Satre from Sud Aviation. When the joint Anglo-French project was confirmed, it was agreed that Britain, with its experience of the Olympus, would take the lead on engines, with a French deputy director, while the French would be in charge of the airframe. Lucien Servanty, designer of the Triton, France's first supersonic jet, was appointed director of engineering with as his deputy Bill Strang, who had worked on the design of numerous Bristol aircraft from the wartime Beaufort and Beaufighter to that post-war behemoth the Brabazon, as well as the 'whispering' Britannia turboprop airliner. In turn, Servanty and Strang headed up a team of six senior engineers. Three were British – Doug Thorne, Doug Vickery and Mick Wilde – and three French – Gilbert Cormery, Etienne Fage and Jean Resch.

Responsibility for each part of the joint project, from engineering and production to sales and marketing, was divided, with the role of chairman and managing director to be held for two years at a time by a French and then a British executive. The first was General André Puget, a former Free French bomber pilot, the second Sir George Edwards of Vickers Armstrong. A charming man who, like all creative people, had an almost visceral loathing of unnecessary meetings, Edwards probably did more than anyone, along with the senior civil servant Sir James Hamilton, to maintain British support for Concorde and maintain good relations with the French. He had to intervene in heated exchanges over the question of whether or not time was being wasted on the development of the medium-range version of the supersonic airliner, a project finally abandoned in 1964. Privately, Edwards believed that 'these international programmes try men's very souls', while Brian Trubshaw noted, 'In simple, straightforward language, no single person was in charge. Recalling some of the paraphernalia attached to the project, it is a miracle that the programme actually happened.' The situation improved, however, in 1968 with the formation of a Concorde Management Board, and especially with Sir James Hamilton's appointment as director general of the Concorde division at the Ministry of Aviation.

Hamilton, a well-tempered and diplomatic Scot, had gone from being a twenty-one-year-old engineering graduate working on special weapons programmes, including the Spitfire Mk V and Mk IX floatplanes, at the Marine Aircraft Experimental Establishment, Helensburgh, via RAE Farnborough, where he was head of projects, to becoming one of Britain's highest-ranking civil servants. Determined to get Concorde built and to prove that the public would not be concerned by its breaking the sound barrier overland, he was known by his colleagues at the Ministry of Aviation – 30,000 of them in 1966 – as 'Boom' Hamilton.

Hamilton was not to succeed in the second of his aims. In his June 2012 *Guardian* obituary of him, Reginald Turnill recalled: 'A year later, as BBC air correspondent, I joined Hamilton on the ministry roof in Whitehall, as Lightning bombers [*sic*] gave Londoners a chance to consider whether they could learn to live with sonic booms. They proved to be much worse than one expert's prediction that they would only sound like the slam of a car door. Responding to political pressure, the government decided to ban supersonic flight over Britain . . . '

As for George Edwards, he was a hands-on engineer and pilot who flew himself between appointments in his own twin-engine Beagle. He had been appointed chief designer with Vickers Armstrong in 1945, and later managing director. Among the many aircraft he designed, inspired or made happen were the Viscount, the world's first turboprop airliner and a great commercial success, the Valiant V-bomber, the VC-10 jet airliner, the TSR-2, Concorde and the Panavia Tornado, a pair of which, seen from my study windows, have been making thunderous low-level practice attacks on the Tain bombing range in Easter Ross as I write. Edwards was much liked and greatly respected, as was his French counterpart, the amiable ex-French Air Force General André Puget.

Puget had been appointed from de Gaulle's general staff to the presidency of Sud Aviation in 1962. During the war, he had been commander of 346 Squadron at 'Little France', as RAF Elvington in Yorkshire was known. He flew Handley Page Halifaxes on missions to Germany and was awarded the DSO. The squadron moved to Bordeaux in October 1945 where it formed the nucleus of the post-war French Air Force. Upsettingly for the British, Puget was removed from his Concorde job and posted to Stockholm as the French ambassador to Sweden. According to Brian Trubshaw, this sudden move was 'supposedly a punishment for the rising costs of Concorde'. He was replaced by Maurice Papon, a favourite of President de Gaulle's.

As chief of the Paris police, Papon was responsible for the death in October 1961 of more than a hundred supporters of a demonstration in favour of Algerian independence. Papon had ordered a curfew. The demonstrators chose to ignore it. Papon's police opened fire on the streets of Paris, and with devastating results. Much later, in 1997, Papon went on trial for crimes against humanity. During the war, he had turned from a fiery socialist to a Nazi supporter. He sent some 1,650 Jews on trains from Bordeaux to their horrid deaths in Auschwitz. He committed other crimes in his career, yet did well under de Gaulle, and although eventually sentenced to ten years in jail, he was released after serving less than four, and died in 2007 at the tender age of ninety-six.

Fortunately, Papon's time with Concorde was brief and the Anglo-French project was to end successfully and largely happily with General Henri Ziegler in the chair. Trained as an engineer, Ziegler was a test pilot and commander of the Free French Air Force in London before becoming managing director of Air France in 1946 and president and CEO of Aerospatiale. A driving force behind Airbus, he was, like Edwards, a big-spirited and popular figure.

Meanwhile, a name for the new airliner was chosen, but its spelling, because of British political cussedness, became something of a pointless joke. The name Concorde was suggested to Sir George Edwards by Charles Gardner, BAC's publicity manager, who had got it from F. G. Clark, the publicity manager at Filton who, in turn, had been offered the name by his son, a Cambridge undergraduate. Edwards loved it, as did General Puget and even General de Gaulle. Concorde it was, except for the British government. Julian Amery, the minister of aviation and a former wartime liaison officer to the Albanian resistance movement, would have none of it. The name was good, but the 'e' would have to go. Edwards refused to give in to such chauvinistic nonsense, with the upshot that all future BAC and Sud Aviation-Aerospatiale publicity material referred to 'Concorde', while British government press releases and official documents insisted on 'Concord'.

This churlish situation was finally brought to an end on 11 December 1967, the chilly day on which Concorde 001, the first prototype, was presented to 1,100 VIPs and other guests at Toulouse. From now on, said Anthony Wedgwood Benn, Britain's minister of technology, to the assembled crowd, the British aircraft also would be called Concorde. The 'e', he said, stood for 'Excellence, England, Europe and Entente'. This seemed rather clever at the time, although, on his return from France, Wedgwood Benn faced the wrath of Scots, Welsh and Ulstermen who baulked at the 'e' standing for England.

One Scottish correspondent wrote to the English minister, 'You talk about "E" for England, but part of it is made in Scotland.' This was the nose cone. Wedgwood Benn replied, 'It is also "E" for "Ecosse"', the French name for Scotland and a clever reminder too of Ecurie Ecosse (literally, Stable Scotland), the Scottish motor racing team that won the 24-hour Le Mans race with supremely fast D-Type Jaguars in 1956 and again in 1957. In later years, the déclassé patrician Labour politician and prolific diarist now known as plain Tony Benn remarked, 'I might have added "e" for "Extravagance" and "Escalation" as well.' But Benn had flying in his blood and did a great deal to see the airliner into production; he was also to be a passenger on the very last scheduled Concorde flight from New York to London in 2003.

Throughout its long development, Concorde was threatened several times by the Labour governments in which Benn served. But not only did he believe in the benefits of technological progress, he had also been a young RAF pilot in South Africa and Rhodesia at the tail end of the Second World War. His elder brother Michael, a fellow RAF pilot who planned to become an Anglican clergyman, was killed in June 1944 flying a Spitfire over West Sussex; a faulty air speed indicator caused him to crash near Chichester. Michael and Anthony's father was the remarkable William Wedgwood Benn, a French speaker and Liberal, who at twenty-eight was the youngest MP following the 1906 general election. Resigning to fight in the First World War, he became a pilot at the age of forty and took charge of co-ordinating operations by the Royal Flying Corps and Royal Navy Air Service in Italy. He was awarded a DFC. And, then, after serving between the wars as a Labour MP, he resigned to join the RAF, flying on operational missions at the age of sixty-three. In 1945, as Lord Stansgate, he was appointed secretary of state for air. 'His physical bravery,' noted the November 1960 *Times* obituary notice of 'Wedgie' Benn, 'was matched by high moral courage, and he stood in awe of nobody.' His younger son was to prove an ideal choice as minister of technology with responsibility for Concorde with an 'e'.

Inevitably, costs continued to rise as the research and production teams tested everything connected with Concorde over and again. Even when the first aircraft took to the air, they flew some 5,500 hours before Concorde was granted the all-important certificate of airworthiness; the 747 had needed about 1,500 hours. It was just as well that the British and French governments, and their taxpayers, of course, were footing the bill for the development of Concorde. Such rigorous testing, however, was necessary not so much because calculations were out in any way, or manufacturing skills in question, but because Concorde and sustained Mach-2 flight were new territories for manufacturers and required new approaches.

Concorde was, for example, the first civil aircraft to benefit from fly-by-wire, the novel method by which the pilot's inputs to controls were sent by electronic signals along wires – there would be no more heroic heaving on 'sticks' pulled back, biceps bulging, into butterfly stomachs. And as Concorde climbed, dived and its attitudes were altered by supersonic flight, so it would be kept in trim – efficient, level flight – not by mechanical tabs on the edge of elevators, which, if they had been fitted, would have caused unwanted drag while raising fuel consumption, but by the pumping of fuel from the front to the centre or the back of the aircraft – a system that was tested on a full-sized rig. Meanwhile, because of the shape of the wings, each separate air intake for the engines was slightly different from its partners. Indeed, there was so much that was new – and, of course, exciting – that no one involved could afford the slightest error of judgement whether in thinking, testing or manufacturing: the world, along with its airlines and politicians, was watching very closely.

As some sixty airlines, as part of a committee chaired by William 'Bill' Mentzer, a senior engineer with United Airlines, became involved in the discussions over Concorde's design, the aircraft became longer and heavier than originally planned. While Concorde's engineers – even the French – agreed that the airliner's galleys could be small, and thus light, because passengers would need less to eat and drink on shortened supersonic flights, the airlines, working with a full-scale wooden model of Concorde at Filton, argued the opposite. Because Concorde was to be a luxurious form of transport, with passengers paying premium prices, galleys would need to be big enough to contain generous stocks of gourmet meals and bottles of various champagnes. So, the take-off weight grew from a planned 270,000 lbs to 400,000 lbs: 175,000 lbs worth of aircraft (engines, 52,000 lbs; airframe, 123,000 lbs), 25,000 lbs of payload and 200,000 lbs of fuel in eleven tanks to lift these 180 tons up to 55–60,000 ft and a Mach-2 cruise across the Atlantic.

Manufacturing, with a Central Programme Office and teams of civil servants in London and Paris to keep an eye on things, was carried out on a production line in Toulouse since used to make subsonic Airbuses and in the vast – and hugely impressive – hangar built for the construction of the Bristol Brabazon at Filton. Effectively, the French built the front section of the wing, the centre of the aircraft, the elevons and landing gear. The British manufactured the nose, cockpit, engine nacelles, rear fuselage, fins and rudder. The French made the leggy landing gear, Britain the alloy wheels, disc brakes (another first on an airliner) and high-performance tyres. The various systems for navigation, fuel, electrics, fire protection and air-conditioning were neatly divided between the two factories.

This duplication of everything and everyone involved in the project naturally made Concorde an expensive aircraft to build, and because of the long gap between the initial go-ahead for production in 1962 and the aircraft's entry into passenger service in 1976, many minor changes had to be made as a result of fresh research and new legislation. There were substantial changes too as Concorde grew in length and put on weight in response to demands by airlines. The giant test rigs at Toulouse and Filton used to heat and cool Concorde's airframes and to test their strength and durability were used to feed data back not only to the Anglo-French manufacturers but also, up until as late as 1983, to the airlines that flew the aircraft. Each new Concorde was expected to make 24,000 flights and to clock up at least 45,000 flight hours in its lifetime: the Filton rig tested the aircraft for 90,000 hours, above and beyond the call of service. The British government funded these development costs until 1984, when British Airways, the sole British operator, took over support costs for its supersonic flagship.

To add to all this expense, parts were shipped between the two factories by road where they could be, although sections of wings and fuselages were flown by those most unlikely of aircraft, the Aero Spaceline 377SGTs, or Super Turbine Guppies. Looking uncomfortably pregnant, these remarkable machines were freighters partly new-built and partly converted from Boeing C-97J Stratofreighters, a military type first flown in 1944 and spun off from the B-29 Superfortress. Fitted with a voluminous new fuselage and Allison turboprops, the Super

Guppies were to fetch and carry for Aerospatiale and Airbus into the mid-1990s. The civil predecessor of the C-97J was the Boeing 377 Stratocruiser, the most luxurious transatlantic airliner of its day. Watching a Super Guppy coming in to land at Filton, it was hard not to think of a Stratocruiser somehow giving birth to her supersonic successor, Concorde.

Engineers, management and eventually test pilots, too, flew backwards and forwards between the two plants set 600 miles apart. This was never going to be an efficient way of building a new aircraft, particularly one of such great complexity. One cost, though, never properly dialled into the project in the 1960s was that of noise and the sonic boom. The project seems to have gone ahead blithely in this respect, as if either no one would really notice sonic booms or, perhaps, they would simply get used to them. The short-range French version of Concorde, finally swept from the drawing boards in 1966, would have boomed its way across Europe and Africa, while at take-off and landing no one involved in the airliner's design expected it to be quieter than a Boeing 707 or a Vickers VC-10, and, fine aircraft as these were, they were noisy.

Ted Talbot tells of early days during development at Bristol when Archibald Russell insisted his team reply to all correspondence concerning matters Concorde. The engineers, with a sense of humour fashioned by the BBC's *Goon Show* and years of austerity, found it very amusing when the public wrote in asking such questions as whether the sex life of bees would be adversely affected by sonic booms or indeed what effect might strong cosmic rays in the rarefied atmosphere Concorde would fly in have on the sexual health of passengers. Replying to a clergyman worried about the damage that might be caused to stained glass windows in his church not far from Heathrow Airport, Talbot suggested that greater damage could be inflicted by the bottom note of the church organ than by a sonic boom.

While this reply appeared to have had a certain ring of scientific proof about it, anyone who was there at the time – or who has watched the brief video on YouTube of a pair of Brazilian Air Force Mirage 2000 jet fighters flying low and very fast over government buildings in Brasilia on 1 July 2012 – will know that windows can be shattered all too easily by aircraft flying in excess of Mach 1. Most of those windows in Brasilia belonged to Oscar Niemeyer's elegant Supreme Federal Court, a concrete and glass building dating from 1958, the year a French Mirage IIIA became the first European aircraft to exceed Mach 2 in level flight. The booms of the aircraft also broke glass in the twin towers of Niemeyer's National Congress building, the seat of Brazil's parliament. Perhaps it was no coincidence that the Brazilian Air Force's fleet of Mirage 2000s was taken out of service a few months later.

The noise surrounding the sonic boom – one created by protestors of all sorts – has still to quieten down, although research work continues into how an aircraft might yet be built that will fly supersonically and quietly. And yet the Concorde project was thrilling to many people, from school children to engineers and senior politicians, while bankers and business leaders could see the benefit of flying around the world in half the time it took in existing jetliners. Airlines, of course, shared in the excitement. Although the French were determined to see Concorde fly no matter what the final bill as a matter of national prestige and while the British tormented the project with questions of cost from the word go, no one had any real idea of how many Concorde aircraft would be built, although the industry talk was of 150 aircraft by 1978. The first options to buy came from Panair do Brasil in October 1961 even before the Anglo-French agreement was made. This was a legacy of Brazil's leap into the modern world driven by the charisma and energy of President Juscelino Kubitscheck, who left office earlier that year having created the new capital of Brasilia with its determinedly modern, if not Mach-proof, buildings designed by Niemeyer.

Pan Am, the first airline to fly both the Boeing 707 and 747, added its distinguished name to the list in June 1963 along with Air France and BOAC, the state-owned national carriers of France and Britain. And with Continental, American, TWA and Middle East Airlines all signing up by the end of that year, thirty-six Concorde aircraft appeared to be on order. This figure rose to more than a hundred, although it dropped to seventy-four by the time of the aircraft's maiden flight in 1969. There was no interest in the medium-range version the French team had been so keen on, not even from Air France, which is why it was finally abandoned in 1966, much to the relief of their British counterparts.

In April 1965, the first metal was cut for the two Concorde prototypes as machinists interpreted the 100,000-plus design construction drawings. Final assembly on 001 and 002 began the following year. New construction techniques were introduced to minimize drag, weight and the possibility of structural failure. Sculpture milling, for example, a method for machining from solid metal, meant it was possible to do away with welds and rivets, while every one of the one million and more parts in the aircraft was checked and checked again for weight. And finally, on 11 December 1967, Concorde 001 was rolled out from the Toulouse assembly line for the newsreel and TV cameras, press and VIPs. The weather was grim. British and French flight crews, freezing in flimsy uniforms but doing their best to grin, looked very cold indeed. This, though, was the first time the public was granted a proper look at Concorde after so many years of planning, research, politics and hype. It looked magnificent.

Despite the deepening conflict in Vietnam and the Six Day War between Israel and Egypt, 1967 had been a year of peaceful optimism, one still looked back on, nostalgically perhaps, for its liberal social reform, Flower Power, colourful clothes and the first albums by Pink Floyd and the Jimi Hendrix Experience. (The Beatles' 'Hello, Goodbye' was top of the pops as Concorde made its French debut.) This was a year, too, of great technological achievement at a time when the notion of teleological progress was still widely acclaimed, and eager audiences tuned in to *Tomorrow's World*, a BBC TV series presented at the time by Raymond Baxter, a wartime Spitfire pilot who had flown daring missions against both German V-1 and V-2 launch pads. British viewers were offered colour television for the first time in 1967. Regular colour broadcasting began on BBC2 in December, although the Wimbledon Gentlemen's Singles had been shown in colour in a test broadcast that July. The Australian player John Newcombe beat Wilhelm Bungert from Germany in straight sets. There was no grunting, pouting, emoting, high-fiving or exaggerated body language on the players' part, and there were no whoops and screams from the crowd: 1967 was a very different world from our own.

But while it was exciting to learn of US test pilots breaking a new speed record with the fixed-wing X-15 rocket plane – Mach 6.7 – and of the launch of the first Saturn V rocket, this was also the year China tested its first H-bomb, France launched its first nuclear submarine, Che Guevara fought US-trained and directed forces in Bolivia and lost, and the *Torrey Canyon*, a supertanker chartered to BP and carrying 120,000 tons of crude oil from Kuwait to Milford Haven, was wrecked off the west coast of Cornwall. Not only was the *Torrey Canyon* the biggest shipwreck in history, but it also caused an environmental catastrophe that did much to encourage campaigners to fight the very world Concorde represented. It took RAF Hunters and Fleet Air Arm Buccaneers and Sea Vixens some while to sink the US-built ship and set fire to the oil that so damaged coasts and sea life.

Elsewhere on the sea, RMS *Queen Mary*, one of the best loved of all liners, made her final Atlantic crossing, while up in the air and very much in the long shadow of Concorde at the time, the Boeing 737 made its maiden flight. By the end of 2014, more than 8,250 of these American 'buses with wings' had been built. Concorde, though, was the focus at the time. Harold Wilson's Labour government was still hoping that its shared investment with the French would finally bring Britain into the bureaucratic fold of the EEC. It was to be disappointed: shortly before Concorde 001 met the public, General de Gaulle said '*Non*' again. Here at last, though, at the end of 1967, was the aircraft that would make flying at Mach 2 as routine for regular airline passengers as it had become for test and military pilots. As Pathé News said, it gave Britain and France 'a three-year lead over America'. And, at the time, this mattered very much indeed.

FOUR

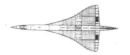

THE RIVALS

TWO days after Pan Am signed up for options to buy six Anglo-French Concorde aircraft on 3 June 1963, the US president, John F. Kennedy, announced federal backing for an all-American supersonic airliner at a speech introducing the National Supersonic Transport Program given at the US Force Academy. Naturally, the American airliner would be bigger, stronger and faster than anything the Europeans could make. Neither the American nation nor its aviation industry was going to be beaten into second place. But, given that Concorde had a head start and was scheduled to fly in 1968, how were the Americans to overtake their transatlantic rivals with an altogether more ambitious project?

In all probability, Kennedy's mind had been made up the previous year when the Anglo-French agreement was signed. Najeeb Halaby, a former test pilot, father of Queen Noor of Jordan and future chairman and CEO of Pan Am, was administrator of the Federal Aviation Agency at the time. He had written to the president suggesting that the US would lose up to 50,000 jobs, along with considerable income and capital, if it allowed the Europeans to make the running. Concorde was a real threat to the United States. In effect, though, the die had already been cast.

On 25 May 1961, the spirited JFK had told a joint session of Congress in Washington DC, 'I believe this nation should commit itself to achieving the goal, before this decade is out, of landing a man on the Moon and returning him safely to Earth.' Six weeks earlier, much to Kennedy's dismay, and alarm, a Soviet cosmonaut, twenty-seven-year-old Yuri Gagarin, had become the first man in space, beating NASA by a month. And even then, while Gagarin had made a complete orbit of the Earth, Alan Shepard – the first American in space – had managed nothing more, or less, than a sub-orbital flight lasting just fifteen minutes.

The Soviets had been first into space with the launch of Sputnik, an artificial satellite, in October 1957, the fortieth anniversary of the Russian Revolution that had brought the Bolsheviks and thus communism to power. In private, President Dwight D. Eisenhower was rather pleased that the 'Reds' were taking the first gamble, but in public his administration, along with the vast majority of Americans, was unnerved, and so much so that the launch of the tiny Sputnik is, rightly, said to have provoked the Missile Gap crisis of the early 1960s – the overriding fear was that the Russkies would blow the US to nuclear smithereens before the Americans could do the same to the USSR – while also triggering the Space Race. When he took office in 1961, President Kennedy was informed confidentially that the Missile Gap was all a bit of a nonsense. Even so, the phrase continued to echo down the decade, and American anxieties were only increased when in 1962 the USSR started shipping ballistic missiles to Cuba, which was only ninety miles from Florida, and by so doing set in motion a full-blown international crisis.

There was, though, something else that was more disturbing, belittling even. The Soviet Union had often been presented to the American public as being somehow backwards, or even backwoods. How galling then to discover that the diminutive Gagarin – he was just 5 ft 2 in – was the son of a bricklayer and milkmaid. He had been raised in a mud hut during the German occupation, and his two older siblings had been transported to Poland as slave labour. One of nineteen military pilots selected as possible cosmonauts, Gagarin clearly impressed his superiors. A space programme doctor's report of 1960 found this popular and handsome young man to be 'modest' with a 'high degree of intellectual development, fantastic memory, well-developed imagination'. He 'defends his point of view', the report went on, and, not surprisingly, given his formative years in Nazi-occupied Russia, 'understands life better than a lot of his friends'. His friends, fellow pilots, chose Gagarin – they had a vote on the matter – as the USSR's first man into space. He was a perfect poster, or propaganda, for the heroic workers' state. He was to die, at the age of thirty-four, when the MiG-15 he was test-flying crashed.

In contrast, Alan Shepard was the son of an army colonel and a pupil at the well-respected Pinkerton Academy, Derry, New Hampshire, where the poet Robert Frost had once taught. A highly experienced navy pilot, he went on to become the oldest man to walk on the Moon. He played a little golf on the lunar surface and, having risen to the rank of rear admiral, left NASA and the US Navy in 1971 to set up, successfully, in business. He was an all-American hero. Yet Gagarin had come from a peasant background and flown into space before him. Now the Americans had to land a man on the Moon before the Soviets and, if they could not get a supersonic airliner into the air before Concorde, then their SST would cruise at Mach 3 rather than Mach 2 and its superiority in long-distance flight would see it take sales from the Anglo-French airliner. Gee whiz – if the projections soon arrived at were right, there would be 500 US Mach-3 airliners in the sky by 1990.

But those darn Reds were to do it again. On 31 December 1968, a bitterly cold day of ice and drifting snow, the world's first supersonic airliner, the Soviet Tu-144, took to the air near Moscow. It flew before Concorde, broke the sound barrier before Concorde and flew at Mach 2 before Concorde, too.

The Soviet Council of Ministers had given its approval for the Tupolev airliner in June 1963, just weeks after President Kennedy announced the US SST programme. This truly was a race, but, although the Russians appeared to have won it, the Tu-144's progress did not go exactly to plan. The aircraft was plagued with problems from the start, and when the first prototype broke up over the 1973 Paris International Air Show at Le Bourget Airport and crashed into a village, killing local people along with its crew, the Tu-144 never really stood a chance. Quite coincidentally, its Anglo-French rival's apparently charmed life was also to be effectively ended by a crash near Paris, when an Air France Concorde came down after taking off from Paris Charles de Gaulle on 25 July 2000, killing everyone on board and four people on the ground.

For a few years in the mid- to late 1960s, it really did seem as though there would soon be not one but three different types of supersonic airliner booming across oceans, and, in the case of the Tu-144, steppes and other sparsely populated Soviet land masses. It was, though, the race – sponsored by politicians and cheered on by national pride on all sides – that was to prove the undoing of both the Boeing and Tupolev. Haste did indeed make waste. And budgets could be an issue too. In his memoir, *Failure Is Not An Option* (2000), Gene Kranz, the former NASA flight director who had flown F-86 Sabres in the Korean War and was to play a crucial role in bringing Apollo 13 safely home, wrote, 'When reporters asked Shepard what he thought about as he sat atop the Redstone rocket, waiting for lift-off, he had replied, "The fact that every part of this ship was built by the lowest bidder."'

While this was not true of Concorde or of the Tu-144, there was always a fear that too much pressure was being put upon researchers and manufacturers to produce these unprecedented aircraft in record time. Some members of the Tupolev team have spoken of working for up to forty-eight hours at a stretch. There had, however, from the mid-1950s been a determination by the USSR, led as it then was by Nikita Khrushchev, a herd's boy and metal worker in his early years, and from 1964 by Leonid Brezhnev, a former metallurgical engineer and wartime political commissar with the rank of major general, to prove that the Soviet Union, with its planned, state-controlled economy, could lead the world in technological advances and even into outer space.

According to Aleksei Poukhov, a Tupolev design engineer, 'For the Soviet Union to allow the West to get ahead and leave it behind at that time was quite unthinkable. We not only had to prevent the West from getting ahead, but had to compete and leapfrog them if necessary. This was the task Khrushchev set us. We knew that when Concorde's maiden flight had been set for February or March 1969, we would have to get our plane up and flying by the end of 1968.'

The American view was equally determined and dogmatic. Soon after Congress endorsed the US SST programme after the publication of a favourable report from a cabinet committee chaired by Vice-President Lyndon B. Johnson, Najeeb Halaby gave a presentation on the supersonic airliner to the American Institution of Aeronautics and Astronautics in Los Angeles. 'It's a challenge,' he said, 'to free enterprise industry to show it can compete and beat nationalized efforts of the French-British, and perhaps the Soviet Union.'

Halaby, then the administrator of the Federal Aviation Agency, was presenting the initial idea for an aircraft that would fly between 125 and 160 passengers over 4,000 miles at Mach 2.2. This was challenge enough, and industry responded by saying free enterprise could only build such a machine with federal help. Despite its rhetoric to the contrary, Washington knew this to be the case. It offered to cover 75 per cent of the development costs, with manufacturers, or the selected manufacturer, footing 25 per cent. No, said American industry. The government came back with a deal promising 90 per cent federal backing. By the time it did so, Kennedy was dead, assassinated by Lee Harvey Oswald in Dallas, Texas, on 22 November 1963.

Three airframe and three engine manufacturers were asked to submit proposals including full-scale mock-ups before deciding where the state investment would be made. This turned out to be at least $1,600 million, or more than was spent on the development of Concorde. The companies involved were Boeing, Lockheed and North American, and Curtiss Wright, General Electric and Pratt & Whitney. Even before the winning partnership was announced on 31 December 1966, airlines, including Pan Am, began placing options on the putative supersonic airliner.

The design competition had closed on 15 January 1964. All three aircraft companies had been researching high-speed commercial flight, Boeing from as early as 1952. Its designers had initially toyed with various delta-wing planes, but by 1959 the swing-wing was beginning to hold sway. In an internal competition held in 1960 for a transatlantic supersonic airliner, a swing-wing design won. A version of this design was duly put forward in 1964, and it also won, even if a public announcement to this effect was not to be made until the end of 1966.

This was no beauty pageant, but an intensely serious contest. In any case, both Lockheed and North American had pushed a long way ahead with the design of Mach-3 aircraft. Lockheed's sensational SR-71 strategic reconnaissance aircraft was later to record Mach 3.3 in level flight on 28 July 1976. Resembling a sort of flying stingray in reverse – fluid dynamics and aerodynamics overlap – and first flown shortly before Christmas 1964, this amazing aircraft was the successor to Lockheed's Mach-3 A-12, which had made its maiden flight in April 1962. Both aircraft had been designed in conjunction with the CIA as replacements for the subsonic U-2 spy plane. (As it was, the U-2 outlived them: just as Douglas DC-3 airliners continue to fly regular scheduled services in Alaska in 2015, so the subsonic U-2 remains operational and on current plans will only be retired in

2016, sixty-one years after its maiden flight.) Lockheed therefore had considerable experience with aircraft that flew at three times the speed of sound. But despite this, its 1964 SST competition entry, the CL-823, was to be less adventurous than Boeing's.

The North American entry was based on the company's XB-70 Valkyrie, the prototype for the USAF's six-engine B-70 Mach-3 bomber and of which two examples were built. The project had in fact been cancelled in 1961 but the two XB-70s were used for research into high-speed flight and in the development of the later B-1 Lancer bomber, which in its B-1B version is still in service with the USAF today. The XB-70 was a beautiful machine, designed by a team led by the wonderfully named Harrison Storms, who had also played a key role in the X-15 rocket plane of 1959, another remarkable and record-breaking North American aircraft.

As it was, North American and the engine manufacturer Curtiss Wright were dropped while Lockheed and Boeing were asked to revise their competition entries. Lockheed's L-2000-7A and bigger 7B designs revealed aircraft similar in many ways to Concorde, and many American commentators have suggested that, if the Lockheed design had been selected, Concorde might have faced a true commercial rival by 1971, the year the SST programme was cancelled. But the winning entry, the stainless steel or titanium Boeing 2707, was a stunner. There could be no doubt about that. With a length of 318 ft from nose to tail – Concorde measured 202 ft – it would have been, and still be, the world's longest airliner by far. The Boeing's twin-aisle cabin would seat between 277 and 292 passengers in a 2-3-2 configuration. Its take-off weight was to be 675,000 lbs, and with four GE turbojets, each producing 63,200 lbs of thrust, mounted below a secondary wing, it would have a maximum speed of Mach 3, cruise at Mach 2.7 and have a range of 4,250 miles. With its swing wings unfolded for take-off and landing, its wingspan would be about the same as a Boeing 747's.

The full-scale mock-up was a seductive thing, and perhaps it was the way the 2707 looked that subliminally swung the SST competition assessors in its favour. After all, the whole point of the exercise was to go one better than Concorde, and the 2707 looked like the future, better than anything yet pictured in magazines, films, comics and even such popular and prescient TV shows as Gene Roddenberry's *Star Trek*, which, from 1966, saw noble twenty-third-century Americans – and one half-human, half-Vulcan – boldly going where no man had gone before in the warp-drive starship USS *Enterprise*.

There was Gerry Anderson's prescient series *Thunderbirds*, too, filmed in glorious Supermarionation: a world of accurately depicted hypersonic airliners, and covetable space rockets, in which puppets made the running in a decade that would take Neil Armstrong and Buzz Aldrin to the lunar surface. First shown in 1965, *Thunderbirds* was broadcast in sixty-seven countries. Gerry Anderson, a Londoner by birth, did his national service with the RAF, while from 1942 Captain Roddenberry flew eighty-nine combat missions with Boeing B-17 Flying Fortresses. After the war, and before moving on to television, he flew Lockheed Constellations for Pan Am. Both must have loved the idea and aesthetic of Boeing's Mach-3 airliner. Indeed, in those days before intense security made plane-spotting difficult, expectant crowds would surely have gathered on the terrace of Heathrow's Queen's

Building and at JFK just to watch this glorious machine taxying out onto the runway, then take off and climb towards Mach 1, its wings now sweeping back to an angle of 72 degrees and merging with the tailplane and its mighty afterburning turbojets.

There was, though, at least one significant problem: that variable-geometry wing. Boeing engineers, led by the appropriately named Walter Swan, found it hard to locate the swing mechanism close enough to the slim aircraft's centre of gravity, while the sheer complexity of the thing spelt trouble ahead in everyday service and maintenance. As the engineers battled on, adding canards – small wings for extra lift – behind the cockpit, the 2707's weight increased, which meant the 2707-200, as it was designated in publicity material, would need more fuel and so would need bigger wings and so on and so forth in an upwards inflationary spiral. As General Jewell C. Maxwell, since October 1965 the director of the FAA's Office of Supersonic Transport Development and himself a highly decorated wartime B-26 Marauder bomber pilot, put it somewhat caustically, 'We had an aircraft that could go all the way across the Atlantic empty, but the airlines would not like that, or it could fly halfway across with a full load, but the passengers would not like that.'

Finally, 2707-200 was ditched and its replacement – the smaller, 234-seat 2707-300 announced in 1968 – featured an ogee delta wing and looked much like both the Lockheed SST competition design and Concorde. Boeing aimed to get this supersonic airliner airworthy in 1974. Work on full-scale mock-ups began in September 1969, by which time no fewer than twenty-six airlines, from Alitalia to World Airways, had placed options on 122 Boeing SSTs. Although there were further and far deeper problems than the question of which wing arrangement was best, Najeeb Halaby, cheerleading the SST programme, could still claim, 'The supersonics are coming, as surely as tomorrow. You will be flying one version or another by 1980 and be trying to remember what the great debate was all about.'

The 'great debate' was about the economy and the environment. Despite concerns about rising costs, the new US president, Richard Nixon, a Republican, supported SST, but there was a powerful environmental lobby concerned not just with sonic booms but also with the effect supersonic airliners might have on the ozone layer. By 1969, there was no question of airlines flying at Mach 1 and above over land. Five years earlier, the FAA had conducted six months of sonic boom tests over Oklahoma City. Citizens were exposed to eight booms a day, and, although the FAA did its best to put a gloss on the results, it received – directly or indirectly – 15,452 complaints and 490 claims for damages, mostly for shattered windows. In rejecting 94 per cent of these and generally behaving in a dismissive and arrogant manner, the FAA lost friends and influence in very high places just as, increasingly, the public began to question and turn its back on the very idea of supersonic commercial flight. Meanwhile, research at the Massachusetts Institute of Technology found that nitrous oxide in the exhausts of high-flying SSTs could indeed damage the ozone layer. Although many of the growing number of criticisms levelled at the American SST project were made by cranks, there could be no doubt that very real concerns for the environment backed by scientific research were powerful ammunition with which to shoot down the Boeing 2707.

The very word 'environment' was new for many people in the 1960s. The US was widely viewed from the outside as the great gas-guzzling consumer society where plump folk would sidle into the plush, buttoned seats of enormous automobiles powered by vast V8 engines that might just return twelve miles to the gallon, before heading off to air-conditioned shopping malls to load up with processed food. While this was not entirely fair, popular concern for the environment was very much in its infancy. The idea of a materialistic progress that would offer people more and more of whatever took their fancy still held sway. Yet somehow – and partly because of those sonic booms – the embryonic supersonic airliner was to become a very public symbol of emerging anxieties. Indeed, the SST programme was damned by what proved to be a shotgun marriage of both environmental and economic concerns.

In April 1970, various groups including the National Wildlife Federation, Friends of the Wilderness, Friends of the Earth, the Committee for Green Foothills, the Citizens' League Against the Sonic Boom and the National Taxpayers' Union banded together under the umbrella Coalition against the SST. The following month, William Proxmire, the Democrat senator from Wisconsin, was appointed chair of the Joint Sub-Committee on Economy in Government. An ardent opponent of both SST and the space programme, Proxmire fired on all cylinders, leading to a vote on the government's funding of the SST project the following year. On 18 March 1971, the House of Representatives voted 215 to 204 against all SST funding, with the Senate rejecting an amendment to restore funding by 51 to 46 votes. The repercussions were immediate. This was the end of the 2707 and with it America's place in the race to supersonic commercial flight. The economic impact on Boeing and subsidiary industries was very hard. Boeing laid off more than 53,000 employees and initially the effect was so hard on Seattle that two real estate agents, Bob McDonald and Jim Youngren, rented a billboard on South 167th Street and the Pacific Highway close to Sea-Tac (Seattle-Tacoma International Airport). It read, 'Will the last person leaving Seattle / Turn out the lights.' It was meant to be amusing.

The fate of the full-scale mock-up of the 2707-300 was quite amusing, too. Between 1973 and 1981, it was on display at the purpose-built SST Aviation Exhibit Center in Kissimmee, Florida. Two years later, the building was sold to the Faith World Church and, until 1990, the Osceola New Life Assembly of God worshipped beneath the wing of the would-be sky god that never reached the heavens, neither on a wing nor a prayer. When the church needed room to expand, the mock-up was sold to Charles Bell, an aircraft restorer, who took it in pieces to Merritt Island. Sold on to the Hiller Aviation Museum in San Carlos, California, it was later moved to the Museum of Flight, Seattle, in 2013 where, back home after its jaunt across the States, it is being restored. Among the museum's exhibits is British Airways Concorde G-BOAG, which made the type's last scheduled flight, from JFK to Heathrow, in October 2003.

If the Americans had continued with the 2707, it would have come third in the race against Concorde and the airliner popularly known as 'Konkordski'. The latter was, of course, the Tupolev Tu-144, which, as we have seen, was the first of the three to fly and the first to break the sound barrier, this in a country where there was precious little concern about noise and the environment and, even if there had been, it would have been treated as dissent and dealt with appropriately.

The Russians had certainly been in a hurry to produce their Concorde lookalike. There was much talk in the Western media of espionage, of how drawings from Filton and Toulouse had been smuggled to Moscow, of spies dressed as priests and, according to one former KGB archivist, of more than 90,000 pages of detailed technical specifications on Concorde and other Western aircraft including the Vickers VC-10 and Lockheed TriStar airliners. James Doyle, a retired electronics engineer and former communist employed as a sub-contractor in BAC's guided weapons division at Filton, went so far as to tell the *Bristol Post* and the Labour prime minister, Harold Wilson, in a letter of how he had easy access to drawings to give to the Russians and of how he had shown Concorde to a KGB agent.

No charge was ever brought against the Glaswegian engineer because nothing could be proved and, as Sir Robert Wall, a long-serving Conservative local councillor and head of costing control for Concorde at Filton, also told the *Post*, 'I know there were two warnings about Russian agents operating at the time [in 1971, when more than a hundred staff were expelled from the Soviet Embassy in London], but the information that was given over must have been virtually useless because the Tu-144 was one of the worst aircraft the world has ever seen.' Julian Amery, the minister of aviation, had his suspicions as early as 1963 when, as part of a delegation to Moscow, he was shown an early model of the Russian design that looked so very much like Concorde. It has been suggested that spoof drawings were made to fox the Russians; perhaps they were, although it seems remarkable that anyone working on Concorde could have spared the time to make them.

As it was, Neil Armstrong's first impression was of 'a fine-looking aircraft – as good as the best kind of products we're putting out'. In the case of the Tu-144, however, the age-old maxim that what looks right is right did not hold up. Aleksei Tupolev's supersonic airliner was indeed very good-looking, but it was rushed and tragedy struck it all too early in its patchy, controversial and brief career. Concorde was put through 5,495 hours of test flying before it went into service: the Tu-144 made do with 800 hours. The difference was to tell, and markedly so.

The Soviet SST was first shown to the outside world, in the form of a scale model, at the 1965 Paris International Air Show. Two years later, Sir George Edwards saw the nearly complete prototype. 'There were so many things that were transparently not right about it,' he remarked, 'that I said to young Tupolev, "You'll have to change a lot of things. You've got the intakes in the wrong place, for one. You've got too unsophisticated a design of wing, with no camber or twist, for two. And although your bypass engines will help you when it comes to airport noise, which I wouldn't have thought in Russia was a very sensitive issue, you'll lose a lot of efficiency when it comes to your cruise performance."'

Edwards was right on all scores, and the next time he saw the aircraft at the 1973 Paris Show, improvements had been made. The Russian public had been shown the light-alloy Mach-2 airliner at Moscow's Sheremetyevo Airport in May 1970. Quite what they must have thought of it is hard to imagine. Although a visible symbol of the USSR's technological prowess, here was an airliner designed to carry the Soviet elite – the aristocracy of labour, perhaps – far above the toiling masses of this workers' paradise. They might also have asked, but for how long?

Although the Tu-144 would fly at Mach 2.2, it could only do this, unlike Concorde, with afterburners blazing at the rear end of its four Kuznetsov NK-144 twin-spool turbofans. This heavy expenditure of fuel would severely limit its range. In addition, along with the aircraft's cooling system, these engines were noisy. A flight on a Tu-144 was not for those with sensitive hearing. Who really cared, though, when what mattered most was the fact that, on 31 December 1968, the Tu-144 took to the air ahead of Concorde? But then, on 5 June 1973, 'Konkordski' fell from the sky, and from credibility and grace as well. The sorry occasion was the Paris Air Show. Concorde was there too, and put on a graceful display for the 250,000-strong crowd, including a soaring climb, afterburners on, to 10,000 ft. The Russians, it seems, were determined, or under instruction, to out-perform their capitalist rival, although, of course, Concorde was also essentially a state project. The Tu-144S – the second production prototype first flown in March 1972 – was in what should have been the capable hands of Mikhail Kozhov, an experienced test pilot and Hero of the Soviet Union, and co-pilot Valery Molchanov. What happened next is historical fact, but quite why it happened remains a farrago of uncertainty, doubt and conspiracy theories.

Kozhov came down towards the runway as if to land, or to touch-and-go, and then blasted up into a rocket-like climb. At somewhere around 2,000 ft, the aircraft stalled, pitched into a dive and, with the airframe under unbearable pressure, broke up, one wing tearing off and then the other. It smashed into a hotel at Goussainville, killing eight villagers and all six on board, among them the Tu-144's deputy chief designer, V. N. Benderov. Why on earth had Kozhov pushed the airliner so very hard? One theory is that he had spotted a French Air Force Mirage flying too close for comfort, and that this was a spy plane. There is no documentary evidence of this, and although no one knows for certain even today – the Russians remained silent – it does seem that Kozhov had reacted as if trying to avoid another aircraft. As he pulled up suddenly, the Tu-144's engines flamed out and, as he tried to re-ignite them in a dive, the aircraft was pushed beyond its structural limits.

The crash did not affect sales of the Tu-144. There was no market, nor was there intended to be one, for Tupolev's SST. It existed solely to beat the West. Even Aeroflot had qualms about it; the national airline would have been happier without the Tu-144 in its fleet. Test flights over the Soviet Union, from Moscow to as far as Vladivostok, continued between 1974 and 1977. Finally, after operating between the two cities, 1,800 miles apart, as a freight and mail plane, the Tu-144S went into weekly service on 1 November 1977 between Moscow Domodedovo and Alma-Ata (now Almaty), which, at the time, was the capital of Kazakhstan.

Just fifty-five return flights were made. These were rarely more than half-full and each flight was a major event and a source of concern. Aleksei Tupolev was required to attend each departure from Moscow, and even then the Tu-144s suffered 226 failures, eighty in flight, meaning delays, cancellations and heart-stopping diversions. It was not even as if the Mach-2 airliner was luxurious. Aside from being inordinately noisy, the cabin was a pretty primitive affair fitted with thin seats covered in garish orange and blue fabrics and with lockers faced in swirling, marble-pattern plastic. There was no underfloor hold. Lighting was erratic and lavatories often out of service. It was as if little or no concern had been given to the very idea that passengers might actually fly in the Tu-144.

Nine Tu-144s flew with Aeroflot. There were seven other Tu-144s: the prototype, a pre-production model and five Tu-144Ds used as freighters. The latter were fitted with improved engines and able to operate on longer-distance flights, as far as Khabarovsk in eastern Siberia. The project was cancelled in 1983, although US finance came to the rescue of the last of the aircraft to be assembled. With just eighty-two flying hours, this modified Tu-144LL was employed jointly by NASA and the Soviet Space Agency in the training of pilots for Russia's Buran space shuttle, which was cancelled after just one flight following the collapse of the Soviet Union, and by Tupolev's Air Development Centre in a high-speed research programme. It made twenty-seven flights in all between 1996 and 1997.

Significantly, perhaps, Tupolev might have produced a supersonic airliner based on an advanced military design, the Tu-135, which was developed under the direction of Sergei Yeger alongside the early stages of the Tu-144. An arrow-like, multi-purpose long-range reconnaissance aircraft and airborne missile platform capable of Mach 2, the Tu-135 was cancelled partly because of cost and partly because Moscow decided it had to follow the lead of the Americans with a swept-wing B-1 clone. (First flown in December 1981, this was the Tu-160 'Blackjack', today the largest and fastest bomber in service with a maximum speed of Mach 2.05.) But Yeger had still managed to work up three civil versions of the Tu-135. He attempted to convince Tupolev that this was the best way to proceed, but there was external pressure to produce an airliner similar to Concorde and the Tu-135 remains one of those haunting 'What if?' aircraft with compelling looks and an impressive specification that never made it into the air.

Military versions of the Tu-144 itself were worked up from the early 1970s. These were to launch ICBMs and, later, cruise missiles from high altitudes, while one of the last attempts to interest the military was a naval reconnaissance and strike aircraft, but the commander of Soviet Naval Aviation, Aleksandr Mironenko, was as unswayed as his air force colleagues: the Tu-144 in whatever guise would be a complex, fuel-hungry and demanding machine unsuited to the needs or mind-set of the military. When he had his first look over a Tu-144, Brian Trubshaw said it felt like a cross between an SST and a Second World War bomber. The Soviet Union encouraged adventurous new technological design even when it insisted on a determinedly traditional and often reactionary view of art, music and architecture. In its frenzied haste to beat the West and to prove that communism was superior to capitalism and a totalitarian state better than a democracy, it tended to push too hard for speed in design and construction, flying, as it were, before it could jump. And all too many designs were planned with military use in mind. When combined, these factors all but ensured that 'Konkordski' would fail. On the part of its engineers, it had been a bold and brave effort, but one that lacked the subtlety, patience and long-term application devoted to Concorde. It had, though, if only for a very short while, been a black eye for the Americans. But now, with the Boeing 2707 and Tupolev Tu-144 out for the count, Concorde had the supersonic skies to herself.

FIVE

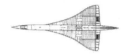

CLEARED
FOR TAKE-OFF

BAD weather had delayed the occasion for several days, but finally on 2 March 1969, the mist lifted, flocks of birds were scattered and Concorde 001 roared into a cold, windy sky above Toulouse. A twentieth-century sky god was born. But although it looked divine from the ground, this first prototype was packed inside with a jumble of weighty scientific and avionic equipment restricting the amount of fuel carried, while its extended crew, captained by André Turcat, were garbed in outfits that looked more suited to a space rocket than the world's most glamorous airliner.

Afterburners on and accelerating hard up to 235 mph, with its distinctly Gallic nose pointing disdainfully towards the ground, Concorde climbed as expected and flew well nigh perfectly, up to 10,000 ft and 275 mph for twenty-seven minutes, undercarriage down throughout. Küchemann's theories on vortices and lifts held, as did the ideas and intensive hard work of so many engineers, mechanics and administrators over the past seven years.

Journalists and TV camera crews from around the world had gathered to witness this special moment. 'She flies! She flies!' exclaimed an emotional Raymond Baxter covering the event for the BBC. As F. G. Clark of BAC noted in his 1975 book *Concorde: the story of the world's most advanced passenger aircraft*, 'In cold blood there may have seemed something faintly ridiculous about his choice of words – what was Concorde mean to do but fly? – but at Toulouse that morning [it was the afternoon, in fact] there were not many cold-blooded onlookers.' And, forty minutes later, Clark reported, 'She came into view and for the first time they [the assembled media] saw that characteristic "sea-bird" swoop in to land. A puff of smoke . . . the nose wheel came down, reverse thrust was engaged and the tail parachute broke from its housing to balloon out behind the aircraft. Safely down! Around the airfield there was a rattling of clapping and applause . . . there were lumps in some throats and tears in some eyes, including those of experienced journalists who one would have thought had seen everything.'

Appearing at the top of the steps, Turcat gave a thumbs up and came down to give reporters his favourable impressions. Put through its paces like no other airliner before it, Concorde 001 was retired less than five years later, in October 1973, and placed in the care of the French Aerospace Museum at Le Bourget. It had made 397 flights and broken the sound barrier 249 times. Turcat himself later gave a moving appraisal of this historic aircraft:

> It was too noisy and smoky. It didn't have the required range for North Atlantic crossing. It was cluttered with test instrumentation . . . the ashtrays were full.

But it had seen a damned lot. It was the first to carry 140 tonnes supersonically. It had flown from 110 to 1,240 knots. It had crossed the South Atlantic in two hours. It had dived, climbed, rolled, yawed and surged more than anyone. Four thousand times, maybe, it had been given modifications. It has been a docile tool in the hands of ten test pilots and twenty airline captains. It has carried the most important persons. It had spent more than one hour in a total eclipse of the Sun [flying faster than the Sun for the benefit of astronomers on board] and no one can, nor will for a long time, beat this unique record. It had measured nitric acid and the stratosphere and seen, at sunset, the ozone layer shadow on the sky. It had given us the biggest thrills of our careers, and heralded a new transport era for the world. In return, we just loved it.

Brian Trubshaw flew Concorde 002 for the first time from Filton on 9 April 1969. He had already flown 001, thanks to an invitation from Turcat. The British maiden flight did not go quite as smoothly as its Gallic counterpart. After three days of trying to take off but held back by faulty instruments, Trubshaw was relieved to get going at last. Unlike Turcat, who enjoyed the long, purpose-built and state-financed runway at Toulouse that continues to serve Airbus so well, Trubshaw had to punch 002 up and away over the A38 at the end of the much shorter English runway. The road was closed, with police holding up traffic. Coming in to land, twenty minutes later, at RAF Fairford, the Gloucestershire air base with a runway built in the early 1950s for heavy, long-range US bombers (B-52s flew from here to Iraq in 2003), a light plane had a near miss with the new supersonic airliner and then at 1,000 ft both Concorde's radio altimeters decided to play up.

'This was definitely unfriendly,' recalled Trubshaw. 'The radio altimeter measures height above ground very accurately and its use was, and is, standard procedure for the last part of any approach.' Experienced, and intuitive, pilot that he was, Trubshaw 'eyeballed the landing' and placed the aircraft a little firmly, but accurately, on the runway. The Filton party returned to base, leaving 002 at Filton. There were presents for the crew, an enormous cake baked by Sheila Scott, the model and actress turned record-breaking pilot. Then it was off to a favourite 'hostelry', and as Trubshaw wrote, 'so ended a memorable day with a thick head to look forward to'.

This was a world before drink-and-driving laws, and thick with cigarette smoke, on board aircraft as well as in country pubs. When, on *Desert Island Discs*, Roy Plomley had asked Sheila Scott to choose one luxury, she plumped unhesitatingly for 'tobacco seeds'. She died from lung cancer. And when Brian Trubshaw was being shown the controls of the Mirage IV used in Concorde testing at Toulouse, his colleague, the French Air Force pilot Gilbert Defer, smoked all the while, dropping cigarette ash into the cockpit of the supersonic jet bomber.

It was also, in Britain at least, a part-comic, part-tragic world of high technological achievement, official ineptitude and fickle politicians with little or no love for design, industry and infrastructure. As Tony Benn – the former Hon Anthony Wedgwood Benn, or 'Tone' to his trade union chums – told Sue

British know-how: cancelled in 1946, the bullet-shaped Miles M.52 could have been the first aircraft through the sound barrier. Its design informed that of the record-breaking American Bell X-1.

British know-how 2: *papier mâché* and sticky tape models, made by W. E. Gray of the Royal Aircraft Establishment, Farnborough, were part and parcel of early wind-tunnel tests for Concorde.

LEFT: First flown in 1961, the pretty HP.115 demonstrated the practicality and efficacy of a slim delta wing in slow-speed flight, essential to the development of a supersonic airliner.

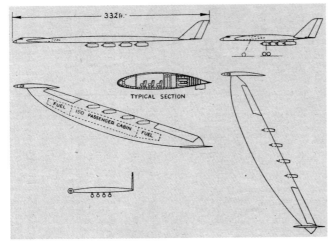

332ft.

TYPICAL SECTION

FUEL   ISO   PASSENGER CABIN   FUEL

LEFT: Proposals for Concorde before the Anglo-French joint development agreement included such radical ideas as this slew or sycamore-wing Handley Page design of 1961. The passenger cabin is in the wing.

RIGHT: The airflow characteristics of Concorde's ogee delta wing were further probed from 1961 by the beautiful and very fast BAC 221, a research aircraft converted from this Fairey Delta 2.

LEFT: Born into the Space Age, Concorde 001 was displayed at the Paris Air Show in 1967: a Braniff Airways hostess models a pink Pucci uniform complete with space-bubble helmet.

BELOW: 'Finally, the big bird flies.' Flown with nose and wheels down by Andre Turcat, Concorde 001 took to the air for the first time from Toulouse on 2 March 1969.

RAF Fairford, 9 April 1969: police halt local traffic as Brian Trubshaw lands Concorde 002 at the end of its maiden flight from Filton, narrowly missing a wayward light aircraft.

Andre Turcat (*centre*) and Brian Trubshaw (*right*) directed Concorde's French and British test flights. Both Second World War veterans handled the media well, shoring up popularity for the controversial airliner.

Seen here on the first scheduled Air France flight from Paris to Rio de Janeiro on 21 January 1976, Concorde's busy cockpit was rather like that of a military jet.

ABOVE: Concorde assembly at Aerospatiale, Toulouse. Talk of the manufacture and sale of hundreds of aircraft proved to be wishful thinking. Ultimately, just twenty Concorde aircraft were built, including prototypes.

LEFT: Concorde was a joint Anglo-French project and yet, with nose cone drooped, the aircraft had a distinctly Gallic profile, like that of a Citroën DS or a superior French president.

Accompanied by a Soviet MiG-21 fighter, a Tu-144 prototype dubbed 'Concordski' took to the air in bitterly cold weather on New Year's Eve 1968, weeks ahead of its Anglo-French rival.

Boeing abandoned its swing-wing Mach 3 2707-200 Concorde rival in 1968. Work on a fixed wing 2707-300 began in 1969, getting no further in production terms than this elegant mock-up.

Lord Nelson and the French might have had their cacophonous run-ins, yet the Anglo-French Concorde, seen soaring over Trafalgar Square, was a triumph of shared technological endeavour and international diplomacy.

MacGregor during the recording of BBC Radio 4's *The Reunion*, 'Concorde's UK debut was a hilarious day. [BAC's] George Edwards was walking around, with a pork-pie hat, like a vicar saying he hoped it wouldn't rain. Trubby [Trubshaw] was saying, "It's the paperwork holding us back." It was really like Biggles or Just William. The whole thing was immensely British and quite unlike the French – the French do it with much more panache.' Indeed, when 001 had been rolled out of Filton on 19 September 1967, there had been no ceremony, no guests, no press and certainly no champagne and smoked salmon as there had been at Toulouse the previous December. There was only the workforce to give the thumbs up. Neither Anthony Wedgwood Benn nor Sir James Hamilton, director general of Concorde at the new Department of Trade and Industry, had been invited.

The two prototype aircraft met for the first time in June 1969 at the Paris International Air Show, where they performed separate displays. The British aircraft was commandeered to fly over Buckingham Palace at 1,000 ft a few days later as a birthday greeting to the Queen, while the French plane went supersonic on 1 October. A week later, pilots from Air France, BOAC, Pan Am and TWA got to fly 001. Its British sibling 002 went supersonic on 25 March 1970. Tested intensively over seven years, it made its last flight to the Royal Naval Air Station, Yeovilton, in July 1976 and has remained on display there ever since inside the Fleet Air Arm Museum.

What had got Trubshaw's goat was the government's amateur attitude towards the rigorous flight-test programme necessary for Concorde to develop from a promising prototype into a fully fledged commercial airliner. Fairford was made available for Concorde test flights only because BAC's vice-chairman, Sir Geoffrey Tuttle, was a friend of Air Chief Marshal Sir Thomas Prickett, C-in-C Air Support Command. There was a lot to be done in terms of new buildings as well as test plants and a hangar. While none of the work itself was slapdash, an air of official indifference hung over Fairford. As Trubshaw noted in his 1998 memoir, *Brian Trubshaw: Test Pilot*, 'The French did not stand still on establishing facilities . . . Toulouse has never looked back and has gone on and on expanding for Airbus until it is now as good a facility as one can see anywhere in the world. This is an illustration of a country with a government determined to have an aircraft industry and one without any degree of consistency.'

The same, of course, had been happening on the railways. While the French state railways pushed ahead with a profitable new high-speed railway network, and TGV (Train à Grande Vitesse) trains have run on it at speeds of up to 200 mph since 1981, British governments played a cat-and-mouse, or stop-go, game with railway finances until the late 1990s, before privatizing them and thus ensuring that investment would be patchy, speeds low compared with other European countries and fares among the world's highest. The TGV might be seen as the Concorde of the rails, even if it lacked any British involvement. The fastest long-distance run to date has been a journey from Calais-Fréthun to Marseilles to launch the TGV Méditerranée in May 2001: the 663 miles were reeled off in three hours and twenty-nine minutes – much the same time as Concorde flew from New York to London – at an average speed of 190 mph.

British governments did their best to give Concorde a hard time. This seemed especially disingenuous given the desire of both Conservative and Labour governments from the late 1950s to join the EEC. Just as the exemplary network of ultra-modern TEE (Trans-Europe Express) trains, linking 130 cities in style and created in 1957, the same year as the Treaty of Rome, was an expression of a new European spirit of unity, so was Concorde meant to be. If Britain was serious about EEC membership, then it had to take Concorde seriously. When, though, Harold Wilson's Labour government took office in October 1964, Concorde was given something of the British Railways' treatment. Now the investment was on, now it was off. No wonder General de Gaulle had little time for post-war British governments, or for perfidious *rosbifs* in general.

By autumn 1964, the British contribution to Concorde had risen from £150 million to £280 million and this in just two years. Roy Jenkins, the eloquent new minister of aviation, was sent to Paris to say that Britain was pulling out of Concorde. While his flight to Paris waited on the tarmac at Heathrow, Jenkins had been handed a Foreign Office telegram that contained the encouraging information: 'The Minister of Aviation should be prepared for the atmosphere of cold enmity with which he will be met in Paris.' And as the *Daily Telegraph*'s Paris correspondent noted, 'If a dispute arises over the amount of compensation which Britain would be required to pay for breaches of contract, France in her current mood would be ready to take it to the International Court at The Hague.' The British wavered.

As it was, De Gaulle was hardly impressed by Jenkins, although in a curious twist of fate, the future Labour chancellor of the exchequer, home secretary and very liberal political opportunist was to become Britain's first, and to date only, president of the

European Commission. The French leader slapped a 'total ban' on meetings between senior French Concorde executives and their British colleagues: this would continue until the British made a firm decision either way. The British government's unacceptable behaviour, said Jean-Jacques Servan-Schreiber, the editor of *L'Express*, risked turning 'a fairly simple technical affair' into 'an extremely unwholesome political conflict', adding, 'The consequences of the behaviour will cost much more than the savings on the Concorde project.'

Jenkins stuck to his guns, although there was nothing he could do to put further political chocks under Concorde's wheels. As he told the Concorde Symposium held by the Institute of Contemporary History at the Science Museum in 1998, 'The Anglo-French agreement had been made in 1962 by my predecessor Julian Amery, with a good deal of, I thought, anti-American rodomontade, and the very tight treaty which had been signed with the French was more suited, again in my view, to a matter concerning a nation's honour than its commercial investment decisions . . . it was a typical example of government rushes of blood to the head.'

Newly re-elected in March 1966 with a majority of ninety-six seats in the House of Commons, Wilson's government turned its guns on Concorde again. Matters began to change the following April when Anthony Wedgwood Benn, the minister of technology, took over responsibility for Concorde. Speaking on *The Reunion*, Tony Benn said that, while Westminster was using Concorde as a key to unlocking the door to EEC membership, Harold Wilson 'didn't trust the French'. It was an absurd and disturbing situation and one on which an increasing number of British jobs – up to a quarter of a million by the early 1970s – depended. 'You can argue whether it should ever have started,' said Benn. 'But what I found so interesting in relation to the criticism of Concorde was you never heard any criticism of supersonic military aircraft and we were building them all the time, and so there was something special about hating Concorde.'

While this is not exactly true, with both Conservative and Labour governments of the time cancelling supersonic military aircraft, there did indeed seem to be something about Concorde that riled a certain breed of politician. (It was to take until July 1974 before Harold Wilson, back in office again, ratified an order for sixteen production aircraft with the French president, Giscard d'Estaing.) But Benn, former RAF fighter pilot and an energetic minister, had adored Concorde from the start and made a point of offering free test flights to shop-floor workers, saying, 'What organization asks people to build aircraft, but never lets them fly?' He remembered one flight around the Bay of Biscay. 'It was lovely . . . we had sandwiches' – although at least one mechanic seemed unsure of his own handiwork: 'One man said to me, rather discouragingly, that he had taken last communion and I thought that as he'd built the plane that was a bit pessimistic.'

The Bay of Biscay was one of Concorde's test-flight circuits, a narrow path between the west coast of Scotland, Ireland, the Cambrian coast and Cornwall another. These routes allowed Turcat, Trubshaw and their colleagues to build up speed, cautiously, until, from November 1970, the prototypes were cruising at Mach 2. On the way to this great speed, low-speed handling characteristics were tested to their limits. The test pilots had a number of causes for concern, among them surging engines, unfamiliar stalls and engine smoke filtering into the cockpit through the air-conditioning system. These matters were dealt with systematically; what everyone agreed is that Concorde was a delight to fly.

As for the French, they appear to have had few doubts about Concorde before it flew. And, if they did, they were not telling, keeping up a united front. As Henri Perrier, former chief engineer of the Concorde division at Aerospatiale, recalled in 1998, there was 'very high pressure of opinion from the left to the right of the political spectrum. This included the Communist Party, which always supported the programme in France, just because the Russians were developing the same type of aircraft in parallel, so there was no argument to say it is only an aircraft for rich people.'

British trade unions were, by and large, dedicated to Concorde, too: during its development and production, Concorde spawned and nurtured tens of thousands of skilled jobs. As Brian Trubshaw remembered: 'I don't think anybody should underestimate the influence that the unions exerted on some people, particularly Wedgwood Benn, because I recall a mass meeting at Filton, all Rolls-Royce, all British Aerospace, which in those days came to something like 10,000 or 15,000 people, and during the course of that occasion, when they were all out on the airfield being addressed by Wedgwood Benn, he received a note which said, "Remember one thing: your job depends on us and we depend on you."'

Flights, meanwhile, were gradually extended – across the South Atlantic from Toulouse to Rio de Janeiro via the Cape Verde islands in September 1971 – while a week before Christmas that year the first pre-production aircraft, Concorde 01, made its first flight as 001 had done from Filton to Fairford. As Concorde flew ever further from Toulouse and Filton, it was clear the aircraft was loved and loathed in equal measure. To young people, the aircraft was a wonder. To older people, Concorde could be a noisome menace. To conservationists, this thunderous machine was an evil angel spreading pollution and destruction; hell, it might even have been a conspiracy to sap and impurify all of our precious bodily fluids. To many American politicians, and certainly from 1971, when the Boeing 2707 was cancelled, Concorde was anathema.

While a somewhat unholy alliance, if not exactly a conspiracy, of the conservation lobby and American chauvinism was to severely delay Concorde's acceptance into New York – its key and economically essential destination – the aircraft did make many friends, even among British politicians. Lord Carrington, the defence secretary in Edward Heath's modernizing Conservative government, was quick to make a test flight with his fellow minister, the trade and industry secretary John Davies. The prime minister himself followed soon afterwards, although not before President Georges Pompidou, who – eyebrows arched, no doubt – had given his approval that same year, 1971, to the winners of the international architectural competition for the design of the radical arts centre in the heart of Paris that would bear his name. The architects were Richard Rogers and Renzo Piano, with Peter Rice as structural engineer. Here was architecture as modern, thrilling and as controversial as Concorde itself.

Prince Philip, a highly experienced aircraft and helicopter pilot, flew Concorde, as did the Shah of Iran, himself a pilot since 1946, when he had flown against the Soviets then occupying the north of his kingdom. The Queen was taken up, as was Donald Duggan, the archbishop of Canterbury, who said as he peered through one of the airliner's necessarily tiny windows over Gander, Newfoundland, 'I have never been closer to God.' On the aircraft's first major international tour, which took in Greece, Iran, India, Thailand, Singapore, the Philippines, Japan, Australia, Saudi Arabia and Lebanon during June and July 1972, Concorde landed back in Heathrow to be greeted by, among others, noisy protestors. Many had written postcards complaining about its noise on arrival; these, it was noted, had been posted a day earlier. Whatever its faults from an environmental point of view, it was clear from early on that Concorde was not going to get a fair trial.

In 1963, the *Observer* printed a two-part piece by Andrew Wilson, its aviation correspondent, under the headline 'The Supersonic Threat'. This was based on a recently published report, *Speed and Safety in Civil Aviation*, by Bo Lundberg, the director of the Swedish Aeronautical Research Institute. Lundberg concluded that supersonic airliners would be a commercial failure, would cause distress and damage property on the ground and would damage the ozone layer. In brief, Lundberg thought supersonic civil aviation unwise. Richard Wiggs, a schoolteacher and habitual campaigner, who proved to be a powerful enemy to Concorde, took up the cause in 1967.

Wiggs was a Quaker from Letchworth in Hertfordshire, the first, idealistic garden city; his parents owned a bicycle shop there. When he was twelve, he led a protest to save a local marshland from being turned into a cricket pitch. At fourteen he became a vegetarian, converting to veganism in later years. A pacifist and conscientious objector, he taught children with learning difficulties while finding his feet as a more or less full-time objector. He campaigned for CND (Campaign for Nuclear Disarmament) before turning on Concorde. As Jerry Ravetz, his obituarist in the *Independent*, wrote, 'When Wiggs launched his attack, the Anglo-French Concorde was still an icon of the technological euphoria of the 1960s. Environmental campaigns were generally dismissed as the province of bearded, be-sandalled vegetarians, all of which stigmata Wiggs bore proudly.'

Wiggs' concern with the dangers of supersonic flight was ignited when, in July 1967, Benn's Ministry of Technology organized that sequence of eleven test flights at Mach 1 plus over London and southern England, with RAF Lightnings performing the dubious honours. The ministry received 12,000 complaints, while Wiggs attracted an impressive array of scientists to his cause – one he promoted vigorously in letters and advertisements in the national press and science magazines – including Fellows of the Royal Society and at least one Nobel Prize winner, the physicist Sir Nevill Mott, who became chairman of Wiggs' Anti-Concorde Project.

'We had allies in the USA,' noted Mott in his biography, *A Life in Science* (1986), 'who successfully opposed the development of supersonic transport there.'

One of these was William Shurcliff, a Harvard physicist who had played an important role in the wartime Manhattan Project, through which the US developed the atomic bombs dropped from the bays of Boeing B-29 Superfortresses on Hiroshima and Nagasaki in August 1945. He was horrified by the destructive power of the weapon he had helped bring into being. As if to atone for nuclear weapons, he became an active promoter of passive solar energy and super-insulation and, in 1967, an associate of the Anti-Concorde Project. At the same time, Shurcliff formed the Citizens' League Against the Sonic Boom; as he told the *Harvard Crimson*, the Ivy League college's daily newspaper, 'We all believe in progress, but some things just aren't progress.' In 1970, he published his *SST and Sonic Boom Handbook*, predicting Concorde's imminent obsolescence.

Wiggs, meanwhile, did everything he could to attract attention to his cause, including driving his 1927 Rolls-Royce – perhaps not the most fuel-efficient car – around the roundabouts at Heathrow, doing his best to hold-up traffic. Concorde, he claimed, was not just an environmental threat, but 'elitist and inherently unsafe', too. Later, after the airliner's one fatal crash in 2000, he suggested that Concorde's total number of flying hours was paltry compared with that of a Boeing and thus its safety record was not as impressive as it might have seemed. Wiggs might have been eccentric but he galvanized a powerful anti-Concorde lobby into action across Britain, the United States and, before too long, many other parts of the world. He even flew across the Atlantic to help organize opposition to Concorde, meeting with Caroline Berman, an aide to New York Democrat politicians and whose home in Nassau County stood directly under the flight path chosen for Concorde, and the Emergency Coalition to Stop the SST.

Quite how divided public opinion was in Britain and France, it is hard to say. Very many people were thrilled by Concorde's progress. Its maiden flights were shortly before the Apollo 11 mission to the Moon and, especially for the young, there was perhaps no intellectual or emotional gap between the sight of Concorde or looking lovingly upon the hauntingly beautiful photographs of the Earth taken by the Apollo 8 crew, which were used almost immediately afterwards in the promotion of environmental causes.

For those living under Concorde's flight paths, however, and for those who revelled in protest, the airliner disgraced itself almost every time it flew. The twenty flights made at Mach 2 from late 1970 between the west coast of Scotland and Cornwall led to reports of panic among local people as well as farm animals along with broken windows and crockery. The government paid damages. When on 13 September 1970, Concorde 002 had been diverted to Heathrow due to bad weather, the airport's switchboard was jammed with calls. Five years later, the noise problem remained unresolved from a technical point of view, although, in Britain at least, it was addressed by an exception made at national level that allowed Concorde into and out of Heathrow despite the noise. This did not satisfy the Greater London Council, but Concorde was not just another civil airliner: it represented the national interest.

Certainly, one problem the prototype aircraft faced was the fact that because of its wing shape and the high angle of approach this demanded as it came in to land at Heathrow, as elsewhere, pilots had to keep the power on until the last moment. This meant louder than normal landings. The following year, 1971, the British Airports Authority admitted as much when it published figures demonstrating that Concorde was twice as noisy as other airliners. It got away with it because it was allowed to do so by the British authorities, although as Andrew Wilson wrote in his book *The Concorde Fiasco* (1973), 'There was no reason why other countries should be so obliging.'

As early as December 1970, commercial supersonic flights were banned over the United States and noise levels restricted at US airports. This was to the satisfaction of many US politicians and environmental campaigners. But as Boeing's design director Lloyd Goodmanson was later quoted as saying in *The Times* of 3 April 1976, 'Much of the official opposition to giving British Airways and Air France landing rights for Concorde was based on pure jealousy of their commercial lead.'

Some months before the publication of Wilson's pugnacious book, Pan Am and TWA cancelled their options for orders to buy Concorde. Even if the airliner was banned from flying over the States, it could always pay its way on routes across Asia to Australia, for example. However, a flight from London or Paris to Sydney would require at least one more stop than a Boeing 747, thus narrowing the gap between supersonic and subsonic airliners, while Charles Gardner, BAC's chief press officer, did little to help Concorde's cause when he suggested that the airliner's supersonic path over the Australian bush would 'only affect a bunch of old Abos'.

The effect of the anti-Concorde lobby was to dramatically restrict the routes Concorde would be able to fly. After much debate in the US, British Airways and Air France were given permission to fly into Washington Dulles International in May 1976. But when, at the same time, a federal ban was lifted on New York for an experimental sixteen-month trial, the city slapped its own on Concorde, a decision that was finally overturned by the Supreme Court the following year. But not before Carol Berman's

Emergency Coalition to Stop the SST had helped inflict serious wounds on the Concorde programme.

When in 2003 news broke that Air France was dropping Concorde, the then seventy-nine-year-old Berman was interviewed by the *New York Times*. Although New York's anti-Concorde lobby had met its match in the guise of the Supreme Court, she claimed, 'We made the [New York] Port Authority agree to limit the number of aircraft to be built to thirteen [*sic*], and obviously, the planes are going to wear out,' adding that 'opponents successfully lobbied to limit the flights to two a day per carrier. And we knew that could never be economically feasible with its small number of seats.'

Where Richard Wiggs had attempted to disrupt traffic at Heathrow Airport at the wheel of his vintage Rolls-Royce, Berman organized two cavalcades of 250 cars driving in both directions through the airport at 5 mph and with the support of Port Authority officials. The *New York Times* reminded its readers that even nuns had protested, with Sister Mary Lou Tressy recalling that when the jets first rumbled over Our Lady of Grace School, Howard Beach, where she was principal, 'she and several students got fifteen gallons of white paint and wrote "Stop the SST" on the roof.' Significantly, though, Jonathan L. Gaska, district manager of the local community board, told the newspaper why he was 'doubly thrilled' at knowing that Concorde was coming down to earth: 'We won't have the noise aggravation, plus the French are losing money.'

The enemies at Concorde's departure gate were joined hand-on-typewriter across the Atlantic. In January 1977, eleven months before Concorde began flying to New York, Peter Gillman, an experienced *Sunday Times* journalist, wrote a two-part article for *Atlantic Monthly* effectively condemning what his American sub-editor labelled 'the benighted offspring of Anglo-French diplomacy and once-and-future dreams of glory in the skies'. Gillman painted a memorable portrait of Gerald Kaufman, Britain's then secretary of state for industry, and his entourage pleading for Concorde at the hearings held by US Transportation Secretary William Coleman in January 1976. 'It was an unusual experience for British politicians and officials to participate in the rough-and-tumble of American political lobbying, or take part in a rowdy debate with Concorde opponents . . . All that they wanted was for Concorde to be given "a chance" . . . let us fly into New York, the British pleaded, and we can pretend that Concorde is not the most disastrous investment decision Britain has made since the war.'

Describing Morien Morgan's STAC report of 1959 as 'a powerful mix of brilliant aerodynamics and disreputable propaganda', Gillman noted how, shortly before his death in March 1976, Dietrich Küchemann described how Philip Hufton, head of the RAE's aerodynamic department, invented the figure for the investment needed for the SST: 'It was done on the basis of let me see, what will the politicians stand. In the whole STAC report, these estimates are the only thing that are rubbish. I have a very bad conscience about that.'

Gillman's aim, while telling a very good story, was to highlight the fact that Concorde was an exceedingly costly act of political vanity. As Morien Morgan told him, Concorde enabled Britain 'to look the Americans very firmly in the eye again'. The aeroplane was too noisy, though, and the attempt by British officials to compare its Jovian voice to that of the Boeing 707 was a little far-fetched and not least because the 707 would soon be reaching the end of its commercial flight path. More than this, not many airlines had really wanted Concorde, although there was a collective expression of interest in the supersonic rush before the industry calmed down and looked again to Boeing, then the world's main producer of civil airliners.

Harold Wilson's Labour governments of 1964–70 had done their best to ditch Concorde, despite the enthusiasm of some of their members such as Wedgwood Benn, while Edward Heath's Conservative administration of 1970–74 was minded to do the same. As Gillman observed, when Heath asked his government's 'think tank', a body of unaffiliated intellectuals headed by Lord Rothschild, and known formally as the Central Policy Review Staff, to deliver a judgement on Concorde . . . when it came it was simple enough. 'Concorde,' it began, 'is a commercial disaster.' But the report did accept that the plane carried considerable importance in terms of diplomacy and foreign relations. It could not recommend cancellation: that was a decision for government.

Like a matador moving in for the kill, Gillman noted that, rather than reduce the cost of passenger flight as all other major leaps in civil aviation had aimed to do, Concorde would increase them 'by up to three times per passenger mile: a ratio disastrously magnified by the actions of OPEC in 1973 and 1974'. It did seem very bad luck, to say the least, that, as test pilots were putting Concorde through its paces and calculating just how far it would fly on its supply of avgas, the Oil Crisis came in to bat and then knocked the developed world for a resounding six.

In response to American technical as well as political support to Israel during the Yom Kippur War, which was fought in

October 1973 against the invading forces of Egypt and Syria with military support from Algeria, Jordan, Morocco, Tunisia and Cuba, OAPEC (Organization of Arab Petroleum Exporting Countries) announced an embargo on oil supplies to the USA along with Britain, Canada, Japan and the Netherlands for good measure. The price of oil rocketed fourfold within months. Petrol rationing was introduced in the States along with a blanket 55-mph speed restriction. There was a rush on toilet paper in Japan – oil is used in its production – followed by another in the US at Christmas. Affected governments held crisis meetings and long-term decisions were made there and then to cut back the developed world's dependency on oil. There would be smaller cars, new forms of energy and an end to gas-guzzling in general.

This was not good news for Concorde, an airliner with a fuel consumption of 17 mpg per passenger mile compared with the 54 mpg of a Jumbo Jet – and the 100 mpg of today's gigantic double-deck Airbus A380. And, for Britain at least, matters took a turn for the worse. At a time of rampant inflation and a dwindling of the real value of its members' wages, the National Union of Mineworkers called for a work-to-rule. Coal supplies fell as the price of oil soared. In response, the government introduced a Three-Day Week whereby electricity would be available for commercial and industrial purposes for restricted hours only on three consecutive days. If you were young or at school at the time, it all seemed a bit of a lark. In January 1974, the miners rejected a pay deal of 16.5 per cent and, the following month, the prime minister, Edward Heath, called a general election over the issue, as he put it, of 'Who Governs Britain?'

The result was that Harold Wilson and Labour were returned to office as a minority government. The Three-Day Week was called off and the miners rewarded with a pay increase of 35 per cent. Wilson won a second general election in October that year, scraping home with a majority of three seats in the House of Commons, and the miners were soon to receive a second 35 per cent rise. But coal mining in Britain did not have a long-term future, whereas civil aviation did. Concorde, though, was out of step, too, and in a new era of awkward austerity risked appearing a singularly expensive throwback to a time of cheap and abundant fuel and of luxury.

Peter Gillman, whose *Atlantic Monthly* feature had spoken of Concorde in the past tense until the final paragraph, was writing not very long after these events, when the Labour administration, now led by James Callaghan, who had served out East as a Royal Navy officer in the Second World War, was still in office, if not quite in power. As for the government's stance on Concorde, Gerald Kaufman at the Department of Industry said the new approach was to be based on profits, not 'prestige, politics or grandeur'. Gillman correctly predicted that no more Concorde aircraft would be built after the last production model – the sixteenth – was sold to Air France or British Airways.

This all seemed very dispiriting, given that Concorde had yet to enter commercial service from London and Paris to New York. Like many other journalists and commentators at the time, Gillman had written off the Anglo-French airliner. 'The present Concordes will fly on the routes for ten years or so,' he wrote, 'then they will probably disappear. After all, the first two pre-production Concordes built in Britain are already in museums.'

While this was slightly disingenuous – the pre-production aircraft had served their purpose – it does seem somewhat tragic that Concorde's obituary was being written while it was entering service and more than a quarter of a century before its retirement. There was, however, as Tony Benn was to recall, something about Concorde that made people from different walks of life want to have a go at it. Gillman himself went on to write in particular on mountains and mountaineering, co-authoring with his wife Leni a well-received biography of George Mallory, *The Wildest Dream*, which was published in 2001. Mallory attempted to climb Everest in the early 1920s; when asked why, he was reported – by the *New York Times* – to have said, 'Because it's there.' As, to Morien Morgan and his colleagues, were both the sound barrier and the prospect of a civil airliner that could cruise at Mach 2 and reach New York from Paris and London. Mallory appears to have failed to reach the top of Everest. Concorde succeeded in climbing a political as well as a technical mountain.

By 1976, however, the airliner's theatre of operation was narrowing. India banned it from flying overland, as did Malaysia. Increasingly, airlines and manufacturers had come to realize that supersonic booms would be as socially and politically sensitive in poor and developing countries as they were in technologically advanced nations such as Britain, Germany and the United States. Sometimes, though, there were other factors at work to make Concorde and its crews unpopular. In early 1973, Brian Trubshaw had taken 001 to South Africa for high-altitude performance trials. This involved landing in Luanda in Angola, then a Portuguese colony involved in a bitter civil war. Perhaps someone was just playing a joke on the crew, but when Trubshaw waved a Union Jack and the national flag of Angola from the flight deck windows, it turned out that he was flying the rebel flag. Honour was somehow restored. 'However,' Trubshaw remembered, 'as we taxied out for the take-off, as per normal procedure, no flags were flown. This unfortunate apparent lack of protocol caused great offence as 002 was suddenly surrounded by soldiers with rifles and machine guns . . . jail was narrowly avoided.'

Meanwhile, the test pilots had been proving Concorde in ever-longer flights even as the Oil Crisis rumbled on and orders dropped away. In February 1973, Concorde 01 made a non-stop flight from Toulouse to Iceland, simulating the Paris to New York dash, cruising at Mach 2 for two hours and nine minutes. The following month, Concorde 02 stretched this to 3,900 miles with a return flight from Toulouse to West Africa, the equivalent of a trip from Frankfurt to New York, in three hours and thirty-eight minutes, and at the beginning of December, Concorde 201, the first production aircraft, took off from Toulouse.

Flight training for Air France and British Airways crews followed in the spring of 1975, certificates of airworthiness were made to both British and French aircraft in the autumn, and on 26 December, an Aeroflot Tu-144 flew from Moscow to Alma Ata – ostensibly the first service flight by a supersonic airliner, it carried freight and mail but no fare-paying passengers. Finally, on 21 January 1976, British Airways commenced its first regular Concorde service from London to Bahrain and Air France from Paris to Rio de Janeiro via Dakar, Senegal. A week later, the Port Authority of New York and New Jersey banned Concorde from its airports.

SIX

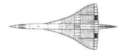

THE SERVICE RECORD

MARGARET Thatcher, who was not yet prime minister, was there to wave off Captain Norman Todd and flight BA300 operated by Concorde 206 (G-BOAA) from Heathrow Airport at 1140 hrs on 21 January 1976. The occasion was the supersonic airliner's first commercial flight from Britain, on its way to Bahrain, an oil-rich state close to the Persian Gulf that had been a British protectorate until 1971. Among the one hundred passengers on board were Sir George Edwards, chairman of BAC, the Duke of Kent, Peter Shore, the secretary of state for trade, Eric Varley, the secretary of state for industry, Sir Stanley Hooker, who had developed the airliner's Olympus 593 engines, and Brian Trubshaw.

Sitting quietly with these royal, industrial and political bigwigs and thirty fare-paying passengers was Leonard Cheshire VC, OM, DSO and Two Bars, DFC, the highly decorated RAF pilot who had flown Armstrong Siddeley Whitleys, Handley Page Halifaxes, Avro Lancasters, North American Mustangs and de Havilland Mosquitoes in some of the most dangerous and successful bombing missions of the Second World War. A witness on board the USAAF B-29 *Big Stink* to the nuclear destruction of Nagasaki and tired of war, Cheshire left the RAF, founded the charity for the disabled that bears his name today, became a devout Roman Catholic and worked to resolve conflicts around the world. He was, wrote Max Hastings in *Bomber Command* (1979), 'a remarkable man with an almost mystical air about him, as if he somehow inhabited a different planet from those about him, but without affectation or pretension'. Like others of his generation, Cheshire told me that he saw Concorde as a harbinger of peace, using military technology for civilized ends while also being utterly thrilling.

Ideally, Captain Todd and his crew should have stopped at Bahrain, refuelled, shot onto Singapore, filled up again and scythed across ocean, desert, bush and forest to Sydney. The route to Australia, however, proved to be nothing more than a dream. Although BA Concorde aircraft did get to fly to Singapore via Bahrain from 9 December 1977, the joint service with Singapore Airlines was cancelled after just three return trips. Once again, noise was the problem. The Malaysian government complained about supersonic booms over the Straits of Malacca after flight times had already been extended because India refused to allow Concorde to fly supersonic over its vast territory while the Saudis were not keen on camel trains and camel breeding being upset by the thunderous passage of Mach 2 airliners. Although the service was re-commenced in January 1979, its flight path avoiding Malaysia, it proved to be unprofitable. Although virtually the entire route between Bahrain and Singapore was flown supersonically, and despite the fact that improvements had been made to allow Concorde to fly further without refuelling, political friction between Malaysia and Singapore meant operation of the service was fraught with difficulty. It was all too bothersome and BA dropped the flight.

It had been interesting, though, to observe that Concorde used less fuel per mile on this route, not least because the aircraft flew in colder air than it did over the Atlantic, and jet engines benefit from such conditions. Air temperature falls up to the tropopause, the boundary between troposphere and stratosphere. This is 10,000 ft higher over the Equator than it is over temperate zones such as the North Atlantic. It allowed Concorde to fly in air cooled to -75° C rather than -50° C. However, this was to prove academic. As for Australia, there were too many cheap subsonic fares available and, in any case, while a subsonic airliner only needed to break its flight once on this long-haul route, Concorde needed to stop twice and so its speed advantage was eroded. The Australian service was a non-starter.

Back on that first BA flight to Bahrain, however, the mood was celebratory. It cruised over Paris, where Air France Concorde 205 (F-BVFA) had departed for Rio de Janeiro, with Captains Pierre Chanoine and Pierre Dudal on the flight deck, at the same time as its British sibling took off, past Pan Am 747s, from Heathrow. And then to Venice and a blast along the Adriatic at Mach 2. Concorde 205 was a marvel. Air Commodore Edward 'Teddy' Donaldson, air correspondent of the *Daily Telegraph*, reported, 'One must sample it to believe it, for here I sit in a comfortable cabin in the calm air at nearly 60,000 ft up, hurtling along faster than the speed of a cannon shell, eating caviar and drinking exquisite champagne that rests without a ripple on my table . . . This without doubt must be the greatest leap forward in air travel the world has ever known.'

In his January 1977 blast against Concorde in the *Atlantic Monthly*, Peter Gillman had noted that Herb Coleman, the London editor of *Aviation Week and Space Technology*, had been 'less sanguine'. Concorde, he said, gave an 'adequate ride . . . if you're used to wide-bodied planes Concorde's cabin tends to close around you – it's like being back in Constellation days. There's a high noise level although not enough to inhibit conversation. Apart from that, it's just another aircraft as far as I'm concerned.'

What must have Donaldson been thinking? Born in Malaysia, he was one of three brothers who flew with the RAF in the Second World War. Joining the service in 1931, he began his career flying 175-mph Bristol Bulldog biplane fighters, a type designed by Captain Frank Barnwell, a First World War fighter pilot-turned-aero engineer. From being in the thick of action in the Battle of France tally-hoing his Hawker Hurricane into packs of Messerschmitt Bf 109s to commanding the first squadron of Gloster Meteor jet fighters at RAF Colerne, Donaldson duly captured a world speed record with a Meteor in September 1946 well before his appointment as deputy commander of air forces in the Arabian Peninsula. He must have been feeling inordinately proud of an aircraft in which the British aviation industry had played such a major role, of a machine developed by engineers many of whom had begun their careers working on successful RAF designs of the Second World War. Now he could relish the sheer luxury of an airliner, and all the chic accoutrements of flight it offered, with the performance of the most powerful contemporary jet fighters.

As for the haughtily dismissive Herb Coleman, he was a former USAAF bomber pilot and recipient of the Distinguished Flying Cross and Air Force Cross with three Oak Leaf clusters who had flown numerous missions over Germany from RAF Chelsworth, Northamptonshire, at the controls of Boeing B-17s. Perhaps, as a God-fearing, all-American Boeing man, he had felt obliged to say something negative about this Anglo-French upstart. I bet he loved it, but this is not what his editor or public would have wanted to read.

Visiting the busy flight deck, after a quiet chat perhaps with Group Captain Cheshire, 'Teddy' Donaldson would have been in excellent and familiar company. Norman Todd had flown four-engine RAF Consolidated Liberator B-24 bombers – American machines – with 355 Squadron from Salbani, West Bengal, against Japanese targets in Burma and Malaya. Cruising at 215 mph at a maximum of 28,000 ft, Flight Lieutenant Todd's missions extended up to fourteen hours and 2,300 miles. He joined BOAC in 1946 and was soon crossing the Atlantic at the controls of Lockheed Constellations, Boeing Stratocruisers and Bristol Britannias. He test flew Vickers VC-10s and Boeing 747s for BOAC and then British Airways before moving on to Concorde.

On the flight deck with Todd were Captain Brian Calvert, who would fly the return leg from Bahrain, and Senior Flight Engineer John Lidiard. Calvert was born in Hankow, China, in 1933 and held captive there with his family by the Japanese for the duration of the Second World War. He undertook his national service with the Royal Navy, flying the Rolls-Royce Griffon-engined Supermarine F.XVII Seafire and Fairey Firefly, along with the bulbous, double-engine Fairey Gannet turboprop. As a purser with P&O, he sailed on liners to Australia, before joining BOAC. By the time he was appointed to the elite Concorde team, he had commanded Stratocruisers, Britannias, Comet 4s, VC-10s and 747s.

Not all pilots made the grade. Concorde was, by all accounts, a joy to fly, but it did require particularly quick reactions as everything happened so much faster than with subsonic airliners and because it had its own particular flight characteristics. Although many of its systems were automatic, adjusting and compensating for a variety of movements in flight with no input from the flight deck, it could be daunting for some pilots to be in charge of a very fast aircraft that had to be powered down to land until the very last moment and that would shoot down the runway at 240 mph before taking off. And yet it must have been reassuring to know that, if all the clever systems between the flight deck and the controls failed, Concorde could be flown manually. It could even fly at high speed if two engines on the same side flamed out or otherwise shut down. Pilots were rigorously trained on simulators before flying Concorde and facing any of these situations. In practice, there was little to worry about: Concorde was a safe, predictable and reliable aircraft, although it did have an Achilles' heel that was to bring it down to earth in flames. (See Chapter Eight.)

According to Christopher Orlebar, who learned to fly in 1965 with the Southampton University Air Squadron (RAF), before joining BOAC and piloting VC-10s, Concorde and later on, Boeing 737s, the total number of British Airways Concorde captains and first officers between 1976 and 2003 was 134; the figure for Air France was 128. On average though between these years, there were twenty qualified British Airways Concorde crews and about the same number with Air France. It was an elite cadre of commercial pilots.

Like so many of his colleagues, Brian Calvert adored Concorde, saying that if there was one frustrating thing about his job it was that he was unable to see the aircraft in action as they were flying it. In retirement, he chose to live in Ashampstead, Berkshire, under Concorde's flight path. Here, the medieval parish church boasts a gloriously cinematic wall painting over the chancel arch depicting the souls of the damned being dragged down to hell and those of the blessed being lifted up to heaven. Whether Concorde was a messenger of heaven or hell depended very much on whether or not those living under its flight path looked on it as a thing of beauty or a machine-age sky demon bent on global destruction.

Meanwhile, Senior Flight Engineer John Lidiard sat facing a wall of analogue switches, dials and controls that would have been more or less familiar to Second World War pilots and especially to bomber crews. When asked by curious visitors to the flight deck what all these switches did, British crews would typically answer, 'Haven't the faintest – they do look rather important, though, don't they?' Visitors to Concorde's cockpit were often surprised at how very friendly and old-fashioned – so very 1950s – the flight deck seemed to be. A decidedly compact workspace, it belonged to an era long before that of glass cockpits with their LCD screens, digital displays and corporate management speak. Crews liked it. Belying its size, Concorde flew smoothly with the ease and precision of the best military jets.

Todd brought Concorde 206 down to land in Bahrain, on time in three hours and thirty-seven minutes at 1520 hrs (local time). Sheikh Isa bin Salman Al Khalifa, Bahrain's absolute ruler, laid on a splendid banquet in his new palace for crew and passengers. A personal waiter in full dress uniform attended each guest. Ryanair or easyJet, this was not. It had been a glamorous and exotic debut, even if it had by no means stretched Concorde to the full; if Concorde had been Pegasus, it would have been seen cantering gracefully through European and then Middle Eastern skies, with the briefest of gallops along the Adriatic furlong.

Air France's flight was delayed in Dakar, arriving in Rio de Janeiro at 1900 hrs, in time, though, for dinner. Among those who had enjoyed a supersonic lunch were General Jacques Mitterrand, chairman and CEO of Aerospatiale, Marcel Cavelle, the French transport minister, and eighty-two-year-old Aurelie Ouille from Toulouse who had booked her ticket in 1967. Five years earlier, Madame Ouille had crossed the Atlantic from Le Havre to New York on the maiden voyage of the liner SS *France*, one of the last of her type. The journey took six days; doubtless, the food was good. On board Concorde, Madame Ouille would have been presented a lunch menu listing:

Petits Hors d'Oeuvres Frise Bouche
Medaillon de Frois Gras Frais
Côte de Veau Richelieu
Pommes Chateau
Coeur de Laitue Braise
Fromages Assortis
Bavarois aux Abricots

The wines offered were a 1964 Chateau Haut Brion, which in 2015 was selling for up to £500 a bottle, or a 1961 Gevrey Chambertin, now worth some £300. Champagne was, of course, on tap, in the form of Veuve Clicquot Cuvée de la Grande Dame. The thinking behind such a menu – and food was good on both British Airways, where it was served on Royal Doulton bone china, and Air France throughout Concorde's twenty-seven-year service – was that, as the aircraft had limited in-flight entertainment or even seats that reclined to an angle guaranteed to upset the passenger behind, then the time could be passed agreeably with good food and wine. Of course, you never knew when Paul McCartney might turn up and, accompanying himself on the guitar, sing Beatles songs from the cockpit with – before 9/11 – the door wide open. Every extra pound in weight Concorde carried – whether screens, headphones or acoustic guitars – mattered critically in terms of fuel consumption and range. But because its flights tended to be brief compared to subsonic airliners, both Air France and British Airways agreed that there was little need for entertainment. In any case, the majority of regular passengers tended to work or read quietly on board; they had no need of further distraction.

Regular flights to Washington Dulles International followed from 24 May, with Brian Calvert and Norman Todd landing immediately ahead of the sibling Concorde service from Paris. The Anglo-French pair drew up to the terminal together, and stopped in unison to ensure their arrival was simultaneous. New York proved a tougher nut to crack, yet when the Supreme Court ruled against the Port Authority of New York and New Jersey's ban on the aircraft, the protest on the ground continued. Noise remained Concorde's great weak point and protesters were determined to prove that the aircraft would fail every decibel test going.

On 19 October 1977, Concorde 201 flew into JFK for a three-day noise-abatement trial. The aircraft's canny crew was Aerospatiale's chief test pilot Jean Franchi, BA's Captain Brian Walpole and Captain Pierre Dudal of Air France. Franchi, who with André Turcat and Brian Trubshaw had led the flight-testing of Concorde from the beginning, enjoyed a challenge. Flying some while earlier with Walpole, he had asked his British colleague if he would like to barrel-roll Concorde, just like a jet fighter put through its paces in an air display. 'You're pulling my leg,' Walpole responded. Whereupon, at 400 mph and 15,000 ft, Franchi rolled the supersonic airliner and then invited Walpole to repeat the manoeuvre in the opposition direction. He did. Walpole was a former RAF Meteor pilot and had been a member of Fighter Command's aerobatic team performing stunts across Europe. Flying Concorde was clearly going to be fun.

Franchi, an air force colonel and former fighter pilot with experience of flying in the USA since 1945 and who lived in a medieval castle, worked out a plan with his colleagues. Concorde would take off from the left-hand of one of the two north-west-facing runways – usually 31L in service – turning left immediately before being flown slowly out to the Atlantic, whereupon the aircraft could be turned again and would climb, full-throttle, to its cruising height and speed.

This was cheating, some protestors claimed. No. It was just wise. Concorde's jet fighter-like abilities meant it could reach for the skies like no other airliner, and the manoeuvre tested on three consecutive days at JFK in October 1977 was to become standard procedure for all Concorde flights from the airport.

On 22 November 1977, BA and Air France were finally able to commence regular flights from London and Paris to New York. This was the route Concorde was destined to fly, allowing it to stretch its wings. Even then, crews needed to keep the beadiest eye on fuel reserves. When, in July 1988, Brian Walpole landed at Heathrow from JFK with twenty-five minutes rather than the required thirty minutes of fuel left in the tanks, he was grounded. He should have diverted to Shannon Airport in south-west Ireland to top up. 'A rule had been broken,' said British Airways in a press statement. 'Captain Walpole has ceased flying duties and will carry on his managerial duties as general manager of the Concorde division until his time (for retirement) comes,' which was the following year.

Walpole had commanded that first BA Concorde flight from London to New York in November 1977. This was just weeks before Norman Todd had flown Queen Elizabeth and Prince Philip home from Barbados at record speed. The 4,200-mile flight took three hours and forty-minutes, an average of 1,134mph. This was the Queen's first flight on Concorde. She visited the flight deck and was happy to be shown the controls by Captain Todd. This was also the year of the Queen's Silver Jubilee. Later, she made her 1991 state visit to the United States by Concorde, and, in honour of her Golden Jubilee in June 2002, Concorde, accompanied by the RAF's Red Arrows display team, was the hugely popular finale of a flypast over Buckingham Palace. The aircraft soared over The Mall as the military band struck up with 'Land of Hope and Glory'. This, though, was a very different

Great Britain than it had been in 1952 and another country from the one in which Arthur Benson, an Eton schoolmaster, wrote the words to accompany Edward Elgar's *Pomp and Circumstance March No 1* sung at the coronation of the Queen's great-grandfather in August 1902, a year before the Wright brothers made sustained powered flight a reality.

The Queen Mother thought Concorde was wonderful, too. In 1985, as an eighty-fifth birthday present, she enjoyed a flight on Concorde with Walpole in command. She had told Captain Jock Lowe – Concorde's longest-serving test and management pilot – that, whenever she heard Concorde approaching Clarence House on its descent over central London to Heathrow, she would go out on the balcony and wave. Lowe had replied that, whenever he flew over, he would flash Concorde's lights in salute. Clearly, the Queen Mother was not concerned about the roar of the supersonic airliner's Olympus engines.

Back in the summer of 1977, though, punk, along with Silver Jubilee street parties, was all the vogue. The Sex Pistols released their single 'God Save the Queen', which was banned by the BBC. The group were arrested and their boat impounded when they tried to play the song live from a boat called *Queen Elizabeth* on the River Thames outside the Palace of Westminster. 'God Save the Queen' reached Number Two in the official charts. It was included in the band's first and only album, *Never Mind the Bollocks, Here's the Sex Pistols*, which was on sale as Concorde flew to New York with British Airways for the first time. While it was possible for a young generation to enjoy both the Sex Pistols and the Silver Jubilee, punk did mark the beginning of a cultural sea change. 'God Save the Queen' tussled for that Number

Two position with Emerson, Lake & Palmer's 'Fanfare for the Common Man', an edited version of a prog-rock interpretation of Aaron Copland's rousing orchestral piece for brass and percussion composed for the Cincinnati Symphony Orchestra in 1942.

Curiously, the Sex Pistols' seditious song was played in *Journey along the Thames*, a short film directed by Danny Boyle as part of the opening ceremony of the 2012 London Olympics attended by the Queen during her Diamond Jubilee. And, while punk had done its best to drown out prog-rock, in 2002 Keith Emerson told the *Guardian*, 'I liked the Sex Pistols. Funnily enough John Lydon [the band's frontman and lead songwriter] became a neighbour in Santa Monica.'

In 1977, however, it seemed that a world of high-tech accomplishment, whether in aerospace or rock music, was being challenged by a culture altogether less acutely skilled, evidently rawer and wilfully populist. Freddie Laker's cut-price, no-frills Skytrain took to the air from London to New York on 26 September, as if cocking a snook at the extravagance – and indulgence – of Concorde. Skytrain was punk to Concorde's prog-rock.

Life for the 'common man', meanwhile, was still a very long way indeed from that of those who could afford to fly Concorde to New York, but also from those for whom flights around the world are commonplace today. As Concorde soared to New York in 1977, half of British homes were without central heating, more than a quarter of jobs were in manufacturing, coal miners were kings of the trade union movement and, at a time of rocketing inflation, firemen called their first national strike. As Concorde crossed the Atlantic at twice the speed of sound, the army responded to fires using Bedford self-propelled pumps known as

Green Goddesses, the last of which had been built shortly before STAC's first meeting in London on Guy Fawkes' Day, and all its fireworks and bonfires, in November 1956. Green Goddesses had no radio, no cutting equipment and just a single ladder. The last was packed off to Africa in 2004, a year after Concorde's retirement.

Concorde flew its first transatlantic passengers from a London subject to terrorist bombing by the IRA, over the newly opened £71m extension of the London Underground to Heathrow Airport, roads increasingly clogged with cars built abroad – more than half of them for the first time that year – and British Aerospace factories, which had been taken over by the state that April. Abba's 'Dancing Queen' enlivened parties and dance floors, *Annie Hall* and *All the President's Men* were the films to watch, five million posters of Farrah Fawcett, co-star of *Charlie's Angels*, flew from the walls of high-street shops as Blondie's Debbie Harry became the next generation's very different all-American pin-up. Elvis died, bestselling books in the bags of transatlantic passengers included *The Shining* by Stephen King, *The Silmarillion* by the late J. R. R. Tolkien and *Success* by Martin Amis. And as Concorde scythed across the Atlantic, the US president Jimmy Carter, no fan of the Anglo-French jet, declared, 'We must face up to the fact that the energy shortage is permanent.'

Concorde flew high above these events and concerns. Serenely, expensively, exclusively. While Air France and British Airways transatlantic schedules were aimed primarily at admirals of industry, senior politicians, diplomats and civil servants, the airliner attracted a growing litany of film stars, musicians, monarchs, popes and celebrities, although there were far, far fewer of the latter in 1977 than there were forty years on. A list of those who did fly Concorde regularly looks rather inevitably like some *Private Eye* spoof: John Lennon and Yoko Ono, Phil Collins, Elton John, Mick Jagger, Joan Collins, Bernie Ecclestone, Richard Branson, Sting, Michael Jackson, David Frost, Tony Blair, Kate Moss, Sir Paul McCartney and Conrad Black. Only Dame Barbara Cartland, the Dalai Lama and Arthur Mullard appear to be missing.

Businessmen and, increasingly, businesswomen were, however, the mainstay of flights between London, Paris and New York. In October 1987, Patrick Mannix, Reuters' international technical manager, became BA's one millionth scheduled transatlantic Concorde passenger. He was presented with a framed certificate, a glass decanter and a complimentary return family ticket. A part of the aircraft's appeal to the supersonic set was that it was possible to fly from London to New York and back in a day, as the broadcaster David Frost, who called Concorde his 'time machine', did many times. Departing Heathrow at a very civilized 1030 hrs, BA 001 was schedule to arrive at JFK at 0925 hrs, getting to New York before it had taken off, or so it seemed going by the clock. Frost was able to record his chat show in Manhattan before leaving on BA 002 at 1330 hrs and landing back in London at 2225 hrs. And as for Sarah, Duchess of York, she commented, 'What's great about it [Concorde] is I'm able to take my children to school at 8.30 in the morning, drop them off, then take BA flight 001 at 10.30 a.m. to New York, and get to New York at 9.30 a.m. in time for my Weight Watchers meetings and speeches.'

It was easy to make your way through even a major international airport quickly in 1977, while, to add to the ease and speed of flying Concorde, the aircraft had its own dedicated departure lounges, complete with telephones, fax machine and secretarial services. As the years rocketed by, the new super-rich, notably footballers, were flown like royalty on board Concorde. In July 1998, a young David Beckham and the rest of the England World Cup team flew from Nantes to Heathrow with the hallowed cup as hand luggage. The following May, the Manchester United team flew Concorde to Barcelona for the Champions League final. 'I was thrilled and honoured to be asked,' said the pilot, '. . . and felt quite emotional as I taxied the Concorde out to the runway, with British flags flying and thousands of people wishing the team luck on the way.'

Times had changed. That pilot was Barbara Harmer, the first woman to fly Concorde in service. Harmer had certainly not been a Second World War fighter or bomber pilot. Born in Loughton, Essex, in 1953, she left school at fifteen to train as a hairdresser. Three years later, she began training as an air traffic controller at Gatwick Airport, Surrey, saving up to pay her way through, first, a private pilot's licence and then a commercial pilot's course. After joining British Caledonian, an airline taken over by British Airways in 1987, she flew BAC 1-11 and McDonnell Douglas DC-10 airliners. Ten years later, she flew Concorde, and the Manchester United team. 'Concorde,' she said, 'is so smooth, it doesn't really get the adrenaline going – but there's nothing like it. Even pilots stop and stare. It has an aura about it.'

Beatrice Vialle, a graduate of the École Nationale de L'Aviation Civile, Toulouse, flew Airbus A320s and Boeing 747s for Air France before moving up to Concorde in 2000. The only female Concorde pilot before Harmer and Vialle had been Jacqueline Auriol, the glamorous daughter of a wealthy French shipbuilder and timber importer. Born in 1917, she studied drawing and painting at the École du Louvre and psychotherapy at the Sorbonne before marrying young and giving birth to two children. She was with the Resistance during the Second World War. In 1947, her father-in-law Vincent Auriol, a socialist who had escaped to England four years earlier, was sworn in as the first president of the Fourth Republic.

Jacqueline moved in to the Élysée Palace with her family, but was soon bored with her new role as a society hostess. Thrilled by a discussion about flying with a test pilot over drinks at the palace, she took up flying in 1947. An accident as a passenger in a seaplane in 1949 saw her in hospital with terrible facial injuries. She went through thirty-three plastic surgery operations before she could face the world. She then took up stunt flying. 'Now that my beauty was gone,' she wrote philosophically in her 1968 autobiography *Vivre et Voler* (published in English in 1970 as *I Live to Fly*), 'I would have to derive a reason for being from the plane which had taken it away.'

Gaining a military pilot's licence in 1950, Auriol became a test pilot with the Flight Test Centre at Brétigny-sur-Orge and, on 3 August 1953, broke the sound barrier with a new Dassault Mystère IV fighter-bomber. This was just three months after the celebrated American pilot Jacqueline Cochran became the first woman to fly at Mach 1, just as she had earlier become the first woman to fly a bomber across the Atlantic and a jet. Her mount, over California, was a Canadair F-86 Sabre borrowed from the Royal Canadian Air Force. On and off through the 1950s and early 1960s, the two Jacquelines competed for the unofficial title of fastest woman in the world; flying Dassault Mirage IIIs, Auriol held the record in both 1962 and 1963. She first flew Concorde as co-pilot to André Turcat.

By the late 1970s, Concorde may have become an aerial business express and a supersonic ferry for players of the beautiful game, but it offered other opportunities and experiences. Aside from regular BA services to New York and at various times between 1976 and 2003 to Bahrain and Singapore, Miami, Washington DC and Toronto (summers only) and Air France flights to New York, Caracas, Mexico City, Rio de Janeiro via Dakar and Washington DC, Concorde was much in demand for both charter flights and celebrations. Although there were never more than fourteen in service, the beautiful aircraft seemed omnipresent. Despite the fears and even hatred of environmentalists, despite naysaying journalists out to prove a point – that Concorde was an abject failure, a total waste of money and resources – and in spite of concerns by airlines themselves that Concorde was, at best, an economic risk and an outsider in a world of wide-bodied jets and cheap flights, millions of people around the world took Concorde to their hearts. They would save for years if necessary to fly Concorde and when affordable charter flights became available – a quick whizz, say, around the Bay of Biscay – these were hugely popular. Concorde was a singular aircraft. It was as if there was only ever one of these compelling machines.

One of the most delightful and appropriate charter flights of all was organized in September 1981 by Concorde pilot Christopher Orlebar and his wife, Nicola. This was to celebrate the fiftieth anniversary of Britain winning the Schneider Trophy, a much-coveted prize for the team that could win the Schneider seaplane and flying boat race three times in five years. The RAF's High Speed Flight came up trumps in 1931, with its third victory. Flight Lieutenant John Boothman flew the course along Southampton Water at a triumphant average speed of 340.08 mph. His aircraft was a Supermarine S.6B designed by Reginald Mitchell, of Spitfire fame, and its engine a Rolls-Royce R, the engine that inspired the Merlin, which powered the Spitfire and was supercharged to brilliant effect by Stanley Hooker, who was key to the development of the Olympus engine that was to take Concorde to Mach 2.

Flight Lieutenant George Stainforth, another of the RAF Schneider team, went on to capture the world air speed record a few days after the 1931 victory with the S.6B, averaging 407.5 mph. The CO of the High Speed Flight, a First World War fighter pilot who had seen much action behind the airscrews and machine guns of B.E. 12s, Spad VIIs and Sopwith Camels, must have been chuffed. He was Squadron Leader – later Air Vice Marshal – Augustus Henry 'Orly' Orlebar.

Orlebar was a distant cousin of the Concorde pilot. As a young lieutenant with the Bedfordshire Regiment, he fought, and was wounded, at Gallipoli in 1915. Transferred to the Royal Flying Corps, he became a successful fighter pilot. From July 1941, he commanded the RAF's No 10 (Fighter) Group and, two years later, was promoted deputy of Lord Louis Mountbatten's Combined Operations, an active 'think tank' that plotted raids against German-occupied Europe up to and including the D-Day landings of 6 June 1944. Sadly, Orlebar died of cancer in 1943.

Among those on board Christopher and Nicola Orlebar's Concorde flights – two of them, on successive days – fifty years on were Air Commodore D'Arcy Greig and Group Captain Leonard Smith, veterans of the winning 1929 and 1931 Schneider teams. Their Concorde aircraft retraced the Hampshire course at 1,000 ft and exactly 340 mph. Aside from the string of technical and human connections between Britain's 1931 Schneider Trophy entry and Concorde's 1981 salute to that important achievement, there was a political element, too. Just as Harold Wilson's Labour government had tried to spike Concorde several times while the aircraft was still in development, so the Labour government of Ramsay MacDonald had done its worst to keep Britain out of the 1931 Schneider Trophy. It might have blamed the Wall Street Crash, but Labour had little interest in the race or what it might do to push forward the design of high-speed airframes and the engines needed to power them. In the event, the British team was able to compete when Lady Lucy Houston, a former dancer and chorus girl from Lambeth known as 'Poppy' who had made four lucrative marriages from the age of sixteen, donated £100,000 to Supermarine, declaring, 'Every true Briton would rather sell his last shirt than admit that England could not afford to defend herself.'

By the mid-1990s, 10 per cent of all British Concorde flights were charters, the majority associated with glamorous travel and adventure. Cunard offered its famous *QE2* to New York and Concorde back to London package. Goodwood Travel could fly you to Istanbul, bringing you back on board the Orient Express and Golden Arrow. Or you could fly Concorde to Jordan for a tour of Petra and a ride on the railway Lawrence of Arabia once did his best to blow up. (In 1929, and disguised as Aircraftsman Shaw, Lawrence had been secretary to Squadron Leader Augustus

Orlebar during the 1929 Schneider Trophy contest.) And you could see the pyramids at Giza – breathtaking structures even today – on a day trip from London.

Some of Concorde's charter flights seem almost comic in comparison. One highly popular day trip was the Christmas Concorde charter to Lapland, from Heathrow to Rovaniemi. This Finnish city lies just six miles south of the Arctic Circle and is the (official) home of Father Christmas. A two-hour flight, with a burst at Mach 2 over the North Sea in each direction, gave passengers eight hours in Rovaniemi's winter wonderland, time enough to cross the Arctic Circle, drink warm reindeer's milk, ride sleighs and, of course, meet Father Christmas. In the late 1980s, Jackie Bassett, founder and president of the Concorde Fan Club, organized Christmas flights, non-stop from Heathrow to Heathrow, complete with dinner but no Father Christmas for as little as £369 a pop. Crackers were pulled as the airliner broke the sound barrier. Despite fears raised during Concorde's development of increased risks of exposure to radiation at high altitude, the public could not get enough of the aircraft, even if this sometimes meant booking tickets for subsonic charter flights, which was not quite the point of flying the Mach 2 airliner.

Subsonic flights, however, had also been available on a regular scheduled basis between January 1979 and June 1980 with Braniff International Airways. These were the only Concorde flights operated by a US airline, but because the route was overland from Dallas-Fort Worth, Texas to Washington Dulles (DC), the maximum permitted speed was Mach 0.95. Braniff, however, was a very colourful airline. Not content with having the artist Alexander Calder paint one of its Douglas DC-8s, from 1965 it had engaged the New York advertising agency Jack Tinker and Partners to give it a radical new image.

The agency's Mary Wells was given the job. She brought in American architect Alexander Girard and shoe designer Beth Levine, along with the Italian fashion designer Emilio Pucci, and devised what became a $2.5m campaign, 'The End of the Plain Plane'. The result was all-orange or lemon yellow or baby blue airliners, kitted out in Hermann Miller fabrics, and served by cabin crews sporting a colourful array of jumpsuits, stylized space helmets, hot pants, high boots and mini-dresses. Braniff's gung-ho president Harding Lawrence loved it all. He fell in love with Mary Wells, too, marrying her in 1967.

What Braniff needed next was an aircraft to match the ambitions of its risqué advertising, jellybean colours and stratospheric hemlines. That aircraft was, of course, Concorde, although it would never fly in Braniff livery. Instead, Air France and British Airways leased aeroplanes over the stretch between Dallas-Fort Worth and Washington Dulles; these then flew on directly to London and Paris, but not before changing both their crews and their registration from American to French or British. And for all its attractions, the service was not a success. Braniff had begun Concorde operations the month after Congress passed the Air Deregulation Act. This meant that Braniff's Concorde aircraft had to compete with low-budget Boeing 727s flown by newly competing airlines over the same route. Given that Concorde was subsonic over America and fares were 10 per cent higher than regular first class, there were often as few as fifteen passengers on board, served by a crew of nine. Braniff was wound up in 1982. It had been a colourful ride.

Its plan to fly Concorde was not, however, so very irrational. The idea had been both to raise the airline's profile and to prepare the way for supersonic routes to South America. British Caledonian had been researching the South American market, too, talking of flights from London Gatwick to various points south of the equator via Houston. The airline was also considering supersonic flights from Gatwick to Lagos, Nigeria and from Gatwick to Atlanta, Georgia, with a stop to refuel at either Gander or Halifax. In 1979, however, rising oil prices put paid to British Caledonian's plans to acquire a pair of Concorde aircraft for these services.

Concorde was magnificent and much loved. But the aircraft, although it had proved itself in flight in its first five years of operation, was hardly profitable. According to figures from Whitehall, British Airways recorded a loss of £10.4m and Air France £36.8m on their Concorde operations. Within and without the industry, and certainly within the walls of the Palace of Westminster, if not those of the National Assembly in Paris, it was seen as more a state than a strictly commercial enterprise. Indeed, when the last Concorde aircraft were assembled in 1978, they were given away to Air France for a nominal sum as no other airline was interested in taking a risk on the costly supersonic jet. Received wisdom had it that Concorde could only continue to operate with the backing of British and French governments. Indeed, not long before it went into service, British Airways had written to the government insisting that Concorde services would lose the airline £20m a year, a considerable sum at the time, and, in fact, pretty much the going rate for a new Concorde.

'All my board members as individuals want Concorde to succeed,' wrote David Nicholson, chairman of British Airways, to Peter Shore, the secretary of state for trade. 'We all share the excitement inherent in a great step forward in aviation technology, but we believe that the financial strength and commercial viability of British Airways are our overriding responsibilities. The difficulty in framing a Concorde policy has been, and remains, that the uncertainties of supersonic operations and marketing of them are so large that they greatly exceed the limits of risk-taking that we are entitled to adopt without some special arrangements for these risks to be underwritten.'

Nicholson, an engineer and industrialist who had repaired ships with the Royal Corps of Naval Constructors while under fire from Normandy beaches on D-Day, was a fan of Concorde. He was, though, rightly worried about the financial risk involved with this expensive and commercially unproven aircraft. Yet the overall Concorde profit and loss figures for its first five years in service conceal the fact that the transatlantic flights were lucrative. And this is the business on which the new chairman of British Airways, Sir John King, decided to focus when he was appointed in 1980. King was a remarkable fellow. Born in Surrey, the son of a postman and seamstress, he left school at twelve. After a spell at a local vacuum cleaner factory, he became a young car salesman and 'repo' man, dealing with buyers who defaulted on their hire-purchase payments. He ran a taxi business, made machine parts for the war effort and went into ball bearings.

King was the epitome of the self-made businessman, and Margaret Thatcher, Conservative prime minister from 1979 to 1990, adored him. His mission when he agreed to chair British

Airways, which lost £140m in 1981, was to prepare for the airline's privatization. He did this by cutting costs ruthlessly, and by 1989 British Airways posted a pre-tax profit of £268m, among the highest in the business. At the same time, it launched its Saatchi & Saatchi advertising campaign, with the slogan 'The World's Favourite Airline' and to the unforgettable lilt of 'The Flower Duet' by Leo Delibes, a nineteenth-century French composer who is often known only, if at all, for this one haunting folk tune.

King recognized that Concorde could be sold as an even more expensive service than it had been to date if it was aimed more categorically at the commercial elite. In future, companies on both sides of the Atlantic signing up to a British Airways loyalty programme would receive Concorde upgrades. Concorde had met its king, and King his fairy-tale princess. He set up a new Concorde division with Concorde pilots – Brian Walpole and Jock Lowe – rather than business executives in charge. In its annual report for 1984–5, British Airways noted, 'Concorde is the undisputed flagship of the British Airways fleet. As such, it is earning not only a valuable return in publicity and prestige, but is making a substantial contribution to our profits in its own right. In the year under review, it earned us revenue of over £100m.'

During 1984, British Airways agreed to take on the full costs, involving those of manufacturers British Aerospace and Rolls-Royce, spare parts and the test rig at Farnborough. It paid the government £16.5m. This was a good deal, but also a bold and necessary move. If British Airways and the government had been unable to come to an agreement, then the Concorde programme would have been cancelled, and the big bird would no longer have flown. Or at least not from Britain. To control costs on its side of the Channel, the French government promised to continue its underwriting of Concorde provided it set the routes it flew. Flights to Washington and South America were discontinued, leaving the daily service between New York and Paris and nothing more: in 1984, Air France Concorde aircraft also turned a profit.

The other good news was that reports showed that the British Airways Concorde fleet was in very good condition. Once these aircraft had been criticized for being in the air for so few hours compared with Jumbo Jets and other subsonic airliners, but now it was realized that their limited, yet profitable, use meant that they should last a very long time. In 1986, British Airways said Concorde would be flying for another twenty years. Jock Lowe suggested 2017 as a final retirement date. As it was, remarkably few upgrades were made between 1976 and 2000; there was little or no need for them and if, for example, glass computer cockpit displays had replaced Concorde's busy analogue instrument panel, then the aircraft would have been out of service for many months because of the technical and legal need for new and exhaustive testing. This would have meant a loss of revenue, and in any case pilots liked Concorde as it was. What it did require, though, was a dedicated team of in-house engineers who understood this very particular aircraft inside out.

In skies dominated by subsonic Boeings and Airbuses, Concorde's magic endured. To celebrate its tenth anniversary in service, four British Airways Concorde aircraft flew in formation from Heathrow to Land's End and out over the Atlantic for a photo-shoot on Christmas Eve 1985, while two days later six of the seven British Airways aircraft – the seventh was in the paint shop – posed together in a fan-like formation outside BA's engineering building at Heathrow. Whether in the air or on the ground, the patterns the airliners made were eye-catching and inspirational. The Christmas Eve flight had witnessed the four aircraft, chased by and snapped from a Learjet, lining up in graceful diamond and swan-like formations in the winter sky above south-west England as if they were not so much civil aviation's answer to the RAF Red Arrows display team but a flock of rare and magnificent mechanical birds.

Concorde – 'Speedbird' was British Airways call sign – continued to break records even when it seemed there were no more to break. On 7 February 1996, G-BOAD, flown by Captain Leslie Scott, and helped by a powerful tail wind, touched down at Heathrow from JFK in just two hours, fifty-two minutes and fifty-nine seconds. This was ninety seconds less than the previous record set in 1990. The fastest Concorde transatlantic crossing of all had been made in just ninety-five minutes, between Hopedale, Newfoundland and the north-west Irish coast by Brian Walpole on 6 September 1987.

Transatlantic crossings by air had been pioneered by Captains John Alcock and Arthur 'Teddie' Brown fifty-eight years earlier flying a modified First World War Vickers Vimy biplane bomber, powered by two Rolls-Royce Eagle engines, from St John's, Newfoundland to Galway, Ireland. Alcock and Brown flew for sixteen hours and twelve minutes, their machine rising to 12,000 ft or falling to just above the crest of fierce Atlantic waves, and eventually nose-diving into the Derrygimla bog near Clifden. They had averaged 115 mph, boosted by a tail wind, and despite that slightly embarrassing touchdown they had defied the ocean that had sunk the *Titanic* just seven years earlier.

What comfort Alcock and Brown had hoped for on their flight was cruelly dashed when the battery powering their electrically heated flying suits failed soon after take-off. Flying into two icy storms, with the aircraft pounded by sleet and snow, they were in danger of freezing to death. They warmed themselves with a supply of coffee laced with whisky, sandwiches and chocolate. They battled through thick fog and, in the second storm they encountered, the Vimy plunged into a spiralling descent, with Alcock – the pilot – only able to level the aircraft out at 100 ft and, even then, he found they were flying one wing up, one wing down. Salt spray whipped the wings as Alcock righted the biplane. When ice threatened to stop the engines, Brown – the navigator – climbed out onto first one wing and then the other to sort things out. He did this five times. No wonder when they finally spotted land – Ireland – through a bank of fog they decided to cut their losses and forego flying on to England. Brian Walpole flew his ninety-five-minute Atlantic stretch in shirtsleeves.

The drama of a transatlantic flight on the warm, air-conditioned Concorde was of a subtle yet distinctive kind. The shape of the airliner remained exciting over the twenty-seven years Concorde was in service, while the cabin, with its six-foot headroom, tiny windows and cramped lavatories resembled that of some elongated executive jet. Pilots enjoyed speaking – but never for too long – about the special features of the supersonic aircraft and few people, even the most impassive global executive buried behind a copy of the *Financial Times*, *Economist* or *Wall Street Journal*, could not fail to be just a little excited as Concorde sped down the runways at Heathrow and JFK – 0 to 240 mph in about thirty seconds – and climbed away like a jet fighter. The left-hand climb out of JFK gave an immediate sense that here was an airliner like no other, a GT among stately sedans.

Throughout transatlantic flights, and despite the cossetting service, hints of just how out of the ordinary Concorde was were never far away, especially in the days before 9/11 when savage killers and zealous killjoys took away such innocent pleasures as a visit to the flight deck, where, in Concorde anyway, the engineering officer would happily show you the gap opening up between his control console and the bulkhead separating cockpit from computer department as the aircraft accelerated beyond Mach 1 and the temperature of the fuselage rose accordingly. There were digital altimeters and mach-meters in the cabin that displayed both Concorde's height and speed. Indeed, it was hard not to anticipate some sort of special drama as the mach-meter signalled Mach 1. Meanwhile, looking out from the tiny, porthole windows, passengers could indeed see the curvature of the Earth and the inky darkness of space seemingly not so very far above them. This was surely the realm of ancient sky gods. And yet, despite the fact that Concorde flew at such immense altitudes, those windows remained unfrosted, such was the heat of the aircraft's skin, and its beautiful wings could still be observed, as captivating as the sails of a racing yacht taut with the wind.

The genius of Concorde was that so much thinking, and testing, had resulted in an aircraft that could fly the Atlantic in three hours at twice the speed of sound without so much as rippling the surface of a gin and tonic. The only way, however, it could make a profit in service was by offering a refined and unashamedly elite service to the very small percentage of airline passengers who were willing to pay a premium to fly Concorde. The dream had been for fleets – for hundreds – of supersonic airliners to make this particular form of transport a part of everyday life. With the benefit of hindsight, it is truly remarkable that the Anglo-French airliner flew in service, and profitably so, for so many years before a subsonic reality caught up with it, pulled it by its elevons and brought it down to ground. By the end of the 1990s, and when a British New Labour government decided to celebrate the Millennium with an ineptly dim and irresponsibly expensive trade show in a hi-tech tent, or Dome, at Greenwich, the era in which Margaret Thatcher had waved off Concorde with so many heroic Second World War veterans on board seemed like ancient history.

SEVEN

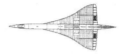

UNPREMEDITATED ART

CONCORDE was a singularly beautiful airliner. Concorde was a ravishingly beautiful machine. Concorde was, as so many people have said from all walks of life and around the globe, as much a work of art as it was a triumph, in its own right, of science, technology, design and manufacturing. The wonder of it is that its beauty, much like that of Reginald Mitchell's captivating Spitfire, was not the work of an artist, but of the artistry of aerodynamics. The subtle curvature of Concorde's wings is alone a study in elegant design and functional beauty, and a thing of beauty is truly a joy forever.

While Mitchell dismissed talk of artistry in the design of aircraft, like other gifted engineers he was able to produce designs of extraordinary beauty. And yet, one must be careful. Mitchell's record includes the ungainly and unsuccessful Supermarine Type 224 prototype fighter, which made its debut just a year before the superb Spitfire, and such competent but ugly-ducking machines as the Supermarine Walrus amphibian of 1933. When sheer speed and performance were what mattered most, then he produced both the Schneider Trophy-winning Supermarine S.6B of 1931 and the Spitfire. It was the forms of such aircraft, and especially the design of their wings, and the maths involved in shaping them, that led to their beauty. So theirs was neither a formally composed nor accidental beauty, but one that emerged through aerodynamic necessity.

The lightweight sports and racing cars of Colin Chapman, the powerful steam railway locomotives of Sir Nigel Gresley, many of them named after racehorses or fast birds, or the lithe grace of clippers and ocean liners in the heydays of sail and steam turbines, were very much of the same breed. Chapman, though, could produce ugly cars as well as very beautiful ones. His first single-seat racer, the Lotus 12, was a bulbous affair, and unsuccessful. Gresley's effective O1 class 2-8-0 heavy goods locomotive of 1914 and his N1 0-6-2 tank engine of 1920 were not exactly *Flying Scotsman* or *Mallard* in terms of looks. Grace of line came with speed and, in all cases, with a growing understanding of aerodynamics. And the beauty of a Lotus Elite or Gresley A3 Pacific, the fastest liners or Spitfire and Concorde is as timeless as that of seagulls and birds of prey.

Concorde has been out of service for more than a decade, and yet it still looks more modern and certainly more graceful than any Airbus or Boeing. In some ways, it was a glimpse of a future that has already slipped into history. It shot across the sky, like a bolt of Olympian lightning accompanied by a thunderous roar.

Concorde moved hearts and minds. Of course, to environmentalists the supersonic airliner was darkness visible, a ring of all too many decibels, a stench of polluting kerosene smoke, destroyer of the ozone layer. Surely, it was the devil's own work, and especially if it was spawned in foul Filton and tainted Toulouse rather than shining Seattle. But if Concorde was in some sense Lucifer, the brightest of the angels and bringer of light who was cast out of heaven – just as Concorde was to be in Paris in the year 2000 – or perhaps the hubristic Icarus, who flew too close to the sun and fell from the heavens, then this was a modern myth with an ancient ending. For Lucifer has long been associated with Venus, the morning star, which still brightens our heavens, just as Concorde's memory and beauty live on and are still widely celebrated.

In March 2006, Concorde was declared the winner of the Great British Design Quest hosted by BBC2's *Culture Show* and the London Design Museum. This was the result of a public poll to find the nation's favourite design since 1900. The results were announced in the cabin of retired British Airways Concorde G-BOAA. Among those on board were Concorde pilots Barbara Harmer and Christopher Orlebar. They were joined at a second celebration at the Design Museum by Alan Whicker, the globe-trotting television presenter, and Tony Benn, the former Labour minister of technology and Concorde champion.

'I'm absolutely delighted that Concorde's won,' said Benn. 'Whenever a Concorde flies, people look at it, it's very graceful, it's very beautiful; it is a symbol of peace and international understanding. It wasn't the most commercial vehicle to start with, but the design and beauty and skill is something that you just have to honour, and I do.' And according to Alan Whicker, 'Concorde was the best passenger plane ever built, I think. If you flew in it or even if you saw her flying overhead she just swept you up. I fell in love with this glorious aircraft that looked as though it was going a thousand miles an hour when it was standing still. And when she was up and away it was a marvellous experience for everyone.'

The BBC had counted on 100,000 voters to give its Great British Design Quest popular credibility. In the event, 211,792 votes were cast, underlining a strong public interest in design and powerful, emotional support for Concorde. Second place went to Harry Beck's famous London Underground map of 1931 and third to Mitchell's Spitfire. Significantly, the list of entries to the Great British Design Quest included the miniskirt, Peter Blake's cover for the Beatles album *Sergeant Pepper's Lonely Hearts Club Band*, the Anglepoise lamp, the World Wide Web, London Transport's Routemaster bus, Jock Kinneir and Margaret Calvert's national road signage and Malcolm Sayer's E-type Jaguar. All these were examples of determinedly modern design, ideas and artefacts that looked lucidly to a benign, bright-spirited, inter-connected and, above all, progressive future.

Harry Beck's Underground map, or 'diagram' as Beck himself preferred, was modelled on drawings of electric wiring circuits. Not only did this allow Beck to ignore conventional geography and re-invent the city as a machine for travelling, but it also meant he was in tune with a new world of crisp, clean graphic design and lettering and a belief in rational technical progress. Initially, Beck's 1931 proposal was rejected by senior management of the London Underground, which was in every other respect a most forward-looking organization. The preference was still for geographically correct maps showing, among other things, how far apart Underground stations were from one another. But as new Tube lines extended far from central London, traditional pocket maps would be unable to include all the new stations – unless, that is, they grew in size to the point where they became unwieldy. For Beck, and indeed for billions of Underground passengers since 1931, this no longer mattered; who really cared exactly how far Leicester Square station was from Covent Garden or Arnos Grove or Rickmansworth, as long as it was clear how you got there? Beck's diagram was finally approved in 1933.

Flying by fast jet has enabled millions to travel quickly and safely around the globe; it has reshaped our world – and our perceptions of it – just as the Underground's new lines and Beck's map reshaped London. Indeed, a Beck-style map of international airports would be a delightful thing to fold into your pocket today: airliners travelling at 550 mph at 35,000 ft all but ignore geography, flying diagrammatic routes across global skies. Concorde, though, had offered a glimpse of outer space, and in so doing had not only ignored but obliterated conventional geography. It flew in very tight corridors of the thinnest air, as if tracing the lines of some strange and entirely novel cartography of the upper atmosphere.

Meanwhile, Jock Kinneir and Margaret's Calvert crisp, rational lettering and signage for Britain's roads were designed as the country's first motorways were under construction. With cars about to travel at much greater speeds on public roads than ever before – well over 100 mph if you drove an E-Type Jaguar, that Concorde of the highways – there was evidently a need for signage that could be seen and understood from considerable distances. Kinneir recalled asking himself a simple question:

'What do I want to know trying to read a sign at speed?' And, as Margaret Calvert stressed, 'Style never came into it. You were driving towards the absolute essence. How could we reduce the appearance to make maximum sense and minimum cost?'

First tested in 1958 on the newly opened Preston bypass in Lancashire – Britain's first stretch of motorway standard road – the signage proved to be highly successful. Calvert and Kinneir went on to design the equally successful Rail Alphabet for British Rail as the state railway launched its bright new Inter-City look for trains, stations, signage and publicity material in 1964. Both design programmes, for BR and the Ministry of Transport, were as good as it got anywhere in the world. Both are rightly hailed as design classics and both are highly satisfying on an aesthetic level – and yet, as Kinneir and Calvert were at pains to point out, their work was strictly functional. How best can the human eye read signage at speed? In this sense, the beauty of their designs evolved in much the same way as what were to be the sensational good looks of Concorde, a machine pared to its structural and aerodynamic essence through its need to break the sound barrier and cruise at Mach 2 at 60,000 ft.

Even the miniskirt had a functional justification. As Mary Quant, the British fashion designer who popularized the miniskirt and made it synonymous with the swinging London of the mid-1960s, told Brenda Polan and Roger Tredre (*The Great Fashion Designers*, 2009), 'It was the girls on the King's Road who invented the mini. I was making easy, youthful, simple clothes, in which you could move, in which you could run and jump and we would make them the length the customer wanted. I wore them very short and the customers would say, "Shorter, shorter."'

Along the King's Road, these lithe young things could run and jump on and off the open platforms of aluminium-bodied Routemaster buses, another elegant yet wholly functional design, researched and tested between 1947 and 1956 before going into service and mass production in 1959. The design and engineering team led by A. A. M. Durrant with Colin Curtis was influenced by wartime advances in aircraft design and technology, the aim being to create the lightest and most fuel-efficient double-deck bus for London while carrying the maximum number of passengers and ensuring the greatest ease of maintenance. Styling, such as it was, was a subtle and almost minimalist affair, with Durrant and Curtis working with the modest and restrained industrial designer Douglas Scott.

There was no attempt to shape a show-stealing design as there would be during the London mayoralty of the ambitious Boris Johnson; such an approach would have appeared pointless and vulgar to engineers and designers of the Concorde, and Routemaster, era. During the Second World War, A. A. M. Durrant had been seconded from the London Passenger Transport Board to head the Ministry of Supply's Department of Tank Design. To Durrant and his team, armies around the world owed the highly successful and long-lived Centurion medium battle tank – derivatives are still on duty – designed originally to outfox and outgun German Tiger tanks. The first full-scale mock-up of the Rolls-Royce Meteor-powered Centurion – the Meteor was based on the Spitfire's Merlin – was made by AEC of Southall, Middlesex, the bus-manufacturing arm of the London Passenger Transport Board.

Mary Quant named her functional, if very sexy, skirt after the BMC Mini, a car she and other King's Road hipsters buzzed around town in. This tiny car had been designed by Alec Issigonis, a Greek-born engineer who had previously created the best-selling Morris Minor, a small, low-cost saloon car with superb steering and road manners built from 1948 to 1971, and still very much a feature of British roads, and those of many other countries, in 2015. The Mini was car design taken to its most functional and almost wilfully spartan while carrying four people and their luggage at 70 mph. It drove like a slot-car racer, won the Monte Carlo rally three times, starred in *The Italian Job* (1969), was owned by anyone from John Lennon to your local hairdresser and remained in production from 1959 to 2000, becoming the best-selling British car of all time. Like the Routemaster, Kinneir and Calvert's signage and Harry Beck's Underground map, the Mini was classless, practical and free of unnecessary convention.

It was both possible, and perfectly feasible, for Great British Design Quest voters to choose between Concorde and the miniskirt, although it might perhaps have made more sense for them to choose between Concorde and the E-Type Jaguar since this lithe and perennially beautiful sports car was designed by a team led by an aerodynamicist. Malcolm Sayer had worked at Filton for the Bristol Aeroplane Company from 1938 and throughout the Second World War. Later on, he tested the aerodynamics of the cars he designed for Jaguar, including the Le Mans-winning D-Type, in the RAE wind tunnel at Farnborough.

Concorde's beauty was, of course, the product of functional, aerodynamic design and dozens of considerations concerning the every practicalities of supersonic flight in regular airline service. But subliminally it was something else, too. On 20 February 1909, the front page of *Le Figaro*, the oldest French newspaper, carried an eye-opening *Futurist Manifesto* on its front page. Written by Filippo Tommaso Marinetti, a thirty-two-year-old Italian poet born in Egypt, it barked:

> We declare that the splendour of the world has been enriched by a new beauty: the beauty of speed. A racing automobile with its bonnet adorned with great tubes like serpents with explosive breath . . . a roaring motor-car which seems to run on machine-gun fire, is more beautiful than the Victory of Samothrace.
>
> We are on the extreme promontory of the centuries! What is the use of looking behind at the moment when we must open the mysterious shutters of the impossible? Time and Space died yesterday. We are already living in the absolute, since we have already created eternal, omnipresent speed.
>
> Standing on the world's summit we launch once again our insolent challenge to the stars!

A century on, it is hard to agree with Marinetti that an exciting but rather ungainly Alco Six or Blitzen Benz is more beautiful than the Winged Victory of Samothrace, a stunning, sensual and dynamic second-century BC Greek sculpture of Nike, goddess of strength, speed and victory. And yet one can empathize to a degree with the fiery poet's desire to strip away the overwhelming weight of the nineteenth century and all its cumbersome design and to reach instead for the stars in the lightest and fastest machines released from the chains of history and stultifying convention. Something of the same spirit was revived in the

1960s, although Marinetti's views on matters political, social and sexual would be abhorrent to the vast majority of those born in the free world after the Second World War:

> We want to glorify war – the only cure for the world – militarism, patriotism, the destructive gesture of the anarchists, the beautiful ideas which kill, and contempt for woman.
>
> We want to demolish museums and libraries, fight morality, feminism and all opportunist and utilitarian cowardice.

As it was, Marinetti was on active service with the Italian army in 1944 when he died in his sixties of a heart attack. A dedicated fascist, he had become a hardened reactionary, lauding a credo for a dismal and lost political and military cause, one destroyed with the help of some of the men who went on to design Concorde, a machine that really can be considered as ravishing as the Winged Victory of Samothrace. In terms of contemporary aesthetics, perhaps Marinetti had been a little too quick off the starting block. In 1909, aircraft – lovely-looking things in their own moth-like way – were fabrications of plywood, canvas and wire, all struts, braces and wires. It was speed that transformed them into highly resolved and even truly beautiful machines.

The American company Douglas shaped what deserves to be called the first modern airliner. This was the DC-3 of 1935, a streamlined twin-engine monoplane that revolutionized commercial aviation. It looked like the future, slashed air schedules across the United States and, in both peace and war, proved to be rugged, dependable and much liked. Examples remain in regular, scheduled airline service in several parts of the world including the United States. As speeds increased above the DC-3's maximum of 230 mph, so shapes became sleeker. With a maximum speed of 377 mph, Lockheed's Super Constellation was perhaps the best looking of all piston-engine airliners, while Tupolev's Tu-114 of 1955, which could reach a very noisy 541 mph and flew in service for thirty years until 1991, was, along with the slower Bristol Britannia, a truly beautiful turboprop. At one point, due to US sanctions, Tu-114s flew non-stop from Murmansk to Havana, although seating was restricted to sixty passengers and an extra fifteen fuel tanks were installed.

Jets offered speeds ever closer towards the sound barrier. The de Havilland Comet 1 (503 mph), the Boeing 707 (550 mph), and the Vickers VC-10 (580 mph) were all graceful machines. But just as Concorde pushed so far ahead of these types in terms of performance and technology – in fact, it was almost as if the aircraft was flying into a realm of sheer, Futurist speed – so it marked an absolute confluence of form and function in airliner design. No wonder so many people flocked to see Concorde at airports and fly-pasts or simply looked up to watch it pass by. Speaking to the BBC's Sue Lawley in a July 2005 edition of *Desert Island Discs*, Paulo Coelho, the Brazilian novelist whose 1987 novel *The Alchemist* has sold more than sixty-five million copies worldwide, chose 'a trip around my island in Concorde' as his one luxury. Concorde's beauty struck a chord in the most thoughtful of writers just as it did with a very wide public.

There was, of course, one minor detail that the BBC's Great British Design Quest could not ignore: Concorde was an

Anglo-French project, and, although this can be argued over until the cows, or *vaches*, come home, the airliner's outline derived first and foremost from the researches of RAE Farnborough. The development and resolution of the design was nonetheless very much a joint effort and it is just as easy to see a non-causal aesthetic link between classic French designs and Concorde, too. The Citroën car company even commissioned a photo-shoot of its late-model DS, a redesign by Robert Opron of the original 1955 Déesse or goddess styled by Flaminio Bertoni and engineered by André Lefèbvre, who had begun his career as an aero-engineer with Gabriel Voisin. Citroën and Concorde did look related. Opron's later SM and CX models for Citroën looked equally comfortable parked alongside Concorde, while the SM in particular was graced with the kind of radically styled and beautifully executed interior Concorde very nearly had at the very last moment, yet lacked for most of its twenty-seven-year career with Air France and British Airways.

When BA and Air France Concorde aircraft made their first fare-paying flights to Bahrain and to Rio de Janeiro respectively, there was, in fact, a curious discrepancy between the refined engineering design of their airframes and the interior design of their cabins. Both were rather dowdy. It would be a cheap shot to say that this was the 1970s, often referred to in Britain as the decade design forgot, an era of brown and orange fabrics, business executives in flared suits, Jason King moustaches, the Morris Marina and bouffant hair. Even such sophisticated British designs of the period as British Rail's Inter-City 125 High Speed Train featured over-lit and soulless interiors reliant on what appeared to be acres of beige-white plastic. It might simply have been, though, that British Airways wanted its revolutionary new airliner to feel more ordinary than it was so as not to unsettle passengers. Contemporary photographs do show what might otherwise be taken for a comfortable meeting venue for grey-suited executives, politicians and civil servants and the equivalent in seat design, fabrics, carpets and overall décor. The French interiors were more colourful, although again rather fusty in terms of thickset seats and heavy-looking fabrics. But new had never had to mean dull or dreary, especially in the air.

When it had been launched in 1930, the sleek, silver transatlantic Zeppelin *Hindenburg*, a masterpiece of lightweight construction, featured ultra-modern furniture and fittings that weighed as little as possible: there were tubular aluminium dining chairs, white plastic washbasins in passenger cabins, and fabric-covered foam walls. The overall aesthetic was a playful version of Bauhaus design, conceived by the flamboyant architect Fritz August Breuhaus de Groot, well known for his ocean-liner interiors and ultra-modern homes for German film stars. The walls of the airship's passenger areas were silk-lined and painted with scenes depicting great historic voyages, the adventures of the *Hindenburg's* older sibling, *Graf Zeppelin*, or else charming capriccios of exotic holiday settings. Not for nothing was the *Hindenburg* described as a 'hotel in the sky'.

Every extra kilogram of weight mattered very much indeed to the Zeppelin company's engineers and mechanics, which is partly why every effort was made to create interiors that, while inviting, weighed as little as possible. More than this, though, the idea was to create an aesthetic sense, an aura of ultra-modern, lighter-than-air travel. The *Hindenburg* met a shocking end at Lakehurst,

New Jersey in May 1937 when it burst into flames. This was not a reflection of its design, but because it was lifted by highly inflammable hydrogen rather than non-flammable helium, a gas the United States refused to supply to foreign countries. And yet, if the ill-fated *Hindenburg* had a lesson to impart to Concorde's design teams, it was clear: shape an interior that reflects the essential nature of the aircraft.

British Airways Concorde aircraft were fitted with new interiors in 1985. This time, the seats possessed a lighter, more modern feel and yet the colour scheme was almost relentlessly grey. Finally, from 2001, a real effort was made by British Airways to give Concorde something like the interior it called for and deserved. Conran and Partners, led by Sir Terence Conran, and Factory Design worked with Britax Aircraft Interior Systems on new seating, fabrics, lighting, lavatories, mach-meters and galleys. As Conran recalled:

> We wanted to create an interior that was as light and elegant as the exterior, and a feeling of comfort and luxury . . . we selected chairs that took inspiration from my idols, Charles and Ray Eames. They were ink-blue Connolly leather with a cradle mechanism, footrests and contoured headrests for comfort and support. We also wanted to make the interior of the passenger cabin brighter with different lighting which would change to a cool blue wash throughout the cabin when the Concorde flew through the sound barrier at Mach 1; that would have been a beautiful sight.

RIGHT: Portrait of Sir Morien Morgan by John Ward (1976). 'Morgan the Supersonic' chaired the Supersonic Transport Aircraft Committee that nurtured the Mach 2 airliner from pipe dream to high flight.

BELOW: Three striking Concorde wind tunnel models from the Royal Aircraft Establishment, Farnborough, in the care of the Science Museum, London, today. Concorde's exquisite shape was the product of exhaustive research.

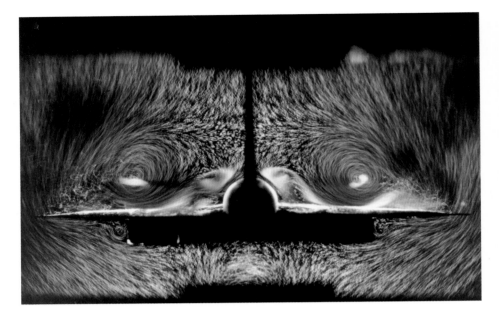

Spectacular image of the vortex pattern on Concorde's wing and fuselage on the approach to landing. These swirling vortexes gave the finely resolved wing tremendous lift on take-off and landing.

Concorde climbing with afterburners on. Only the very fastest jet fighters could keep pace as Concorde shot across the Atlantic at Mach 2 in a haze of kerosene and champagne.

Has an aircraft ever been more beautiful than this? The graceful, dart-like lines of Concorde were the product of intense research into aerodynamic forms and strictly purposeful technological artistry.

Summer, 1985. Concorde G-BOAG salutes QE2 over the English Channel with a cast of Red Arrow Hawks. The Cunard liner made its maiden voyage two months after Concorde first flew.

A remarkable photograph taken on Christmas Eve 1985 showing the first and only time Concorde aircraft flew in formation, a piece of cake for experienced British Airways pilots.

Timeless beauties. Concorde G-BOAA flies past the white cliffs of Dover with Mk IIa Spitfire P7350 on 6 June 1990, commemorating the fiftieth anniversary of the Battle of Britain.

Cossetted passengers in Concorde's understated cabins were oblivious to the supersonic drama conducted around them. Their only sensation of speed was measured through mach-meter read-outs on bulkhead walls.

Crowds gathered on and beside Isambard Kingdom Brunel's sublime Clifton Suspension Bridge to welcome Concorde G-BOAF home to Filton on 26 November 2003. This was Concorde's very last flight.

One future for high-speed flight is space tourism. Virgin Galactic promises to take whooping passengers on zero gravity sub-orbital trips, their SpaceShipTwo aircraft launched from a twin-fuselage White Knight Two mothership.

Unleashed from a Boeing B52-B on 16 November 2004, an unmanned NASA X-43A hypersonic test plane flew briefly at Mach 9.65, the highest speed yet recorded by a powered aircraft.

'What man-made machine will ever achieve the complete perfection of even the goose's wing?' Even the most magnificent aircraft have yet to match the subtlety of a bird in flight.

The apotheosis of Concorde. Final flight, 2003.

It would indeed, but sadly it never quite happened as Conran, who had designed Mary Quant's first shop, Bazaar, on Chelsea's King's Road in 1955, had hoped. The subsequent decision to withdraw Concorde prematurely meant that only a part of this fitting scheme was executed, but not the new blue-wave lighting or the smart new lavatories, which were known as 'washrooms' on board Concorde out of politeness to American passengers. There had been, though, a practical as well as aesthetic reason for these new interiors: they were intended to save around 880 lbs in weight, offsetting the additional weight of the Kevlar and rubber liners, which had to be installed in Concorde's fuel tanks in 2000–1. (See Chapter Eight.)

Air France Concorde aircraft were treated to four interior design schemes, the first by Raymond Loewy, the godfather of modern industrial design and styling. Born in Paris a decade before the Wright brothers' first successful powered flight, Loewy was an aircraft, automobile and steam railway locomotive enthusiast. His first successful design, at the age of fifteen, was for a model aircraft powered by a rubber band that won a James Gordon Bennett Cup prize in 1908. It was put into production the following year with the trade name 'Ayrel'. Thirty years later, Loewy, who had moved to New York after serving with the French army's corps of engineers during the First World War – he rose to the rank of captain, decorated a trench with Parisian wallpaper, had his uniform tailored and received the Croix de Guerre with four citations for bravery under fire – designed a 'flying penthouse' interior for Howard Hughes' private Boeing 307 Streamliner.

Loewy's ability to win publicity and, more particularly, increase companies' turnover and profitability through design was to become legendary. He was featured on the cover of *Time* magazine's October 1949 issue as 'Designer Raymond Loewy: He streamlines the sales curve'. And yet Loewy's interiors for Concorde were rather conservative, too. His silverware – yes, silverware – was adventurous, and the porcelain and glass were of the best quality, while the beige and brown seats and décor, with a splash of green here and there, were relaxing, if uninspiring. Loewy had another go in 1985, the year before he died, with plush Bordeaux-red seats, fit no doubt for a French president in all his pomp but perhaps better suited to a wide-bodied transatlantic jet than the sylph-like Concorde.

Pierre Gautier-Delaye, a former director of interior architecture at Loewy's design studio, produced a new style for 1988, making use of a much lighter palette of white, yellow and grey. Five years later, Andrée Putman's Ecart studio gave the French aircraft yet another treatment, with taupe fabric seats crowned with generous but tightly fitted white antimacassars. The look was one of restrained elegance and chic, and appeared comfortable too, even if it again seemed detached from the aesthetic and achievement of Concorde's supremely beautiful airframe.

Putman said the look she created for her design studio had been inspired in part by the summer holidays she spent in her formative years at Fontenay Abbey, Montbard, the former Cistercian monastery founded in the early twelfth century and a private home since 1906. While there are no flying buttresses at Fontenay, the serenely beautiful Cistercian aesthetic can indeed be spoken of in something of the same breath as Concorde. Why? Because Cistercian monastic architecture was elemental, pure and functional, built to serve the modest material needs yet richly spiritual purposes of the medieval religious order. As a result, the beauty of Cistercian monasteries is an expression of a way of thinking, believing and building rooted in necessity, and pared to its elegant bones, or stones. Add anything to the architecture of Fontenay and its sibling monasteries and their carefully balanced harmony would be destroyed; take anything away and the loss would be immediately apparent. All these things are true of the design of Concorde.

There was a tantalizing link in the late 1990s between Andrée Putman and the British approach to the design of Concorde's interiors. In 1999, Putman designed a delightful shop in a Mayfair mews for the fashion designer Joseph Ettedgui, his wife Isabel and the Connolly family, the well-known English leather-makers. The result was an inspired aesthetic balance between Putman and Connolly's approach to a functional yet refined and reassuring elegance. However, up to the end of Concorde's career, the British and French aircraft offered what had become two quite different ways of looking at the same challenge: how to create a look and an ambience that was at once modern, luxurious and, as far as possible, in tune with both the engineering design and the look of Concorde and the emotional as well as intellectual spirit that sent it soaring into the stratosphere at twice the speed of sound. The British favoured a slightly racy image expressing the idea of scintillating speed seen through the lens of hi-tech design and styling, while the French opted for a kind of cool, modern hotel chic, as if supersonic speed was something to be enjoyed with studied insouciance.

As Concorde's interiors improved over the decades, so did the airliner's external liveries. British Airways Concorde aircraft went into service in 1976 dressed in a slightly dull Union Jack paint scheme. Although the main body of the airliner had to be white, ostensibly to reflect heat from its fuselage in supersonic flight, the blue band along the window line and the tail-fin logo were a little awkward and even perhaps frumpy, much like the interior design of the cabin. In fact, the BOAC livery that would have graced Concorde if the airliner had gone into service in the late 1960s or early 1970s had been very much better, and was possibly the best of all those proposed by the many airlines that had placed options on orders for Concorde before cancelling them.

Landor Associates, a big international design and branding agency based in San Francisco, came up with Concorde's second British Airways colour scheme, which was seen on the aircraft from 1985 to 1997. It was white again, of course, and featured a red speed stripe under the windows and a tail logo that spoke of corporate efficiency; it was businesslike but as dull as a grey-suited corporate executive. While such executives were indeed the mainstay of Concorde's transatlantic flights, the airliner cried out for something altogether more transcendent. The need was answered in 1997, when the London design agency Newell and Sorrell produced a new colour scheme for British Airways aircraft – a scheme famous, or infamous, for its no fewer than twenty-eight different tail-fin designs based on ethnic art from around the world, most memorably from Africa and Asia.

These decidedly colourful patterns split public opinion. British Airways' chief executive officer, Robert 'Bob' Ayling, believed that the previous Landor livery was 'remote and aloof'. As British Airways was a global airline, it should reflect global cultures. The former prime minister, Margaret Thatcher, was not amused. 'We fly the British flag, not those awful things,' she growled as she pulled out a hanky and draped it over one of the offending designs. Among the many new tail-fin patterns, one stood out for its patriotism and flowing good looks. This was a logo that played very successfully with both the Union Flag and the White Ensign, flags once flown by the Royal Navy and the ships it built, among them Admiral Nelson's flagship, HMS *Victory*, at Chatham Dockyards on the north Kentish coast. The Chatham Dockyard Union emblem was applied to the tails of Concorde aircraft, now otherwise painted pure white, and it looked just right, a fluttering, slipstreaming flag at the tail of the fastest airliner to ride the world's airwaves. In due course, from 2001, this emblem replaced the controversial ethnic tail fins on all British Airways aircraft.

Air France retained just the one livery throughout Concorde's long service with the airline: white with a French flag in the guise of a red, white and blue barcode. Introduced in the mid-1970s, this simple livery was applied to all other Air France airliners. It outlived Concorde and has been modified only slightly since. The only other livery Concorde wore in service was very much a one-sided affair. The port side of G-BOAD was painted in Singapore Airlines colours – a blue speed stripe through the window line followed by a tail emblazoned with a stylized yellow Silver Kris, a mythical bird, on a deep-blue background – while the starboard side bore British Airways livery. This was the Concorde that flew the London to Singapore route between 1977 and 1980.

There were, though, two more colour schemes in later years, although these were one-offs, worn for very short spells. One was the dark-blue, red and white paint job given to Air France

Concorde F-BTSD in 1996 as part of a \$500m relaunch of Pepsi-Cola. Given the American hostility to Concorde just two decades earlier, Pepsi's endorsement of the Anglo-French airliner was a sign that it had made friends in the intervening years, at least around the soft drinks-consuming world. Despite its enthusiasm, Pepsi was not able to have things entirely its way. When Air France was awarded the contract, it discussed the proposed all-blue paint scheme with Aerospatiale. The French manufacturer agreed to a blue fuselage, yet insisted the wings should be painted white to keep fuel tanks cool in high-speed flight. Even then, the airliner was not to fly at Mach 2 for more than twenty minutes.

Painted in secret at Air France's maintenance hangar at Orly, the Concorde was wrapped in brown paper to hide its identity before being flown clandestinely at night to London Gatwick on 31 March 1996. Two days later, the aircraft was unveiled to a party of journalists and celebrities before shooting off on a ten-day tour of European and Middle Eastern cities. Opinions on this advertising colour scheme remain divided, yet there is little doubt that Concorde looked uncomfortable, and whatever it might have done for sales of Pepsi-Cola, the trick was never repeated.

The most spectacular, and oddest, paint scheme Concorde endured had been unveiled in an Aerospatiale hangar at Toulouse on 2 March 1989. This was to celebrate the twentieth anniversary of the airliner's maiden flight. A production test aircraft, F-WTSB, retired in 1985 was sprayed in glittering, star-spangled reds, whites and blues by local art students and displayed to a large gathering under a flashing light display accompanied by a musical piece performed by players apparently sealed into transparent boxes in front. The occasion was as nominally avant-garde as the paint job was bizarre.

Concorde wore a fictional white and red livery in the American disaster movie *The Concorde . . . Airport '79*. While the plot and flying sequences were pure hokum, and the cast – Alain Delon as the French pilot, Sylvia Kristel of *Emmanuelle* and *Private Lessons* fame as the purser – was a comic joy, the Concorde seen now under attack from a SAM missile, now by a rogue F-4 Phantom II, was quite real. It took Jennings Lang, the film's producer, several years to persuade Air France that this was a suitable role for their star airliner. Was it worth it? No. The film flopped, losing money at the box office. Critics panned it, with *Variety* calling it an 'unintentional comedy'. The aircraft chosen for this gloriously silly film was F-BTSC, leased to Air France by Aerospatiale at the time and bought by the airline for one franc in 1980. In May 1989, she flew Pope John Paul II into the heavens. On 25 June 2000, she was the Concorde that crashed in real life, killing all on board.

Curiously, *The Concorde . . . Airport '79* was the film that spelt doom for the long run of *Airport* disaster movies, which were directed by David Lowell Rich and began with *Airport* in 1970, starring Burt Lancaster and Dean Martin – their surnames evoking British and American Second World War bombers – and a Boeing 707. Lancaster described the film as 'the biggest piece of junk ever made', although it was a box-office hit. The script was based on Arthur Hailey's best-selling thriller of the same name published in 1968. According to an *Independent* obituary by Peter Guttridge, 'Although he [Hailey] suffered from airsickness, he served as a pilot in the RAF during the Second World War, flying fighters in the Middle East and transport aircraft in India. He achieved the rank of flight lieutenant.'

Hailey scripted what is probably the first aircraft disaster movie, *Zero Hour!*, a creaky 1957 outing for a Douglas DC-4, while twenty years later David Lowell Rich directed *SST: Death Flight*, a TV film that spelt doom not for Concorde but for a fictional American supersonic airliner – the world's first, of course – based not on the Boeing 2707 but on the less well-known Lockheed L-2000. The scale model used in the filming was given Boeing 747-style engines mounted in pods under the wings: at Mach 2, these alone would be enough to cause a tragedy. The film was widely mocked, but not so much as Rich's *The Horror at 37,000 Feet*, a CBS Television shocker from 1973. Demonic forces terrify passengers on board a Boeing 747 flight from London to New York. In one sequence, William Shatner, of *Star Trek* fame, enters the luggage hold at the back of the aircraft brandishing a flaming torch before the ghost of an evil Druid sends him hurtling from the airliner.

In 1980, the fast-paced satire *Airplane!*, starring Leslie Nielsen as a doctor on board a 707 in which virtually everyone including the crew fall ill from food poisoning, and Peter Graves – Jim Phelps from *Mission Impossible* – as a pervy pilot, put an end to this particular genre of daft, if often hugely popular, films. And although F-BTSC was to meet a terrible end in real life, Concorde went on to play passing roles in a number of less grisly films. In *The Parent Trap* (1998), twin girls, played by a young Lindsay Lohan, one living with her English mother (Natasha Richardson) on one side of the Atlantic, one with her American father (Dennis Quaid) on the other, bring their separated parents together again. When, in the final scene, shot in the States, it seems that the mother has decided to fly back to London with her English daughter and without her husband and American daughter, these two manage to get to London first to welcome them home, and they all live happily ever after. But how could they possibly have got to London first? They flew Concorde, of course, the world's most beautiful airliner bringing beauty and joy back into their lives.

EIGHT

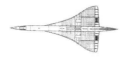

PHOENIX RISING

ON 27 August 1783, Benjamin Franklin, founding father, American minister to France and popular polymath, was among a 50,000-strong crowd gathered on the Champ de Mars, where the Eiffel Tower rises today. The occasion was the flight of Le Globe, the world's first hydrogen-powered balloon. Invented by the French mathematician and physicist Jacques Charles and built by the brothers Anne-Jean and Nicolas-Louis Robert, the unmanned red and yellow balloon rose quietly, if spectacularly, above the rooftops and treeline of pre-revolutionary Paris. It disappeared from sight, sailing on for another forty-minutes before it began to descend over a village some ten miles north-east of the city centre.

From all accounts, the local peasantry were alarmed. As this demonic visitation touched down on their cornfields, they tore into its delicate rubberized silk fabric with axes, knives and, of course, pitchforks. One of the world's first flying machines had come down to earth only to be destroyed. In Gonesse.

On 25 July 2000, Air France special flight 4590 prepared to take off from runway 26 (right), Charles de Gaulle Airport, Paris. It was close to 5 p.m., local time, and Concorde F-BTSC was packed to the gunwales with a full complement of nine crew, 100 passengers and their luggage. Ninety-six of the passengers were German, mostly from Monchengladbach, heading to New York, where they were booked on board MS *Deutschland*, a 22,400-tonne cruise liner launched in Kiel in 1998, for a sixteen-day tour to Ecuador, stopping off in Cuba and the Bahamas. Some had planned to sail on to Sydney for the 2000 Olympics.

On board Concorde, Captain Christian Marty opened up the throttles. Within twenty seconds, and now committed to take-off, the airliner ran over a seventeen-inch-long and one-inch-wide shallow strip of titanium that had detached from a thrust reverser cowl door of one of the three engines of a Continental Airlines DC-10, which had departed five minutes earlier on the same runway bound for Newark. The strip burst one of the Concorde's tyres. Debris flying through the air at over 300 mph – notably a 4.5-kg lump of tyre – caused a hydraulic shock that blew out a section of the aircraft's No 5 fuel tank.

Kerosene pouring out under pressure burst into flames. The live cable to the brake cooling fans might have arced when cut by debris. This arc ignited the fuel. The intensity of the fire caused the on-board fire warning from the No 2 engine to sound. Flight engineer Gilles Jardinaud responded by shutting it down. It was a fatal decision. Perhaps if the engine had been allowed to run, there might have been sufficient power to give Marty the speed he needed for a safe take-off and climb away from Charles de Gaulle. Now, though, he had neither the speed nor sufficient runway left. Flying at 230 mph, the aircraft climbed to 200 ft. The port wing was on fire, the starboard wing lifted and the crew throttled back in an attempt to level out the aircraft. But it was simply too late. Concorde fell to earth.

Fifteen years later, no one is quite sure what happened. Reporting from Paris for the *Daily Telegraph*, Patrick Bishop and Harry de Quetteville interviewed, among others, Darren Atkins, a British businessman who was on board a plane waiting to take off shortly after Flight 4590. 'It was already smoking as the plane accelerated down the runway,' Atkins recalled. 'As the aircraft drew level with us – this is before it started to take off – the left-hand engines were burning very heavily. On the tarmac was some debris that had fallen off the engine[s]. It was still on fire after the aircraft had departed.'

Sid Hare, an American pilot, told the reporters that the plane's engines seemed to be racing two or three times louder than usual. 'It was a huge fireball, like a mini atomic bomb. One of the engines obviously had a catastrophic failure. It was trailing flames two or three hundred feet.' Flightdeck crew and some of the passengers on an Air France 747-400 that had just arrived from Tokyo and was waiting to cross the runway watched the terrifying spectacle, too. One of those witnesses was Jacques Chirac, the president of France. The Concorde veered sharply towards its left on its take-off run, missing the Jumbo Jet, so witnesses said, by just twenty feet. 'Watch out,' Concorde's first officer had said.

Less than ninety seconds from take-off, Captain Marty informed Air Traffic Control that he was trying for Le Bourget aerodrome, where in 1927 Charles Lindbergh, the first pilot to fly solo non-stop across the Atlantic, had brought *The Spirit of*

St Louis safely down to land. The 3,600-mile venture had taken thirty-three and a half hours. Fifty-five years later, Christian Marty had windsurfed his way across the Atlantic without assistance. This daring voyage had taken thirty-seven days. His supersonic transatlantic flight to New York in July 2000 lasted less than two minutes.

'We saw it lose altitude,' said fifteen-year-old Samir Hossein, who was playing tennis under the Concorde's fiery flight path. 'It chopped off some trees and headed to the ground. The pilot tried to bank, but the plane rolled over and smacked into the hotel nose first and turned over. We saw flames shoot up 120 feet and there was a huge boom.' The stricken aircraft hit the all but empty Hôtelissimo Les Relais Bleus, killing four members of staff, and ploughed to a halt, a blackened tangle of charred metal, in cornfields surrounding the village of Gonesse. All on board were killed outright.

Many more might have died. It is possible that the Concorde might have hit the Air France flight from Tokyo with its payload of 400 passengers including Mr and Mrs Chirac and their close political entourage. Meanwhile, a group of sixty-four young musicians from Suffolk had been booked into the Hôtelissimo Les Relais Bleus that afternoon to meet up with fellow students. Altogether, 200 were to have gathered here for a meal shortly before Concorde crashed. Luckily, they were running a little late after a Channel crossing from Dover to Calais.

Concorde had been brought down to earth by accident for the first time in its thirty-one-year flying history. Its safety record had been second to none. That July evening, Air France grounded its Concorde fleet, and from then on it was the British who worked hardest to keep the supersonic airliner flying. While the French had lost money throughout much of Concorde's career, British Airways had made its supersonic operation into a profitable and much-coveted asset. Out of respect to Air France and all those who died, however, British Airways cancelled its Concorde flights, but for that day only. 'We have complete confidence in our Concorde aircraft,' Mike Street, British Airways' customer services and operations director, told the press, 'and we believe there is no technical, safety or operational evidence to suggest that Concorde should not operate safely into the future.'

The following morning, BA 001 was off from Heathrow to New York as usual, although with only forty-nine of the seventy-eight passengers who had booked flights on board. Steven Bacher, a South African stockbroker, told reporters, 'It's my first and I hope not my last flight on Concorde. I will be nervous for the first five minutes, but after that I'll be fine.' Brian Pople, an electrical contractor from Watford, added, 'Lightning doesn't strike twice. It's only happened once in thirty years. If I thought it wasn't safe, I wouldn't be going.'

The air authorities, however, thought differently. Whether or not British Airways Concorde aircraft were safe, the aircraft's certificate of airworthiness was withdrawn in mid-August. While everyone concerned agreed that a burst tyre had caused the crash at Gonesse, no single burst tyre should ever bring down an airliner. An official investigation was set up under the auspices of BEA (Bureau d'Enquêtes et d'Analyses pour la sécurité de l'aviation civile). It would determine the fate of Concorde, and the longer it took, the less likely it would be that the big bird would fly on into the new millennium. British Airways defended Concorde without hesitation. As its chief executive Rod Eddington told the press, 'We have been flying this aircraft in commercial service for twenty-five years. It's done 50,000 flights with us and it has a terrific record.' This, though, was not enough to save a loss of face on 15 August when the Concorde about to depart on BA 001 to New York was towed back to its terminal at Heathrow and its passengers transferred on to a subsonic flight as the ban on the Mach-2 airliner came into force.

The crash led to a discussion in the aircraft business as well as in the specialist and national media concerning just how safe Concorde really was. For a short spell, paranoia was the order of the day. And yet, there had been genuine cause for concern and, as it turned out, for many years. Concorde's tyres – those fitted until 2000 – proved to be a serious weakness. As early as November 1981, the American National Transportation Safety Board (NTSB) had been in touch with the French BEA concerning its own investigations into four serious incidents regarding the tyres of Air France Concorde aircraft. According to the NTSB, these incidents had been 'potentially catastrophic'.

The most serious of the four incidents had occurred in June 1979, when two tyres burst during a take-off from Washington Dulles, puncturing three fuel tanks, damaging No 2 engine, severing hydraulic lines and electrical wires and tearing the aluminium skin on the top side of a wing. In February 1981, an Air France Concorde on a flight from Mexico City to Paris was forced to land at New York's JFK Airport after tyres blown during an earlier take-off from Washington caused engine damage. The NTSB was particularly concerned that Air France crews appeared perfectly willing to take off after tyre bursts. Altogether, between

1976 and 2000, there were fifty-seven cases of tyre failure with both Air France and British Airways Concorde aircraft. Six of these had caused damage to the aircraft's fuel tanks. But the issue had not been ignored: modifications were undertaken after June 1979 with the fitting of stronger tyres – and wheels too. Furthermore, should a tyre deflate at a speed of up to 155 mph, the failure was now signalled to the flight crew and take-off was stopped. From 1993, according to one Concorde captain, tyre incidents were practically eliminated.

Significantly, British investigators into the Gonesse crash noted that the aircraft's landing gear had been loose, causing uneven movement during take-off and, as a result, uneven pressure on the tyres. The French investigators found that Captain Marty and his flight crew had done the best they could do in truly impossible circumstances, and they also found that the strip of metal from the Continental DC-10 was neither manufactured nor fitted in accordance with McDonnell Douglas guidelines. This finding prompted a criminal investigation of Continental Airlines, while in 2008 charges of involuntary manslaughter were brought against John Taylor, a Continental mechanic, Stanley Ford, a Continental maintenance manager, Claude Frantzen, who had worked for the French civil aviation authority, and Henri Perrier, the distinguished former chief engineer of the Concorde division at Aerospatiale.

While there appeared to be a case worth investigating against Continental, the legal pursuit of Perrier, an engineer and a man of great integrity, was ill-founded. What could be said about Concorde's design is that it was experimental, it was a venture into unchartered territories, and yet it had been designed with safety uppermost in mind and had proved to be one of the safest of all aircraft. A verdict was finally announced in Paris in December 2010. While Perrier, Ford and Frantzen were exonerated, Continental was fined 200,000 euros, ordered to pay Air France one million euros and instructed to pay 70 per cent of the cost of compensation claims by families of the Gonesse crash. John Taylor, meanwhile, was given a fifteen-month suspended prison sentence, but in November 2012 all convictions were overturned by a French court of appeal.

It was perfectly feasible for Concorde to have still been in service that same year, 2012. Certainly, as far as British Airways was concerned, there was no particular reason why the aircraft should have been retired before 2017 or 2018. In April 1999, Frank Debouck, Air France's deputy vice-president in charge of Concorde's North American route, was quoted in the *Los Angeles Times* to the effect that each French Concorde would soon undergo a year-long mechanical overhaul, which was expected to extend its flying life until 2015. 'A second overhaul could keep the planes airborne until 2030,' Debouck added, 'but after that, civil supersonic air travel remains a question mark.' The newspaper commented, 'For now, the Concorde is among the world's safest planes. Its only major scare came in 1979 when a bad landing blew out a plane's tires.'

On both sides of the Channel, however, the Concorde fleet was in fundamentally good shape, although further lists of faults logged over the years could not be ignored. Archives of the independent Aviation Safety Network note a British Airways Concorde on a charter flight to the Bay of Biscay turning back to Heathrow in January 2000 when a warning light flashed in the cockpit. At the end of that month, a Concorde on a BA flight from Barbados suffered an engine failure on its approach to Heathrow. The previous year there had been an emergency landing at Heathrow and an immediate return of a flight from JFK after take-off caused by problems with nose-gear and hydraulics. Along with a number of engine shutdowns, the archive also reveals an incident in October 1993 of brakes locking on a BA Concorde taxying at Heathrow leading to a burst tyre and damage to a fuel tank, while that July brake seizure on a BA Concorde landing at Heathrow caused a burst tyre and damage to both the wing and No 3 engine. And as early as June 1979, two tyres of an Air France Concorde had burst as the aircraft took off from Washington Dulles. Unable to retract the landing gear, the crew had turned back to the airport, where they found that debris from the tyres had caused hydraulic and fuel leaks.

Upper sections of rudders had broken off in flight on three occasions. An elevon had broken off on another, while fine cracks had been discovered in Concorde's slim wings. Ultimately, though, all these particular problems were satisfactorily resolved and the aircraft had flown safely with no loss of life throughout its long career as a test plane and in commercial service. And yet the suspicion there might be something wrong with the fleet continued to nag away.

For David Rose, an investigative journalist with the London *Observer* at the time, there was something else to worry about. In a dramatic article published on 13 May 2001, and after interviewing Sir Malcolm Field, chairman of the Civil Aviation Authority, Rose suggested that the real cause of the accident that had witnessed Concorde roaring down the runway at Charles de

Gaulle 'like a recalcitrant shopping trolley with a jammed wheel' was a lack of maintenance and care on the part of Air France. Not only were the wheels of the ill-fated Concorde's main landing gear out of alignment, but the aircraft was also overloaded and, with its centre of gravity unbalanced and a tail wind behind him, Marty should not have taken off as and when he did.

According to John Hutchinson, a British Airways Concorde pilot, Captain Marty would have found himself trying to save a 'onetime thoroughbred', which was 'responding like a flying pancake, like a sack of potatoes'. And as Rose pointed out, 'The fact that Marty had to rotate his plane 11 knots below its stipulated rotation velocity was always going to make it difficult to save. In the event, he never got close to V2, the 220-knot airspeed that would have represented stable flight. For a few seconds in the agonizing minute between take-off and catastrophe he got up to about 210 knots only for No 1 engine – which had begun to recover – to fail for a second time.'

As John Hutchinson told Rose, 'The accident appalled me beyond belief. The images of the plane and the crash will live in my mind forever. But it now seems that a single failing may not have caused the accident. In simple terms, if all the procedures and drills had been followed, if there had not been shortcuts and blind eyes, the crash might not have happened.'

Hutchinson had begun his career with the RAF in 1955 and flown Avro Shackleton long-range maritime patrol aircraft from Singapore before joining BOAC in 1966 and piloting Boeing 707s, Vickers VC-10s and Jumbo Jets before Concorde. At Heathrow on 8 April 1968, he himself had survived an engine failure on take-off that had led to a major fire and the loss of life. The aircraft involved was the heavily loaded Boeing 707 *Whisky Echo* en route to Sydney, and Hutchinson was on the flight deck but not flying the aircraft. Seconds into take-off, there was a loud bang as No 2 engine failed. 'Bloody hell!' exclaimed Check Captain Geoffrey Moss, who was on board to review the performance of the pilot in command, Captain Cliff Taylor. 'The wing's on fire.' Taylor was able to take off and, despite losing the burning engine – it fell into a gravel pit – made a controlled emergency landing back at Heathrow. Now that the Boeing itself was on fire, passengers made their escape any which way they could. One of the five people on board who died was air stewardess Barbara Jane Harrison, who had gone back into the blazing cabin to rescue those too slow to save themselves. She was awarded a posthumous George Cross.

Hutchinson knew that a failure by the crew to switch off the fuel to the stricken engine had been a major cause of the blaze that caused the death of Harrison and four passengers. It is not hard to imagine how deeply affected he must have been by the sight of the Air France Concorde on fire as it struggled to take off from Charles de Gaulle more than thirty years later. Like other Concorde pilots, he remained intensely loyal to the supersonic airliner. Appearing on the BBC's *Breakfast with Frost* on 30 July 2000, hosted that day by Peter Sissons, Hutchinson was asked whether or not passengers would now desert Concorde, hastening the day the aircraft was finally taken out of service.

'I can only say that I spent fifteen years flying that aeroplane,' he replied. 'I regard it even now as the safest aeroplane flying in the skies. I do not view this accident as some sort of virus infection that's about to run through the entire Concorde fleet . . . I believe that Concorde had another ten or maybe fifteen years of life in it and I hope that public confidence will be restored in the aeroplane in spite of that ghastly tragedy.'

Sissons asked if there was going to be 'a son of Concorde', or whether the aircraft's eventual, or even imminent, passing would mark the end of supersonic flight. Hutchinson, who in retirement flew a 1950s Auster Aiglet, which cruises at 110 mph and can keep flying at anything above 29 mph, replied:

> Well, I tell a story often about an elderly American lady I flew in about 1979 from Heathrow to Washington. I got her up on the flight deck and I'm chatting away to her – she was aged about eighty-five – and I said, 'You've obviously been very interested in airlines and the aviation industry . . . when did you first see an aeroplane?' And she said, 'I first saw an aeroplane in 1908 when one of the Wright brothers landed at Savannah, Georgia.' I said, 'When did you first fly?' And she said, 'I first flew in 1911.' And that really says it all. So in one lifetime we've gone from the Wright brothers to flying at twice the speed of sound in Concorde. And I cannot believe that in another sort of two or three generations from now people will be saying to their children, 'Well, yes, darling, we did fly supersonic at the tail end of the twentieth century and beginning of the twenty-first century, but it's all too difficult now.'

The following three years would be unsettling for anyone who flew, maintained, scheduled or simply adored Concorde. On the one hand, a special effort was made to resolve any technical problems and safety issues arising from Gonesse; on the other, plans were afoot – notably in France – to rid the skies of this supersonic albatross.

On 27 July 2000, a memorial service attended by 1,200 was held in Paris for those who died on board Flight AF4590 at the monumental Madeleine church facing the Place de la Concorde. This is where three years earlier, a service had been held for Diana, Princess of Wales on the evening of the day she had been killed in a car accident minutes away from this vast neo-Roman building designed by Pierre-Alexandre Vignon for Napoleon Bonaparte as a temple to the glory of his Grande Armée. So many dreams had been dispelled behind its daunting Corinthian portico. In Germany flags flew at half-mast, while red roses were strewn across the crash site in Gonesse.

A time for mourning was followed by modifications to the Concorde fleet on both sides of the Channel. Initially, progress was slow, bogged down by legalistic bureaucracy, but in November 2000 a group of six key members of the Concorde team met to cut to the chase. These were Jim O'Sullivan, British Airways' technical and quality director, the chief Concorde engineers from Airbus UK and Airbus France, John Britton and Alain Marty, Hervé Page from Air France, Roger Holliday, chief airworthiness engineer from Airbus UK, and Mike Bannister, BA's chief Concorde pilot. The key plan of action they produced was almost startlingly straightforward: Kevlar synthetic-fibre linings for the fuel tanks and new Kevlar-reinforced Michelin NZG (Near Zero Growth) tyres that were nearly immune from disastrous failure when damaged.

Even though the plan was simple, the results would need to be tested and retested before Concorde could fly in service again. But as the cost of doing nothing – lost revenue, a need for extensive maintenance if the aircraft sat on the ground for many more months – was high, and the modifications themselves were relatively cheap, it had to be worthwhile. To show it meant business, British Airways lined up all seven of its Concorde aircraft for a one-off photo-shoot and then work began on designing, making and fitting the Kevlar linings. Each aircraft would require 124 of these, but as each Concorde was very much a bespoke aircraft there were minor differences in each of them – as anyone who has restored Mk 2 and E-Type Jaguars, for example, will understand all too well.

In practice, fitting the Kevlar liners proved to be a challenging task. There was no other way to do the job other than getting the smallest and trimmest engineers to crawl into the tanks and to install the liners as if they were laying carpets in the lowest and most claustrophobic rooms imaginable. While the liners added to Concorde's weight, this was offset by the new British Airways interiors installed at the same time. The new blue leather seats, for example, were significantly lighter than their pseudo-armchair predecessors: every fraction of each pound and ounce mattered.

Down in the undercarriage, new wiring shields were fitted to prevent electric arcing – should it occur – from igniting leaked fuel. An Air France Concorde, F-BVFB, was used as a test mule at Istre-Le Tube air base, Marseilles – heavily bombed by the RAF during the German occupation of France – powering up and down the runway to study flow patterns of coloured water pumped from under the wings, simulating fuel loss. When she flew from Charles de Gaulle to the south of France in January 2001, F-BVFB had been vectored by radar away from what would have been its normal flight path over Gonesse.

Rolls-Royce, meanwhile, tested an Olympus 593 to destruction at the Ministry of Defence's Proof and Experimental Establishment at Shoeburyness on the Thames Estuary. Guns, engines and secret weapons have been put through their sonorous paces here since the Crimean War. Signs bear such intriguing legends as 'Do not touch or attempt to remove any unidentified object'. Red warning flags fly, and strange bangs and unfamiliar echoes are commonplace. What Rolls-Royce and the Concorde team were concerned to know was how the Olympus would behave if it ingested fuel or gas from an external source such as a leaking Concorde fuel tank. The answer was remarkably well; even if the engine surged, it would recover.

In France, Michelin had come up with a Christmas present for Concorde in December 2000 in the guise of a new tyre, one designed for the then up-and-coming double-deck Airbus A380, that would be ideal for the supersonic airliner. And yet, it was July 2001 before British Airways was able to issue a press release announcing the first fully fledged test flight with a modified Concorde. This was G-BOAF, which finally shot off from Heathrow on a strangely dark summer afternoon with Mike Bannister in command accompanied by Captain Jock Reid of the Civil Aviation Authority and a team of engineers monitoring various aspects of the aircraft as it headed out to the Atlantic on a loop to RAF Brize Norton, Oxfordshire. Crowds waved G-BOAF off from Heathrow and, despite the grim weather, three hours and twenty minutes later more crowds waved it back again into Brize Norton.

Speaking to the press after a pukka landing, an ebullient Mike Bannister said, 'It was absolutely fantastic to get behind the controls. I have been flying Concorde for twenty-two years, but this was the best flight ever. The initial reaction is that the aircraft performed brilliantly.' G-BOAF spent a summer holiday of sorts in Ireland, helping to re-familiarize Concorde crews flying in and out of Shannon Airport. In France, F-BVFB under the command of Edgar Chillaud, chief pilot of Air France's Concorde division, made a debut three-hour test flight from Charles de Gaulle on 23 August; Concorde crews were retrained at Chalons-Vatry Airport, ninety miles east of Paris. (This is the airport named Paris-Vatry-Disney by the low-budget airline Ryanair despite the great distances separating it from both Place de la Concorde and Disneyland Paris. Speaking to the *Independent* in April 2012, Michael O'Leary, Ryanair's pugnacious chief executive, said, 'I have myself driven from Vatry to Paris in just over an hour' – presumably in a road-going Concorde.)

On the morning of 5 September, Mike Bannister was filming a TV programme for the Discovery Channel with G-BOAF at Heathrow. He took a call while doing so; it was the go-ahead from the French and British civil aviation authorities: Concorde was back in business. Bannister and his team had more than a hunch that the revived Concorde service would be successful; throughout the refit and tests, British Airways had kept in direct contact with its core Concorde passengers, feeding them news and even organizing trips around its engineering base at Heathrow to observe the work as it was carried out.

A full test flight with British Airways staff doubling as passengers followed. This was a Mach-2 loop from Heathrow around the North Atlantic, complete with fine food from a new menu and the best champagnes. Staff enjoyed the new Conran-designed departure lounge at Heathrow, the comfortable new Connolly leather seats on board the aircraft and Concorde's entertainment system. Was it all too good to be true? Perhaps it was. That same day – 11 September 2001 – demonic spirits in the guise of al-Qaeda operatives crashed a pair of Boeing 767 airliners into the twin towers of Manhattan's World Trade Center, killing thousands and changing the nature of civil aviation from one of commonplace convenience to one of apprehension.

It was hardly a propitious start to the revived transatlantic Concorde service. And for a dark spell many people were indeed put off from travelling 'across the pond' from fear of further acts of terrorism. New York, though, would soon be back in business. Indeed, as President Calvin Coolidge had told the Society of American Newspaper Editors in January 1925, 'The chief business of the American people is business,' adding, 'of course, the accumulation of wealth cannot be justified as the chief end of existence. But we are compelled to recognize it as a means to well-nigh every desirable achievement.'

And just as one of those desirable achievements was a skyline of buildings as high as 1,350 ft, as the twin towers had been, so another was flying between two great commercial cities across the ocean that separated them at 1,350 mph. It had been this same fusion of trade, newly accumulated wealth, emerging technology and a belief in something beyond material existence that had forged the world's first determinedly tall buildings as well as the earliest machinery.

As far as we know, the first of those buildings were the baked mud-brick ziggurats of Sumeria, rising between the twin Rivers Tigris and Euphrates in what was once Mesopotamia and is southern Iraq today. The desire to reach for the sky while celebrating both wealth and the gods (or god), combined with the inexhaustible ambition of masons and architects, led on to the pyramids of Ancient Egypt, the spires of medieval cathedrals and eventually to skyscrapers sprouting from the streets of New York and Chicago in the late nineteenth century, when steel frames and safe lifts, or elevators, made living and working 1,000 ft above sidewalks a perfectly sane and profitable reality.

There had been warnings, however, from the earliest days that this reaching up to the realm of the new alpha (and omega) male sky gods, or the one God of Abraham, was somehow blasphemous. According to the King James Bible, generations after the Great Flood came to the land of Shinar (Mesopotamia), where they said, 'Come, let us build ourselves a city, and a tower whose top is in the heavens; let us make a name for ourselves, lest we be scattered abroad over the face of the whole earth.' But an all-powerful God decided that this was an ambition too far on the part of mere humans. So 'the Lord scattered them abroad from there over the face of all the earth, and they ceased building the city. Therefore its name is called Babel, because there the Lord confused the language of all the earth and they ceased building the city.'

God did his best to keep people apart and to confuse them, but both religion and trade have often brought them together again,

and many of the world's finest and most thrilling buildings –
Salisbury and Ulm cathedrals among so many others – reached
as high towards the heavens as their patrons could afford and
their architects could invent. Today, the world's tallest building,
the Burj Khalifa, is in the Middle East, the pinnacle of a society
that worships a single god and is a dab hand at trade, too. This
elongated, latter-day Tower of Babel in Dubai is 2,722 ft (828 m)
high. From its vertiginous viewing galleries, visitors look down
on the great commercial city spread below them and across to
the seemingly boundless dunes of the Empty Quarter, a shifting
sea of sand evoking a world before the very first ziggurat. And,
as if to reinforce the point that towers and trade bring peoples
together, the Burj Khalifa was designed by SOM, architects of
One World Trade Center, the new twinless tower in New York.

For many decades, the tallest building in the world was the
Empire State Building. Rising above mid-town Manhattan in
the Great Depression of the 1930s, it was a symbol of better
days to come. It even survived an aircraft crashing into it – a
North American B-25 Mitchell bomber lost in fog – in July 1945.
At a press conference held in Chicago in October 1956, Frank
Lloyd Wright unveiled his design for The Illinois, a mile-high
skyscraper designed as a challenge to New York. A skyscraper too
far, it never happened.

And yet despite talk that after 9/11 the skyscraper would wilt
and die, developing countries around the world are flexing their
economic muscle and, as they do so, investing in ever taller
buildings. Today, the People's Republic of China boasts hundreds
of skyscrapers, which are usually defined as buildings more
than 500 ft (152 m) tall. The skyline of Pudong, Shanghai's new

commercial centre, is a forest of extravagant skyscrapers, and when it opens in 2015, the twisting Shanghai Tower, designed by the US firm Gensler, with Jun Xia as lead architect, will be – at 2,073 ft (632 m) – the world's second tallest building. The Chinese, though, are likely to want to go much higher than this, while oil-rich Middle Eastern states, kingdoms and emirates are competing with them and other countries keen to display their newfound wealth have joined in this slightly inane numbers game. Where will it all end? Significantly, perhaps, the tallest new building in Russia is named after a space rocket. This is Moscow's Vostok Tower at 1,224 ft (373m), designed by nps [sic] and partner Schwegger Associated Architects, and due to open in 2015.

After the Burj Khalifa and the Shanghai Tower, the world's third tallest building is the curious Mecca Royal Hotel Clock Tower, a mixed-purpose skyscraper complete with a vast, four-sided clock-face, that looms over the Grand Mosque and the Kaaba, one of Islam's holiest sites, said to have been built by Ibrahim (Abraham). The Mecca tower, designed by Dar Al-Handasah architects, is 1,972 ft (601m) high. Clearly, the upward look to the heavens, along with ambition, competition and trade, remain the driving forces behind a building type that, despite terrible divine or man-made events, will aim ever higher in the twentieth-first century and even beyond.

Given this spirit, Concorde – a machine that flew so very high above not just every skyscraper but every other airliner flying between these high-rising global cities – had its place in the new world order after the shocking events of 11 September 2001 when American Boeings in the hands of psychotic men were used as tools to bring the tallest American towers down to earth. Concorde's own fall in flames over Gonesse the year before had seemed to some a message of sorts that, like Icarus, this was a human invention that had reached that bit too close to the heavens. And yet, Concorde did fly again and profitably so. This was because there was a demand by high-flying business executives to trade face-to-face between New York, London and Paris, and a subliminal collective desire in liberal Western democracies with their belief in freedom, including that of worship (or not), to stand up to savage bullies and their single-minded desire to drag the world down into some new dark age of perverted religion.

While British Airways prepared itself for the born-again transatlantic Concorde service, New York began work on designs, initially by the Polish-American architect Daniel Libeskind, for a Freedom Tower commissioned to take the place of the twin towers destroyed by men who believed neither in life and liberty nor happiness. This was to be 1,776 ft high, a symbolic reference to the US Declaration of Independence of 1776. The original draft, with its famous line 'We hold these truths to be self-evident, that all men are created equal, that they are endowed by their Creator with certain unalienable rights, that among these are Life, Liberty and the pursuit of Happiness', was written by Thomas Jefferson, founding father, third president of the United States and one of the finest architects of his era.

Jefferson crossed the Atlantic to Paris in 1784, a year after the signing of the Treaty of Paris that marked the end of the American War of Independence between Britain and its former colonies. In Paris, Jefferson was met by his fellow countrymen and trade ministers John Adams, who was later the second president of the United States, and Benjamin Franklin. All three believed that enlightened human reason and knowledge would improve the human condition; all three watched balloons ascending over Paris, carrying men high into the air and the future.

Air France and British Airways Concorde flights to New York resumed on 7 November 2001. New York's mayor, Rudolph 'Rudy' Giuliani, said, 'Concorde's return is symbolic of how all New Yorkers feel about rebuilding this great city.' What a change this was from a quarter of a century earlier, when Concorde was widely viewed by Americans and New Yorkers in particular as some malevolent force invading the city.

'We hope Concorde's return will play a major part in rebuilding confidence in New York,' British Airways' chief executive Rod Eddington told the American press, 'and demonstrating that it is business as usual between the UK and the USA. We have received tremendous support from our regular business customers over the last year and we look forward to carrying them supersonically across the Atlantic once more.' Jean-Cyril Spinetta, chairman of Air France, shared the sentiment, saying, 'Concorde's return to New York is symbolic of Air France's tribute to the people of this city, to their strength and their strong resolve to rebuild. Within our own ranks, we have not forgotten the show of sympathy and support of many New Yorkers in the hours and days following the Concorde accident of July 25, 2000.'

No more than ten Concorde aircraft were to fly across the Atlantic from 2001. The British fielded five of its seven supersonic airliners, the French four with one in reserve. This says much about the power of Concorde in terms of its great symbolic value to transatlantic commerce and cordiality. While fleets of Boeings were crossing and re-crossing the North Atlantic safely each day, Concorde represented the joining of hands in the air between France, Britain and the United States in a way that no other aircraft, or invention, could match.

By November 2001, e-mail had become a commonplace form of communication, with progress in the development of such technology evolving in winking, bleeping leaps and bounds. Perhaps there was no longer a need to fly the Atlantic at immense speed, and yet the desire to meet colleagues in person before signing a deal has remained a constant, and the sheer glamour and excitement of racing the sun across the Atlantic has never failed to lose its allure. 'I'm no use at video conferencing,' Neville Bain, chairman of the Royal Mail Group, told Valerie Grove from *The Times*. 'It's not the same. I need to eyeball people, and touch them on the elbow' – and, as Grove added, 'You do not get Krug and caviar in a video conference.' From November 2001, tickets for Concorde would be very expensive indeed, and yet they continued to be in high demand: 7,000 seats had been booked by the beginning of the month.

Simultaneous Concorde flights departed Heathrow and Charles de Gaulle at 1044 hrs (local times). Air France carried captains of industry, and British Airways both these and, of course, 'celebrities', a breed of shiny people that had grown as if exponentially over the previous decade and were soon to be defined as 'people you have never heard of'. Concorde itself was pure celebrity. 'We have put Concorde back where she belongs,' purred Captain Mike Bannister over the Tannoy. 'Sit back and relax. We're glad to be back.'

At JFK, the two airliners, F-BTSD and G-BOAE commanded respectively by Captains Chillaud and Bannister, were positioned nose-to-nose outside the BA Terminal. Company bigwigs, airline executives and transport ministers gave and listened to congratulatory speeches; in the evening they were invited to a slap-up dinner at the New York Stock Exchange. It was business as usual. Or was it? Late that same afternoon (GMT), a British Airways Concorde nicknamed 'Blair Force One' for the day, took off from Heathrow heading not for a civil American airport but to Andrews Field, the USAF air base at Washington DC. 'Blair' referred, of course, to Tony Blair, Britain's New Labour prime minister, his trip by Concorde a symbolic gesture in his extraordinarily close alliance with George W. Bush, the newly elected Republican president of the United States. A month earlier, American and British forces had unleashed aerial attacks – the opening shots of Operation Enduring Freedom – against Taliban targets in Afghanistan. The aim was to 'smoke out' the Taliban and destroy its haven for Al-Qaeda and its own founding father Osama bin Laden, the Saudi Arabian son of a billionaire construction magnate, who had plotted the destruction of the World Trade Center. Blair's fast flight to Washington DC would also lead to the 'shock and awe' invasion of Iraq in March 2003. According to Bush and Blair, this grave misadventure was 'to disarm Iraq of weapons of mass destruction, to end Saddam Hussein's support for terrorism, and to free the Iraqi people'. As was well known before the invasion, except apparently to Bush and Blair, there were no weapons of mass destruction, nor did Saddam Hussein support terrorism, nor did Operation Iraqi Freedom free the Iraqi people. When it returned to service on 7 November 2001, Concorde was indeed flying into more turbulent skies.

The supersonic airliner itself remained a symbol of a more optimistic world. Its presence, although loud and a thorn in the side to unforgiving environmentalists, was somehow reassuring and, soon enough, Concorde would be described as an 'icon' and 'national treasure'. If not quite a pet, it was clearly cherished in its last two years of operations. And when pomp and circumstance demanded it, Concorde was there to put on a show, to represent Britain, especially in moments of national celebration and display. On 4 June 2002, Concorde G-BOAD flown by Mike Bannister concluded a fly-past, accompanied by the RAF Red Arrows display team, and behind an aerial flotilla of military aircraft, at 1,500 ft over Buckingham Palace. The occasion was the finale of the Queen's Golden Jubilee celebrations. More than a million people had gathered to watch from St James's Park, Green Park and The Mall. Of other British aircraft, only the Supermarine Spitfire, the Avro Lancaster and, perhaps, the delta-winged Avro Vulcan were held in such fond esteem. After so many years, people in the crowd that day still pointed up, exclaiming, 'There's Concorde!'

On 10 April 2003, British Airways and Air France announced jointly that Concorde would retire that year. To the public at large and to Concorde passengers in particular, this came as a surprise. In February, however, an Air France Concorde on its way from New York to Paris had been diverted to Halifax, Nova Scotia, after its No 3 engine was shut down after a fuel leak. In March, an Air France Concorde lost a part of its lower rudder. When the airline made its decision public the following month, Air France chairman Jean-Cyril Spinetta said, 'Air France deeply regrets having to make the decision to stop its Concorde operations but it has become a necessity. The worsening economic situation in the last few months has led to a decline in business traffic which particularly weighs on Concorde's results. Maintenance costs have substantially increased since its return to service. Operating Concorde has become a severely and structurally loss-making operation. In these circumstances it would be unreasonable to continue operating it any longer.'

British Airways' Rod Eddington sounded a little less specific, perhaps even less certain. 'Concorde has served us well,' he said, 'and we are extremely proud to have flown this marvellous and unique aircraft for the past twenty-seven years. This is the end of a fantastic era in world aviation but bringing forward Concorde's retirement is a prudent business decision at a time when we are having to make difficult decisions right across the airline. The demise of the Concorde will indeed be a sad day in aviation history, even the end of an era. If you have the means and the time, don't miss a last chance to fly aboard its majestic splendour.'

But if Concorde was so very special, then why the apparently out-of-the-blue decision to ground it? Noel Forgeard, president and chief executive of Airbus, gave little away when he said, 'The Airbus predecessors, Aerospatiale and British Aircraft Corporation, created the Concorde some forty years ago and we are proud of this remarkable achievement. But its maintenance regime is increasing fast with age. Thus, as an aircraft manufacturer, we completely understand and respect the decision of Air France and British Airways, especially in the current economic climate. It goes without saying that, until the completion of the very last flight, we will continue to support the operators so that the highest standards of maintenance and safety are entirely fulfilled.'

Richard Branson, the publicity-conscious chairman of Virgin Airways, offered to buy British Airways' seven Concorde aircraft for a pound each, the nominal price, he believed, the government had sold the aircraft to the airline. Virgin would fly them to New York, Barbados and Dubai. When British Airways denied the claim and rejected this chirpy offer, Branson upped his game to a £5m bid while at the same time putting forward a proposal for the establishment of a charitable trust that would keep two Concorde aircraft flying on a semi-commercial basis. At the time, British Airways was toying with the idea of keeping a Concorde of its own in flying condition for air displays and special trips, but again it turned Branson down. What stopped both Branson and British Airways from flying a Concorde, or Concorde aircraft, into the future, however, was not ultimately a lack of resolve, but the simple fact that Airbus was unwilling to provide, much less manufacture, spare parts for the supersonic airliner beyond the agreed retirement date of October 2003.

For Donald L. Pevsner, a US lawyer born in New York, and a self-confessed 'aviation enthusiast since I first saw the first BOAC Comet 4 aircraft leave Idlewild Airport/IDL [later JFK] for London/LHR on October 4, 1958', the decision to retire Concorde prematurely was nothing less than a betrayal. Between 1985 and 2000, this ardent steam railway locomotive enthusiast and Concorde buff had chartered the supersonic airliner for numerous and sometimes spectacular flights. These included two record around-the-world flights, eastbound in 1992 and westbound three years later. At the time, Pevsner was regarded widely as the Ralph Nader of the aviation industry; where Nader had campaigned for safer cars in the 1960s and shot to international fame with his 1965 book *Unsafe at Any Speed: The Designed-In Dangers of the American Automobile*, Pevsner championed the rights of air passengers. He was, though, very much in love with speed if this involved an express steam locomotive, or Concorde.

'The saga,' Pevsner wrote, 'of the secret betrayal of Concorde by senior executives at both Air France and British Airways, and the secret collusion between the Chairman of Air France and the President of Airbus to ensure Air France would not have to suffer the "loss of face" that would ensue from its unilaterally retiring its Concorde fleet, thereby leaving British Airways with a monopoly on supersonic transatlantic service, is a nasty litany of hypocrisy, cowardice and "corporate politics".'

Pevsner's accusations had in part been fuelled by Rob Lewis's book *Supersonic Secrets*, published in 2003. Pevsner and Lewis's contention was that Airbus was keen to get shot of Concorde. It was busy developing the enormous Airbus A380, a sedate aerial cruise liner to Concorde's sleek racing yacht and antithetical to it in so many ways. Air France, or at least its chairman Jean-Cyril Spinetta, clearly felt the same way, while support for Concorde from the very top had been damaged to an unknown degree by the fact that the Boeing 747 carrying President Chirac came all too close to Captain Marty's stricken aircraft as it attempted to take off from Charles de Gaulle on 25 July 2000. For its part, British Airways decided to cut maintenance costs by reducing the number of Concorde aircraft available for service at any one time to five and pulling out of the charter market.

Meanwhile, the idea that Concorde was an 'old' aircraft and should be retired on that basis alone was gaining ground among subsonic management on both sides of the Channel. Pevsner, for one, was having none of this. 'Just look at the Boeing B-52 bomber, which has been flying for sixty years, and the McDonnell Douglas DC-8 60/70 series, which has been flying for forty-seven years [he was writing in 2010], as only two relevant examples. Plus, the highest-time BA Concorde (G-BOAD) retired with just 23,397 total hours: about the same as a five-year-old Boeing 747-400. The highest-time AF Concorde (F-BVFA) retired with just 17,824 hours: about the same as a four-year-old Boeing 747-400.'

When Airbus announced a sharp rise in the price of keeping Concorde flying, the die was cast. If Air France retired its Concorde aircraft, then the entire cost would fall on British Airways, making its own too expensive to keep in service despite high fares and high passenger demand. When the joint announcement was made concerning the final retirement of Air France's Concorde fleet on 31 May 2003 and British Airways' on 24 October, significant costs had to be written off, although because Air France had not refitted its aircraft to the extent British Airways had, the cost to the French was significantly lower. To recoup the £84m retirement cost of its Concorde aircraft, British Airways, says Pevsner, 'packed its planes with "supersonic tourists" over the next six months, and realized about £92m in revenue as nearly every flight departed with all one hundred seats filled with fare-paying passengers'.

Passengers wanted Concorde, but neither Air France nor Airbus did. Even British Airways' plan to retain a solitary Concorde for special flights was scuppered when Airbus refused point-blank to continue technical support of the aircraft after 31 October, ensuring that its certificate of airworthiness would be withdrawn. Not all senior British Airways managers were so mustard-keen on ridding the skies of Concorde. They knew full well the extent to which the British public had taken the supersonic airliner to heart. In those final six months, countless people came to Heathrow, or as close as they could in a post-9/11 world, to watch Concorde take off and land. And for those who watched Concorde flying across central London daily, the clock was ticking all too quickly. Peter Marlow, the distinguished Magnum photographer, published a book, *Concorde: the Last Summer*, three years after Concorde's forced retirement. It shows the sheer variety of people of all walks of life, nationalities and classes, if perhaps not creeds, who came to look up wistfully into damp skies and pay quiet homage to the aircraft.

In 1997, the talented German photographer Wolfgang Tillmans had published a book that sits naturally alongside Marlow's on the bookshelf. *Concorde* is a collection of poetic shots of the airliner. Like Marlow's, these were not for the out-and-out aircraft enthusiast, but for all those who found it rather hard to express quite why this thunderous machine that had been such an affront to so many professional campaigners, compulsive naysayers and righteous environmentalists in earlier decades was so compelling, heart-rending even. As Tillmans himself put it in his introduction, 'For the chosen few, flying Concorde is a glamorous but cramped and slightly boring routine whilst to watch it in air, landing or taking off is a strange and free spectacle, a super-modern anachronism and an image of the desire to overcome time and distance through technology.'

Today's airliners have their transcendental moments, not least when seen shimmering in high flight on azure summer days, their pure white contrails etching painterly skies. Concorde, though, offered the drama of a sudden sighting of an osprey among seagulls, a soaring eagle over cawing rooks, an operatic hot air balloon over the densely packed central streets of eighteenth-century Paris. No wonder the virus of twenty-first-century management took against it. Furthermore, Concorde was perceived by its detractors as being a machine from the analogue era, a time as distant as the Jurassic Period to aspiring global executives riddled with a rampant and apparently incurable addiction to digitalia and what appeared to be an unforgiving allergy to manufacturing, engineering, craft and skill.

Dials, switches, turbines, cogs, levers and anything that hinted at analogue had become things to pass by, eyes averted, while clutching the latest, and instantly obsolescent, smartphone in one hand, the other pressing a small Seville orange, as once did the Tudor cardinal Thomas Wolsey, to the delicate executive nasal passages to dispel the odour of working machinery and any hint of workshops and factories. These were, after all, ghastly things and best left to the dutifully productive Chinese and ragged children in developing countries far away of which little was known beyond the luxury suites of a few five-star resort hotels. And these destinations were anyway reached by subsonic Boeings and Airbuses crammed with every digital gizmo going and managed in flight by crews whose main job was to kowtow to Captain Computer and in-flight control systems that must be obeyed, even when an airliner was in danger of tumbling from the skies and only the quaint, old-fashioned, pre-digital flying skills of its pilots could save it.

Or, as Donald L. Pevsner, put it, 'No longer can we cross the North Atlantic Ocean in 3 hours 23 minutes at 56,000 ft; nor experience the jet-fighter blast down the runway at take-off; nor climb at up to 12,000 ft per minute on special occasions (which I did out of Lisbon/LIS for Paris/CDG the day after we captured the Westbound Around the World speed record); nor revel in the ultimate mode of high-speed luxury transportation. Instead the actions of those persons (Air France, Airbus and to a lesser extent BA management) . . . have resulted in the first backward step in aviation since the Wright brothers first flew on December 17 1903.'

Lord Colin Marshall, British Airways' chairman, was a Concorde enthusiast, as was his CEO Rod Eddington. Speaking to *The Times* in May 2003, Marshall said, 'Concorde can't keep flying unless the manufacturer is willing to go on producing the parts. Airbus said they were not willing to support Concorde beyond the end of October. We might well have considered continuing if they hadn't. It would have been much more difficult for Airbus if Air France and British Airways had presented a united front in supporting the continuation of scheduled services.'

Both real and crocodile tears were shed when flight AF 001 (F-BTSD) left New York for Paris on 31 May 2003, commanded by Captain Jean-François Michel and bringing with it sixty-eight passengers, eleven crew members and a dog. 'Concorde will never stop flying,' said Jean-Cyril Spinetta, chairman of the loss-making French airline, 'because it will live on in people's imagination.' A charter flight around the Bay of Biscay and over the Channel Islands that day proved to be the final commercial flight by an Air France Concorde to take off from Paris. Flown by Jean-Louis Chatelain and Beatrice Vialle, F-BVFB landed an hour after AF 001 arrived from New York.

'Every flight is a moment of delight,' said the French skipper Chatelain. 'It is the Formula One of aviation, with the performance of a jet fighter.' Chief stewardess Joelle Cornet-Templet told the press, as well she might, 'It is a magic aircraft. The pleasure of flying in it is almost a carnal one.' A week earlier, a Spanish couple claimed to have joined the Mile High Club, making love on board British Airways flight 001 from London to New York. An unabashed British Airways spokesman commented, 'We only hope that the earth moved for them at twice the speed of sound.'

The British love of Concorde continued unabated. Concorde made a farewell tour around North America, followed by flights to cities in England, Northern Ireland, Scotland and Wales in October. There was a flight for a fiver (£5) in association with the *Daily Mirror*, a simultaneous landing at Heathrow by Concorde aircraft flying in from Manchester and New York, and then on 24 October, the arrival at Heathrow of the last three British Airways Concorde aircraft in commercial service, one behind the other, from Edinburgh, the Bay of Biscay and, of course, New York.

That final transatlantic flight was a curious affair that somehow summed up the airliner's anomalous existence. The aircraft concerned was G-BOAG, captained by Mike Bannister, and, in terms of the big picture that day, the flight was moving – at Mach 2 it could be nothing less – and undoubtedly a momentous occasion. It was my second flight on the supersonic airliner, and so very different from my first, rather more subdued Atlantic crossing years earlier. I wrote up my record of the flight for the next morning's *Guardian* standing in front of the aircraft:

> The sky seems a little lower this morning; a cathedral without a spire, a mountain without wolves. Yesterday Concorde, the Anglo-French sky goddess, drooped her nose for the last time in commercial flight, coming in to land among commonplace Boeings and Airbuses at Heathrow airport.
>
> And then she turned and pirouetted slowly into her hangar to meet and greet the massed ranks of waiting TV cameras, as 100 celebrities, captains of industry, competition winners, newspaper editors and at least one ballerina and a fashion model emerged from her nipped and tucked fuselage.
>
> The last trip on Concorde G-BOAG from New York yesterday was not exactly as elegant as it should have been. The cabin was host to a media scrum, and for all the fine foods and wines, the journey felt rather like a trip back from a rugby match. As noisy as the aircraft's engines, and then some.

This was such an exquisite aircraft, a triumph of aerodynamic and engineering design. And yet from inside, its final flight had been something of a rough ride. Burly media men with ruddy faces squeezed into suits a size too tight exchanged Anglo-Saxon insults as they drank champagne and, implausibly given their girth and Concorde's Size 8 frame, even squared up to one another. One big fellow threw a glass of water over another. Other chaps, broad of beam and brimming with vintage bubbly, guffawed loudly enough to drown out even the Olympus turbines.

Mike Bannister took it all in good stead, speaking like a BOAC or RAF pilot of yore. 'His speech pattern and choice of words,' I wrote, 'were those of the age in which Concorde was nurtured. Spitfires had gone out of service with the RAF in the Far East just two years before the supersonic programme that launched Concorde took flight.' And as it was, the hard facts of a more modern commerce were the shots that finally brought Concorde down to land after 50,000 flights, 100,000 supersonic flying hours, 1,000,000 bottles of champagne, 2,500,000 passengers and 140,000,000 miles.

There were a few non-paying flights as Concorde aircraft were dispersed to museums across Britain and France and around the world. Mike Bannister took G-BOAG back across the Atlantic on 3 November, and two days later – the forty-seventh anniversary of that first STAC meeting in London – made a record-breaking flight from New York to Boeing Field, Seattle, in three hours, fifty minutes and twelve seconds. The flight path had been over northern Canada, where the Speedbird flew supersonically for ninety-four minutes. On loan from British Airways, Alpha Golf stands in front of the Raisbeck Aviation High School outside Seattle's Museum of Flight.

The last flight of all – by the last Concorde built – was from Heathrow to Filton on 26 November, three weeks short of the centenary of the first powered flight by the Wright brothers. Christopher Orlebar parked his car on the central reservation of the A3044 directly under the flight path to watch the great aircraft he knew so intimately well thunder over and up into the wet Middlesex sky. 'Just as the Wrights had settled who would become the world's first pilot by tossing a coin,' Orlebar wrote, 'so it was resolved who would be the last to land Concorde. Paul Douglas flipped the coin; Les Brodie called heads and won. As he put it, "It was the Queen who decided."'

Flying out to the Atlantic, Brodie took G-BOAF up to Mach 2 before turning for the Channel Islands, Southampton, the M4 corridor and so to Bristol. He flew the airliner at 3,000 ft over Isambard Kingdom Brunel's Clifton Suspension Bridge, thus conjuring a meeting of two hauntingly beautiful examples of engineering genius. The bridge was lined with Bristolians who spread out up onto the Downs, among them, as Orlebar noted, those who had built this very aircraft and others who had spent the bulk of their careers caring for her. From late 2017, if all goes to plan, G-BOAF will be the centrepiece of a purpose-built visitor centre, with major backing from the Heritage Lottery Fund, at Filton; the organizers hope to attract 120,000 visitors a year, the equivalent of 1,200 Concorde flights with every seat sold.

Not every last surviving Concorde was packed off to a museum. G-BOAB, which last flew into Heathrow in August 2000, remains parked in and around the British Airways engineering building, a ghost of future past. There have been rumours to the effect that the BA-owned airliner will be scrapped, flogged to some tourist venue in Dubai – berthed, perhaps, alongside the sorry hulk of the elegant Cunard liner QE2, which made her maiden voyage two months after Concorde first took to the air from Toulouse – or even saved and flown again.

The Save Concorde Group is determined to see a Concorde back in the air, while Heritage Concorde, a group of former Concorde engineers, is actively engaged in looking after Concorde airframes around the world and the French Olympus 593 group is involved in a long-term collaboration with the British ventures. In 2010, the Air and Space Museum at Le Bourget said that it hoped to restore F-BTSD to a condition where it could at least taxy up and down a runway, although this would be both a little frustrating for anyone involved and heavy on the brakes.

It is not impossible for Concorde to return to the skies. Armchair critics who were determined to believe that a Rolls-Royce Olympus-powered Avro Vulcan would never fly again must have been disgruntled when XH558, *The Spirit of Great Britain*, did just that in October 2007 thanks to the Vulcan to the Sky Trust. It goes without saying that the challenge for Concorde enthusiasts is enormous, and yet if they do manage it, Concorde might once again make every other passenger aircraft look old-fashioned.

The splendid 80-ft-long model of a British Airways Concorde that greeted passengers to Heathrow Airport for many years was replaced in 2008 by a model of an Emirates Airlines Airbus A380. As the model was an advertisement, British Airways had to pay a substantial sum to keep it in place, but since the airline was scheduled to move into its own dedicated terminal, the Richard Rogers-designed Terminal Five, in March 2007, it agreed to donate the model to the Brooklands Museum, Surrey – a treasure trove of historic aircraft, racing cars, motorcycles and London buses gathered by the world's first purpose-built race track – where, since 2012, it has been the museum's gate guardian.

This was a fitting decision as not only were major components of all Concorde aircraft built a few minutes from here at BAC's Weybridge workshops, but Brooklands is also home to the first British production Concorde, G-BBDG. Although this particular aircraft, last flown in 1981, never entered passenger service, today it is a hugely popular exhibit, offering simulated flights at just £5 a head.

For rather more you can have a crack at the Concorde flight simulator. This was dismantled and moved from Bristol to Brooklands in 2004. Gordon Roxburgh, an electronics expert and Concorde enthusiast, used off-the-shelf computer software to resurrect this thirty-year-old training box. Although lacking hydraulic jacks, the visual system creates a convincing sensation of movement. The revived simulator has a 165-degree field of view collimated to infinity and thus a clear and realistic view from the 'cockpit'. As former Concorde pilots serve as instructors, this is as close as you can get to flying the aircraft without leaving the ground or, of course, turning back the clock. And then there are the lunches and talks with one of the museum's most popular trustees, Mike Bannister, while for some visitors, Concorde is nothing less than a romantic experience: a notice on the museum's website on New Year's Day 2015 read: 'Due to a wedding in Concorde on Friday 2 January, the first flight will be 1225 p.m.'

Passengers using Paris Charles de Gaulle Airport will have passed by Concorde F-BVFF many times in recent years; the airliner is mounted on a mound above a roadway and positioned at an angle evoking both take-off and – sadly – that day at the beginning of a new century, a new millennium, when the big bird's fate was sealed. Concorde might have risen like a phoenix in 2001, but in effect it had made it into the twenty-first century by the skin of its long nose. The spirit of Concorde will forever be haunted by the ghosts of Gonesse.

NINE

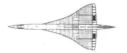

SUPERFAST
FUTURES

THERE had been a Plan B. Concorde was never meant to have been a one-off design. As Dudley Collard of Sud Aviation, and later Aerospatiale, recalled in 1998, 'Concorde is a very undeveloped aircraft. Directly it was developed enough to perform its mission, development stopped.'

The original aim had been for sales of perhaps 500 Concorde aircraft, while the development of a new model, and production of new supersonic airliners from other countries, pressed ahead. Proposals for a B model were drawn up immediately after Concorde went into service in 1976. This was not a new design, but a blueprint for an improved aircraft. Concorde B would be quieter, burn less fuel and fly longer distances, up to 5,000 miles. The plan was for the new aircraft to be in service from 1982. Existing Concorde aircraft could then be upgraded to meet the new specifications and routes opened up such as New York to Tokyo, with a stopover at Anchorage, for example, or Hong Kong to Los Angeles via Honolulu. Sydney and Cape Town would also come within Concorde's reach.

Poor sales of the A model Concorde, together with a sharp and continuing rise in the price of fuel in the 1970s, put paid to progress on any successor. And yet there remained an underlying belief both within the aviation industry and among the public at large that in the not too distant future we would be flying very much faster indeed. Supersonic? How slow and quaint this would seem to hypersonic (Mach 5 plus) passengers flitting between London and New York in under an hour or Tokyo and London in no more than two.

How quaint, too, were some of the design compromises – or the sheer ingenuity – that had enabled Concorde to perform as well as it did. Concorde captain Jock Lowe told an insightful story about Concorde's hidden workings:

> The engine is round, the intakes are square, so at the corner of each engine there is a little gap. So we have secondary air doors, as they are called. I think it is the only Heath Robinson system on the aeroplane. It is driven by one motor and one cable, and we have had more turn-backs because of this purely incidental system. The doors have to be locked for take-off because the engines are so powerful they would suck the exhaust gas back in; they have to be open for supersonic flight, because the air has to cool the engine. And they have given us trouble. I flew the Prime Minister [Tony Blair] earlier this year to meet President Clinton, with Mrs Blair on board, and on

take-off, if these doors don't open, you have to keep the speed back to keep the air loads off so you can try to open them. We have a senior flight engineer sitting there, Mr Blair sitting behind me, we have just taken off with all the bands and fanfare and Mr and Mrs Clinton are waiting, and the engineer says 'Can you just keep the speed back to 250 knots, Jock?' He whispered it, and I knew he could only be saying that for one reason: the secondary air doors had not opened.

It took a minute to re-set the circuit breaker, and from then on the flight went to plan. The Heath Robinson device had worked, but if it had failed, there would have been no Plan B.

Whether or not anyone really wants or needs to fly this fast remains a question to be answered by future generations. Perhaps we will end up using hand-held *Star Trek*-style transporters that beam us to any point in the world in nanoseconds. Perhaps we might want to slow down instead and take life easy. Nevertheless, the technology to fly so very much faster than Concorde had been in development since the 1940s. Safely ensconced in the United States after the Second World War, Werner von Braun and his team appear to have achieved hypersonic flight with V-2 ballistic missiles a year before *The Eagle*, an English boys' comic with a circulation not far short of a million, was launched in 1950.

The Eagle, whether bought newly printed from contemporary newsstands or handed down in lovingly bound collected volumes, informed, educated and entertained overlapping generations of boys and young men – girls, too – with its underlying message of a decent, good-humoured and technologically sophisticated world represented at its ideal best by its long-running *Dan Dare: Pilot of the Future* comic strip. The Concorde team, on the English side of the Channel, loved this, as did a whole generation of scientists, architects, engineers and designers. Pilots, too. Dan Dare's fictional career and the superb artwork that propelled his ventures convincingly around the world and into space caught the mood and set the tone for a broadly optimistic and technologically advanced future, both on Earth and the other worlds we would explore. Excepting Venus, of course, home to the dastardly Mekon and his terrible Treens.

Born in Manchester in 1967, three years after the first lunar landing, *The Eagle*'s Dan Dare read Mathematics and Astrophysics at Trinity, Cambridge before post-graduate studies at Harvard. He joined Space Fleet, flying from its British headquarters near Formby on the Lancashire coast. The architecture of this Space Fleet base, as with so many of the other worlds and extra-terrestrial cities depicted in *Dan Dare*, was realized with imagination, panache and a real understanding of what might come to pass if only the notion of progress had not given way to one of insatiable and wilfully unsustainable mass consumption.

Where did Frank Hampson, Dan Dare's creator, get his ideas? 'A lot of it came from his head,' says Don Harley, who drew the *Dan Dare* strip in later years. 'He must have known a lot about architecture. You can see the influence of Frank Lloyd Wright. We looked at magazines . . . *Life* and *National Geographic* . . . Frank had also seen V-2 rockets close-up during the Allied push into Germany.'

A star pilot, and very much in the mould of the best RAF pilots of the 1940s, Hampson's Dan Dare led the first manned mission to Venus in 1995–6 and his colourful photogravure adventures in *The Eagle* were set in the late 1990s. The point here is the implicit inference of the Dan Dare timeframe and its inspired storylines and illustrations. It was all but impossible for absorbed *Eagle* readers to believe that by 2015 manned rockets would not have landed on Mars and well before then not shot off into intergalactic space. And surely, hypersonic flight would be commonplace too? The idea that people might instead be fighting on CCTV in supersized shopping malls over cut-price 55-inch plasma idiot boxes, mugging one another for the latest shiny digital gewgaw or training shoe, or that others might be using jet airliners as merciless tools for amoral creeds bent on murdering fellow human beings in their thousands, was unimaginable.

Superfast military aircraft had been researched and developed from the end of the Second World War, yet the kinds of speeds that would be familiar to decent, civilized sorts in Dan Dare's world were – and still remain in the second decade of the twenty-first century – difficult to achieve and sustain in the realm of civil aviation. While Lockheed, for example, continues to pursue the development of its Mach-6 SR-72 unmanned spy plane, capable of flying around the world in six hours, turning this military design into a credible daughter of Concorde will be no easy task.

What should such an aircraft be made of? At hypersonic speed, the skin of an airliner would heat up to 1,000° C. To date, the most likely material would be carbon fibre embedded with titanium crystals. If the airliner could fly ionospherically at 250,000 ft, this would aid cooling to some degree. It sounds exciting. But how far, and just what, might you see from this immense height? Nothing. To help shield the cabin from intense heat, and given the state of current materials technology, there would be no windows. But as fewer and fewer people look out of windows when travelling today – their eyes are glued to iPads and similar devices – perhaps this would be perfectly acceptable. As for the crew – always assuming airlines of the future will need pilots or want to pay for them – they really will need to keep their eyes on screens: to ensure a hypersonic airliner is efficiently streamlined, and to keep the flight deck as cool as possible, cockpit windows will be anathema. It may well be that new forms of windows will emerge over time; it would be a shame for pilots and passengers who like to see where they are going and what lies beyond them, on earth as in space, to be sealed into a world of seatbacks and digital displays. That Pan Am Space Clipper – presumably hypersonic – which shuttled silently between the Earth and a giant space station ('Change here for the Moon') in Kubrick's *2001: A Space Odyssey* offered passengers and crew views out as well as the latest in flight-deck instrumentation.

Beyond the question of materials and heat, a hypersonic airliner will need immensely capable engines. Currently, one way of flying hypersonically is by scramjet or supersonic combusting ramjet. A scramjet sucks in and compresses air supersonically throughout the engine's combustion cycle; there is no need, as with Concorde's Olympus power plants, to slow down the flow of air before combustion. This advantage means that a scramjet might fly as fast as Mach 24 (16,000 mph). It has no rotating parts; in fact, it has very few parts whatsoever. What could be better? British and American scientists and engineers worked up the idea in the early 1960s, although the first successful flight of an unmanned scramjet was made in Russia in 1991.

The first fully manoeuvrable scramjet was NASA's X-43A, a 12-ft-long, unmanned machine looking very much like the sort of paper aeroplane launched across any number of school classrooms. On 16 November 2004, the third of these experimental planes achieved a new world speed record for an air-breathing, as opposed to rocket-powered, aircraft. Launched at 43,000 ft on the back of a Pegasus rocket over the southern Californian coast from a Boeing B-52 bomber, the X-43A was carried up to 110,000 ft before its engine was ignited. Off it went, quickly accelerating to Mach 9.7 (6,600 mph) in level flight.

This was a terrific achievement, although the X-43A was not exactly the prototype of a future airliner. The record-breaking aircraft was essentially all engine, its wing-body doubling as an air-intake and exhaust – so no room there for the drinks trolley. It was unable to land; instead it fell into the sea and that was the end of its flying days. Its scramjet engine could only ignite and perform at speeds of above Mach 4, meaning that the X-43A was incapable of taking off from the ground under its own steam. This is not to belittle an impressive accomplishment, but to highlight what steps would still be needed to be taken before commercial hypersonic flight could become anything like a realistic proposition.

The development of the hypersonic jet has been slow, partly because it requires a level of funding governments have found hard to justify and private enterprise is unable to provide, and partly because it is very difficult. And yet, rather like supersonic flight itself, the idea had been around for a long while and from time to time had gripped the public imagination. In the first episode, filmed in 1966, of Gerry Anderson's *Thunderbirds*, that memorable television puppet show for children, a villain known as The Hood attempts unsuccessfully to kill all those on board Fireflash, an atomic-powered hypersonic airliner making its first commercial flight from London to Tokyo in, yes, two hours, cruising at Mach 6 and 250,000 ft. The model, by Derek Meddings, was a wonderful thing. This episode of *Thunderbirds* was broadcast three years before Concorde's maiden flight, and ten years before the Anglo-French airliner went into service. Fireflash could take off and land under its own power. Half a century on, this remained the main stumbling block for real-life hypersonic airliners.

Between 2005 and 2010, several hypersonic airliner projects made the news, although few appeared to solve the problem of how to operate such an aircraft in everyday commercial service. In 2009, the German Space Agency (Deutsches Zentrum für Luft und Raumfahrt) received European Union funding for research into plans for a fifty-seat hypersonic rocket plane capable of flying from Frankfurt to Sydney in ninety minutes. The fifty-seat Mach-24 Spaceliner would be coupled to a liquid hydrogen rocket that would blast it off into space. Passengers would experience several minutes of weightlessness after the rocket had fallen back to earth before gliding down to the other side of the world hypersonically. The falling rocket would be collected by an unspecified aircraft and guided down to land before re-use. 'Maybe we can best characterize the Spaceliner,' Martin Sippel, the project's co-ordinator, told *TechNewsDaily*, 'by saying it's a kind of second-generation Space Shuttle, but with a completely different task.'

This sounded all very complicated and fraught with the possibility of misadventure. There was also something about it all that smacked of German Second World War rocket projects and all those last-ditch Nazi designs for jet- and rocket-powered interceptors and bombers. Besides, any such Spaceliner would need its own dedicated launch pad, and getting it off the ground would be a noisy affair – too noisy for towns and cities. So where could you locate such a pad, or pads? Perhaps at the isolated site of Peenemunde on the Baltic coast, where von Braun and his rocket men once infamously developed the V-1 and V-2. And if so, then how would you connect Spaceliner passengers to other flights and services? There would surely need to be major new investment in public transport links, and in accommodation for those who worked on the pads and serviced the Spaceliners. And what about commercial infrastructure? Would there be enough custom here for yet another of the vast and hugely profitable shopping malls that have long since become synonymous with airports, to such an extent that departure lounges and airliners have come to seem little more than accessories, a necessary nuisance? Or would potential developers prefer to invest more safely elsewhere, or just to play the Frankfurt money markets?

The Spaceliner posed as many questions as it did solutions to the idea of hypersonic flight, especially as it was not expected to fly until at least 2050, by which time it might seem more than a little outdated. The European Space Agency, meanwhile, launched its LAPCAT (Long-Term Advanced Propulsion Concepts and Technologies) programme in 2005. Funded by the European Union, this was conducted in two stages between then and 2012. The most relevant idea that emerged in terms of the future of civil aviation was a project for a liquid hydrogen-powered long-range Mach-5 (3,700-mph) airliner. This was the A2, developed principally by Reaction Engines based in Culham Science Centre, Oxfordshire. In theory, the proposed airliner, 469 ft long with a wingspan of 135 ft and a take-off weight of about 880,000 lbs (the same as a Boeing 747-400), would use existing airports and fly from, for example, Brussels or Frankfurt to Sydney in around five hours. The route would be over the North Atlantic, North Pole and Pacific Ocean where few humans, although many sea mammals, would be disturbed by sonic booms.

Illustrations of the A2 revealed an aircraft in very much the same spirit as the Fireflash in *Thunderbirds*. But where Fireflash's atomic engines had been a dubious proposition, the A2's Scimitar engines were well thought through. A development of the team's earlier Sabre rocket engine, designed to take a spaceliner up to an orbiting station where passengers – i.e. scientists and astronauts – would switch to another craft to take them on to Moon, exactly as in Kubrick's *2001: A Space Odyssey*, the Scimitar would be a combination of a turbofan and pre-cooled high by-pass jet, suiting it to both subsonic and hypersonic flight. No one expects it, or anything like it, to fly before 2035.

Members of the Reaction Engines team, formed in 1989 by Alan Bond, a mechanical and aerospace engineer, had previously been involved in HOTOL (Horizontal Take Off and Landing), an unmanned British space plane 'of Concorde length' designed to carry 15,500-lb payloads into space and, like the Space Shuttle, to return from missions and land on runways. From 1982, British Aerospace and Rolls-Royce were given government funding to research and develop HOTOL, which they expected to unveil in twelve years' time. Asked for its view, RAE Farnborough thought twenty years was more realistic and that the project would be very costly. Funding was cancelled in 1988, by which time it was clear that the design had a number of technical shortcomings that might not even be worth putting right. However, what did interest the aerospace insiders, notably in the United States, was Alan Bond's classified engine design.

Bond had long wanted to go much further than from Brussels to Sydney over the North Pole or from a rocket launch pad to the Moon. Between 1973 and 1978, he led Project Daedalus – the design for an unmanned starship – for the British Interplanetary Society. This scientific probe was to have flown as close as thermally possible to Barnard's Star, a red dwarf six light years distant and one of the Sun's closest neighbours, within a human lifetime. It will take the NASA probe Pioneer 10, launched in 1972, and the first man-made artefact to escape the Solar System, approximately 10,000 years from now to pass within 3.8 light years of Barnard's Star. Daedalus was to overtake Pioneer 10 at quite some speed: it was scheduled to get there in just fifty years.

Contact with the American probe, then seven and a half billion miles from Earth, was lost in January 2003, while Daedalus remains the stuff of a compelling research paper, if not of science fiction. For many years the chairman of the British Interplanetary Society, which had proposed a multi-stage Moon landing in the early 1930s, was Arthur C. Clarke, author of 'The Sentinel', the 1948 short story that inspired Kubrick to make *2001: A Space Odyssey* and create its Concorde-style Pan Am Space Clipper, just as Kubrick's interest allowed Clarke to extend 'The Sentinel' into a full-length novel. Since its publication in 1968, the book has sold more than three million copies.

Other projects seem more likely to become reality. Since it was first founded in San Francisco as the Alco Hydro-Aeroplane Company in 1912 by Allan and Malcolm Loughead, Lockheed has built very many thousands of aircraft, including the P-80 Shooting Star, the USAF's first jet fighter to enter service, the F-104 Starfighter, the world's first Mach-2 fighter, and the breathtaking Mach-3 SR-71 reconnaissance aircraft, along with such famous airliners as the piston-engine Constellation. These were all designs led by Clarence 'Kelly' Johnson, who began his career with the company as a tool designer in 1933 and in January 1939 saw the first of what were to be 10,037 of his P-38 Lightning, a highly distinctive twin-boom, twin-engine long-range fighter, take to the air; it was the only US fighter manufactured throughout the Second World War.

Johnson's SR-71 first flew soon after Lockheed had started work on its revised L-2000 proposal for the US supersonic airliner programme. A contemporary of Concorde's and always painted a blue so dark that it was often mistaken for black, it remained in service with the USAF from 1966 to 1998, retiring from NASA the following year. On 1 December 1974, Majors James V. Sullivan and Noel F. Widdifield hurtled a Blackbird from New York to London in one hour, fifty-four minutes and fifty-six seconds, making even Concorde seem slow. They had cruised at 80,000 ft above the Atlantic at Mach 3.2. It was an astonishing performance for a gas turbine-powered aircraft. The SR-71 still holds the record for the fastest manned air-breathing aircraft, although twelve of the thirty-four built were lost in accidents.

Lockheed had become very adept at developing aircraft that flew at the very margins of what was considered possible at any one time. As we have seen, the SR-71 itself had been intended as a military development of the CIA's U-2 spy plane, another extraordinary Kelly design. This lightweight subsonic jet, with its enormous wingspan and glider-like flying characteristics, was designed to fly at 70,000 ft on missions over the Soviet Union and other Cold War enemies of the US. (One, piloted by Gary Powers, was notoriously shot down over the USSR in 1960.) But while it was able to fly so very high, and frugally so, its pilots were all too well aware that the aircraft's stall speed at this great height was just 12 mph above its 'never exceed' maximum speed.

From August 1971, U-2s flew from Moffett Field, California, as atmospheric research aircraft for NASA's Airborne Science Program. The aim was to sample air pollution, the depth of the ozone layer, radiation and other factors affecting and affected by supersonic airliners, including Concorde and its possible successors. A civilian version of the high-flying aircraft, the ER-2, replaced the U-2s from 1981 onwards; these flying laboratories operate from NASA's Neil A. Armstrong Flight Research Center at Palmdale, California. Their work is key to the future of civil supersonic flight.

Meanwhile, Lockheed's proposed SR-72 offers higher and faster flight than these Cold War predecessors. Working with Aerojet Rocketdyne of Sacramento, California, Lockheed could potentially have this, the first practical hypersonic aircraft, in the air by 2030. Its engines will be dual-mode turbine-ramjets, enabling it to take off from existing airstrips, fly on missions at Mach 6 and land back at base like any other military jet.

Lockheed, however, has not made airliners for a long while. The last was the L-1011 TriStar, a wide-bodied jet that, despite a number of special features including the ability to land itself in zero visibility and a better than average safety record, was launched too late behind the rival McDonnell Douglas DC-10 and Boeing 747. The delay was due to financial and technical problems with the airliner's Rolls-Royce RB-211 engines, and the L-1011's struggle onto the market was only made more difficult when senior Lockheed executives were forced to resign after it was discovered they had bribed the Japanese prime minister, Kakuei Tanaka, and other members of his government to buy twenty-one TriStars for ANA (All Nippon Airways) when the airline had intended to purchase DC-10s. Lockheed – or Lockheed Martin as it is today – has designed and built some astonishingly innovative aircraft over the decades, and is as well placed as any other company to go hypersonic. But while the idea of a Mach-6 airliner is exciting and increasingly possible, development costs will be enormous and, although it is always hard and unwise to predict too far ahead, there is no guarantee that airlines in decades to come will want these next-generation Concorde aircraft.

The view back in the 1970s was that research should continue. In the United States, this was led primarily by NASA in association with the major American aircraft manufacturers. British Airways suggested NASA use one of its Concorde aircraft for test purposes; in the event, this role went to a re-commissioned and re-engined Russian Tu-144. From 1982, the space agency's Supersonic Research Programme – one championed by President Ronald Reagan, even if he had to withdraw funding some years later as part of sweeping government budget cuts – examined how the range of supersonic airliners might be extended by employing new forms of lightweight honeycomb titanium and polycarbonate airframes that could withstand higher temperatures at greater speeds than Concorde, and, most importantly, how to reduce the noise of such aircraft by a half. A report published in 1995 looked at the potential of a 300-seat Mach-2.4 airliner with a range of 5,000 miles.

This research at first went hand-on-slide rule with research into a National Aero-Space Plane, the American equivalent of Britain's HOTOL, funded by NASA and the US Department of Defense. Reagan was particularly keen on this project after he had experienced an exhausting subsonic flight back to the States from Japan. In fact, in his 1986 State of the Union address, the president called for 'a new Orient Express that could, by the end of the next decade, take off from Dulles Airport, accelerate up to twenty-five times the speed of sound, attaining low earth orbit or flying to Tokyo within two hours'.

Although this scramjet project accelerated further research into, among other areas, new materials and new methods of cooling the skin of hypersonic aircraft such as passing hydrogen over it, it proved to be an unrealistic proposition, although it did pave the way for the unmanned X-43 project. Ronald Reagan never got to fly to Tokyo within two hours. And when, in 1998, Boeing pulled out of a long development programme with NASA for a new supersonic airliner that over the years had drawn in the most advanced thinking from Italy, Japan and Russia, the whole idea of a successor to Concorde stalled, although Boeing itself was to continue research with NASA into unmanned scramjets. On 1 May 2013, the Boeing X-51 flew successfully at over

Mach 5, although this test flight lasted just over six minutes, with three and a half of these at hypersonic speed. Although it had flown for longer than the super-fast X-43A, the aircraft also ended up in the Pacific Ocean once it had burnt up its limited fuel supply. So, by 2015, hypersonic flight was clearly still in its infancy, while the future of supersonic airliners seemed, at best, uncertain.

If such aircraft do have a future, it seems that, at first, this will be as either executive jets or as playthings for joy-riders in search of something more exciting than the fastest roller-coaster or black ski-run. In 2004, Richard Branson, the daredevil British entrepreneur who hoped to take over Concorde flights over the Atlantic after British Airways, under pressure, had pulled out from the route the year before, founded Virgin Galactic. This long-running venture – and saga – aims to shoot reels of Hollywood celebrities, along with Stephen Hawking, the British theoretical physicist and cosmologist, and others who have pre-paid $250,000 for a ticket, into space from a spaceport in the Californian Mojave Desert designed by the distinguished British architect Norman Foster. For six whole minutes they will experience weightlessness before gliding back to Earth and, at some point in their two-and-a-half-hour flight on a Virgin Atlantic SpaceShipTwo, they will certainly break the sound barrier.

The 'spaceships' have been designed by Burt Rutan, an inventive Californian aeronautical engineer, and were built at first by Rutan's company, Scaled Composites, and then by the Spaceship Company, a Californian corporation owned jointly by Rutan and Richard Branson. The six-seater, rocket-powered SpaceShipTwo was first flown on 7 December 2009, launched at 50,000 ft from between the twin fuselages of a Scaled Composite White

Knight Two four-engine carrier jet, which was itself first flown in December 2008. They certainly made a remarkable sight, these two 1950s-style science-fiction-film machines, taking off from the Mojave. They could easily have caused a new Roswell Incident, the occasion in summer 1947 when the crash landing of a USAF research balloon near a ranch in New Mexico sparked an entertaining and long-running conspiracy that 'proved' an alien spacecraft had fallen from the sky at a time when aliens were only ever interested in flying over the United States. Perhaps they had hoped to catch Ronald Reagan on screen at an open-air drive-in movie theatre.

On 29 April 2013, the SpaceCraftTwo VSS *Enterprise*, named after Captain James T. Kirk's starship in the TV series *Star Trek*, flew at Mach 1.43 at 69,000 ft. The aim – delayed, year after year – had been to send the *Enterprise* soaring sixty-eight miles into sub-orbital flight; sadly, on 31 October 2014, the machine broke up in flight and crashed, killing one of its two crew, test pilot Michael Alsbury. As Burt Rutan had said in 2008, commenting on his SpaceShipOne, the world's first privately funded spacecraft, 'This vehicle is designed to go into the atmosphere in the worst case straight in or upside down and it'll correct. This is designed to be as least as safe as the early airliners in the 1920s . . . don't believe anyone that tells you that the safety will be the same as a modern airliner, which has been around for seventy years.'

Concorde, though, was safe and very much so until the spectacular accident at Gonesse damaged its reputation and, to an extent, its commercial viability. Richard Branson, however, remained gung-ho; if people wanted to fly into space, then so they would, even if it might take some extra while to get them there.

And yet, perhaps a far more impressive achievement was the non-stop circumnavigation of the Earth by Burt Rutan's piston-engine Model 76 Voyager in December 1986. This lightweight twin-fuselage aircraft was flown by Rutan's brother, Dick, a veteran of 325 missions during the Vietnam War, and Jeana Yeager (no relation to Chuck Yeager, the first pilot to break the sound barrier) at an average speed of 116 mph. Their aerial voyage lasted a little over nine days. In that time, no extra fuel was taken on board and Voyager arrived back safely at Edwards Air Force base, California, with 1.5 per cent of its fuel to spare. Somehow, this truly extraordinary demonstration of fuel economy, and flying skills, was far more impressive than the prospect of sending whooping celebrities on roller-coaster flights into space. Increasingly, though, this kind of super-enhanced funfair ride appeared to be the future of supersonic commercial aviation.

A strikingly beautiful wind-tunnel model of a supersonic passenger jet unveiled by the Japan Aerospace Exploration Agency (JAXA) in 2013 promised no more than fifty seats at the very most if the real thing was to go into production and service. Its extremely long pointed nose should help to reduce the aircraft's sonic boom, or so Takashi Ishikawa, director of JAXA's Aviation Program Group, hopes. 'So far,' says the scientist and engineer who spent much of his childhood making model aeroplanes, 'no one has managed to substantially reduce the sonic boom. If Japan becomes the first to test this technology successfully, we will be far ahead of everyone else. No single nation can develop supersonic transport on its own, since this requires an enormous amount of capital, and the integration of many advanced technologies. Japan is no exception . . .

developing core technology for supersonic aircraft will be our ticket to participation in such an international project. Supersonic transport will come to fruition sooner or later.'

There have been other transport technologies where one nation has tried to take a lead too early in the day for them to be a success, especially when finances have been limited, the media has been hostile and government support either stop-go, topsy-turvy or simply non-existent. When in 1981, for example, and under government pressure, British Rail introduced three Advanced Passenger Trains (APT) into service on the state-owned network's West Coast main line between Glasgow and London, these radical express trains were not ready for service. Their design incorporated an active tilt system, which enabled the trains to race around bends on existing tracks at unprecedented speed without disturbing passengers. Capable of 155 mph, the trains were also fitted with hydrokinetic brakes and could stop from very high speeds within the distance allowed for by existing signals. What these inventions added up to was a train capable of rivalling the high-speed exploits of the French TGVs and the Japanese Shinkansen 'Bullet' trains, both of which ran on dedicated and expensive new lines. APT would be British Rail's Concorde.

Sadly, although the trains did work well during much of 1984, their first outings with the press and politicians aboard were rather sorry affairs, characterized by breakdowns, sticking brakes and what was perceived to be a seasick-inducing ride, although it was said that the latter was mostly experienced by Fleet Street journalists over-indulging in British Rail's on-board hospitality. British Rail abandoned its APT, selling its technology to Italy's

Fiat Ferroviaria, which had been developing its own tilting train. With the vital British contribution, the Fiat ETR 450 was born, entering service with Italian State Railways between Milan and Rome in 1988. Since then, Pendolinos have been sold to many railways, including those running in China and the United States. And in 2002 Virgin Rail, the British train operator owned by Richard Branson, ushered in its latest Class 390 Pendolinos on services from Glasgow to London which ran on the same 1981 schedule as British Rail's APTs.

One day, British airlines may well buy supersonic passenger aircraft based on Concorde from American and perhaps even Chinese manufacturers. The British public will no doubt gawp at these aircraft and gladly travel in them on international shopping sprees or other leisure pursuits, not much minding, or caring, that the UK can no longer manufacture such wondrous machines. In fact, the supersonic passenger jets most likely to come onto the market in the foreseeable are both designed by US companies. Neither aircraft will push the boundaries of aviation, but they could be successful. This is because the Spike Aerospace S-512 and Aerion AS2 are both business jets designed for executives who need to be seen to be in a hurry and, understandably, do not wish to be caught up in the interminable queues, brusque rudeness, bullying and banality of all too many contemporary international airports.

Vik Kachoria, who has spent thirty years in the aerospace industry, is president and CEO of Boston-based Spike Aerospace. His enthusiasm for advanced technologies is undimmed and he has said that, if it were possible, he would like to develop a VTOL (Vertical Take-Off and Landing) supersonic business jet capable of operating from city centres. His description of his early career on Spike Aerospace's website is as enjoyable as it is informative: 'Early in his career, he conducted research at NASA and MIT on the Solar-Terrestrial Magnetosphere and designed an early pattern recognition software. He built a prototype Mag Lev train in the 1980s, contributed to a proposal on asteroid mining and investigated anti-particles/anti-gravity. He currently serves as an advisor or investor in several early-stage technology companies. Mr Kachoria has a pilot's license and is working towards his commercial rating.'

It is this spirit of enthusiasm, and inventiveness, that has driven many of the most imaginative and significant leaps and bounds in the world of aviation as in other forms of transport, new technologies and business ventures. It is difficult, though, to know the extent to which companies like Spike Aerospace are flying a kite in terms of developing aircraft that will excite a certain sector of the global business sufficiently for it to want to pay out what will necessarily be very large sums of money for a form of aircraft banned, for example, from flying across the United States and very many other countries. But for the record, the Spike Aerospace S-512 is a twelve- to eighteen-seat twin-engine jet – powered by two Pratt & Whitney turbofans – designed to cruise at Mach 1.6 and with a range of 4,000 miles. Its design features a very discreet windowless cabin lined with digitally active walls that can transform into views of real landscapes, starscapes or films.

Spike Aerospace, however, is not alone. The Aerion Corporation of Reno, Nevada, was founded by the businessman and philanthropist Robert Muse Bass, its name inspired by a mythical

Greek horse we know from Homer's *Iliad*: 'There is no man shall catch you by a burst of speed, neither pass you in pursuit if you were driving Aerion, the swift horse of Adrastus (King of Argos), that was of heavenly stock.' Aerion was also endowed with the power of speech, although clearly no relation to America's best-known talking horse, Mister Ed. In one 1965 episode of the enormously popular television show of the same name, a beautiful palomino was seen, complete with flying helmet and goggles, flying a Boeing C-97 Stratofreighter. Mister Ed flew upside down. He looped the loop. He flew backwards and after losing control came down to land in a lake by parachute.

The Aerion experience should be a little smoother, not least because the AS2 will be fitted with passive laminar-flow wings. Dating from the Second World War – North American P-51 Mustangs benefited from a small degree of laminar flow – these wings smooth the flow of the air itself over their surface. In practice, and as proved by NASA test flights with a Lockheed Martin F-16XL between 1988 and 1996, and again for Aerion in 2013 with an F-15B fitted with laminar-flow wings, friction is reduced by up to 50 per cent and, along with it, heat, fuel consumption and, to an extent, noise as well. The AS2's thin wings, curved on both upper and lower surfaces, are also to be fitted with high-lift flaps that should enable pilots to take off and land at speeds similar to those of current subsonic business jets.

Aerion aims to sell the AS2 on the basis first and foremost of sheer speed. Its website is very enjoyable in an unashamedly all-American way. 'Get there first.' 'If fast is better, fastest is best.' 'Flying Mach 0.85 is like flying dial-up in a broadband world.' This reminds me of Farquharson, the American traveller Robert Byron meets in his wonderfully funny, and erudite, travelogue *The Road to Oxiana*, which was published in 1933, two years before the Douglas DC-3, the world's first modern airliner, took to the skies. While in Teheran, Byron is given to understand that he might have to take on Farquharson as a travelling companion to Oxiana, a near-legendary land on the Russian hem of Afghanistan. Any such journey, today as then, would take a long while and be full of interest, archaeology, danger and revelry. 'There are one or two points I'm *vurry* anxious to discuss with you,' Farquharson tells Byron. 'I want to make it clear that if I do go to Afghanistan I shall have to make a *vurry* hurried trip . . . I'm pressed for time.'

In September 2014, Aerion teamed up with Airbus Defence and Space, bringing the AS2 that bit closer to reality. The AS2 differs from the Spike Aerospace S-512 not only in its wing configuration, but also in employing three rather than two engines. Again, this is to reduce noise by spreading the maximum output needed for take-off. What seems true, even if it is not a guarantee for the sales of supersonic business jets given the current restrictions placed on them, is that the very idea and the sheer excitement of supersonic travel is still very much abroad more than a decade after Concorde's last flight. On 15 October 1997, and some four hours' drive north-east of Reno, Nevada, Wing Commander Andy Green, an RAF fighter pilot, broke the sound barrier for the first recorded time on land while wrestling – or so it looks on video – very calmly with the 'wheel' of Thrust SSC, a ten-ton jet-propelled car created by a team led by Richard Noble, an English businessman, and aerodynamicist Ron Ayers and built by G-Force Engineering at Fontwell, Sussex on the edge of the South Downs.

Green's maximum speed along the floor of the Black Rock Desert was 763 mph, and his engines were a pair of afterburning Rolls-Royce Spey turbofans as previously fitted to British F-4 Phantoms and, in less potent guise, to subsonic Grumman Gulfstream business jets. The British team's follow-up project is the Bloodhound SSC, a 7.5-ton vehicle powered by a Rolls-Royce EJ200 afterburning turbofan and a Norwegian-Finnish Nammon HPT hybrid rocket. The machine is due to make its first test runs in 2015 with the aim of racing along a desert track at over 1,000 mph. A new location will be needed, as the engine will not develop maximum thrust at sea level, and in any case the racing stretch along Nevada's Black Rock Desert has been pitted by the sulphurous activities of the curious annual Burning Man Festival held here since 1997. This involves the burning of a giant wooden man. The purpose, unlike the immolation within such a frame of a hapless Scottish policeman in Hammer Films' deliciously sinister film *The Wicker Man* (1973), has something to do with art. Meanwhile, the Black Rock Desert has also witnessed the launch of the world's first successful amateur space rocket: this was the Space Shot 2004 'Go Fast' prepared by the Civilian Space eXploration [sic] Team, a group of enthusiasts founded by the Minnesota-born inventor and rocketeer Ky Michaelson in 1995. The 'Go Fast' made it into space on 17 May 2004.

As for the airliner industry itself, the lure of supersonic flight had not wholly lost its charm by 2015, although the pressures to banish it wholly from its mind had grown inordinately from the 1980s. (See Chapter Ten.) Research into possible new fuels for superfast flight ignited discussions concerning the practicalities of electricity, nuclear fusion and forms of advanced power sources that were, as yet, more theoretical than practical. In 2014, Lockheed Martin, working in association with NASA, showed the press illustrations of its N+2 supersonic airliner. Looking like a machine that would be perfectly suited to the navigation of a 1970s prog-rock album cover design by Roger Dean, the N+2 was perhaps most of all a device to enable the aircraft manufacturer to raise key issues concerning high-speed commercial flight.

'To achieve revolutionary reductions in supersonic transportation aircraft noise,' said Michael Buonanno, manager of the N+2 programme, 'a totally new kind of propulsion system is being developed.' This, though, was top secret, although Buonanno was able to say, 'We are also exploring new techniques for low-noise jet exhaust, integrated fan noise suppression, airframe noise suppression and computer-customized airport noise abatement.' In other words, supersonic flight is noisy and all that can be done, given existing science and technology, is a slight reduction in that noise, rather as if we might still be able to listen to the radio while a thunderstorm rages directly overhead without having to crank up the volume.

'Though it is not practical to completely eliminate noise, these advancements,' according to Buonanno, 'would result in a sonic boom that sounds much more like a distant thump than a sharp crack.' The Lockheed Martin design would seat eighty passengers with 'sonic booms one hundred times quieter than the now-retired Concorde. It's all about the design details. You need to be able to manage the progress of volume and lift to create a series of closely timed small shocks rather than one big one . . . the aircraft would have to be very long, so that the volume and the lift of the plane are allowed to gradually build up and then decrease.' But, as part of this quietening process, the airliner would be slower than Concorde, using turbofans with their lower exhaust velocity rather than Concorde's pure jets. The dream for both Lockheed Martin and Boeing, which has also been working with NASA on the same research programme, is for a commercial jet than can cross from the east to the west coast of the United States in half the time it took in 2014 without falling foul of the Federal Aviation Administration (FAA), the public at large and artistic folk burning wicker men in the Black Rock Desert.

NASA has been exploring 'low-boom' supersonic aircraft booms for many years. Its belief is that the FAA could be persuaded to relax its transcontinental ruling over supersonic booms at some time in the 2020s if these could be 'tuned'. 'Engine installation is a critical part of achieving an overall low-boom design,' says Peter Coen, the manager of NASA's High Speed Project. 'If we mount the engines in a conventional manner, we need to carefully tailor the shape of the wing to diffuse the shock waves. If we mount the engines above the wing, the shock wave can be directed upward and not affect the ground signature. However, such installations may have performance penalties.' After extensive NASA wind-tunnel tests on models made by both Boeing and Lockheed Martin had been completed, Coen felt able to say, 'We've convinced ourselves that we have the design tools and we've validated the level we need to design to. We've reached a point where quiet, low-boom overland supersonic passenger service is achievable.'

This, though, is not saying that low-boom overland supersonic passenger services will be necessarily desirable. To executives bent on making '*vurry* hurried' trips, they may well be. But to anyone down on the ground, will such future airliners really sound like the occasional passing bumblebee? Could we get used to them, just as people who live not so far from motorways with their continuous low-frequency thrum seem to have managed? And anyway, why give a decibel in favour of hurried executives and gurning celebrities who, aside from charter flights and passengers who have saved up for special occasions, are likely to be the only people on board rumbling their way over the Midwest?

The real boom in the aviation industry of 2015 was the apparently inexhaustible demand for new airliners. According to Alan Tovey of the *Daily Telegraph*, talking to Airbus in late 2014, 'More than 31,000 new airliners and air freighters will be needed over the next twenty years, primarily driven by growing middle classes in emerging economies taking to the skies. The European aircraft manufacturer forecasts these new jets will be worth $4.6 trillion (£2.8 trillion) to the aerospace industry as passenger numbers grow up to an annual rate of 4.7 per cent from three billion passengers a year [in 2013] . . . Asia is expected to be the biggest market for the new aircraft, taking 39 per cent, more than the total of the next biggest regions, Europe at 20 per cent and North America at 18 per cent.'

And, even more significantly, what the airlines said they wanted was bigger aircraft. Not eighty- or 100-seat supersonic transports, but flying towns. The biggest market of all by 2025 was predicted to be China's internal aviation market, and perhaps the Chinese authorities might be perfectly happy for supersonic jets to boom across the Gobi and Taklamakan Deserts, or even across provincial towns and cities. China operates the world's fastest futuristic trains – the Shanghai Maglev from the city's Pudong International Airport to the edge of its new skyscraper zone, which reaches speeds of 268 mph on its 18.6-mile trip – and, for two years before a collision caused by defective signals, it ran the world's fastest conventional railway, the 573-mile Wuhan–Guangzhou High Speed Railway. The line was built in four years and from 2009 non-stop trains sped from one end to the other four times faster than existing express services at an average speed of 194.2 mph. China Southern Airlines, based in Guangzhou and with a large fleet of Boeing 737s and short- to medium-haul Airbuses, complained to Beijing about unfair competition. Might this airline be in the market for a transcontinental supersonic American airliner?

Boeing's prediction for the future was for an even greater number of new jets, 42,180 of them by 2025. In fact, all these, should they come to be built and delivered to their new owners, will be subsonic. The sheer volume of airline traffic in coming decades might well encourage a desire by those who can afford it, or are willing to save up for tickets, to seek forms of exclusivity, if only to get away from what the English actor Ernest Thesiger famously described, when asked at a dinner party about his experiences as a soldier in the thick of the Battle of the Somme, 'Oh, my dear; the noise, and the people!' Such exclusivity might take the form of flights on board Mach-1.7 business jets or, perhaps, on altogether slower and statelier forms of transport. Images of Concorde flying in company with the *QE2* when that fine ship was still a fast turbine liner rather than a cruise ship show these two possibilities operating hand-in-silk glove. But the lure of low-cost universal flight and airbuses as opposed to airliners may rule the skies for a very long time to come, keeping advanced forms of aircraft design, even if they could be quietened, at bay.

The year 2016 will mark the sixtieth anniversary of the first meeting of STAC in London that ignited the Concorde project. The following year will mark the seventieth anniversary of Chuck Yeager's breaking of the sound barrier. And still there will be no Plan B. Perhaps it is no longer an option.

TEN

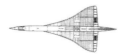

AN END TO ADVENTURE

ALERTED by urban explorers, a happy breed of inquisitive people whose mission is to track down, explore and record our secret, forgotten or otherwise abandoned architectural and industrial heritage, in 2006 I went to see what was left of the National Gas Turbine Establishment at Pyestock close to Farnborough. Here were purpose-built government sheds and warehouses laced with stirring, period-piece test equipment erected, installed and used to richly effective purpose for the most part between the 1950s and the 1970s. In shadowy interstices between control rooms – all analogue dials, switches and imperial measures – and miles of ducts and wiring, I could almost make out the sterling figures of John Steed and Emma Peel – The Avengers – and other Cold War chimeras and spooks thwarting plots to spirit the latest Top Secrets to nefarious foreign regimes bent variously on world domination, slaking the demands of mad gods and the destruction of personal freedom.

This is where Concorde's Olympus jets – its gas turbines – were tested as if in flight at speeds of up to 2,000 mph and where the engines of V-bombers, Harriers and Tornados were put through their paces, along with those that would power Royal Navy warships. This is where engines snaffled from the Soviets were reported on and, when useful, reverse-engineered. For at least a quarter of a century, NGTE Pyestock was at the forefront of jet technology. It was one of the largest – perhaps the largest – and most advanced research stations of its kind. Its very existence harked back not just to the early days of jet propulsion, but also to those of early nineteenth-century British industrial manufacturing and know-how. Concorde flew from the shoulders of giants.

The NGTE was born in 1946, the brainchild of the Attlee Labour government's shotgun marriage of Frank Whittle's pioneering Power Jets Limited and the RAE's Turbine Division, both of which had been nationalized in 1944. The first chairman of Power Jets, and scientific adviser to, at first, the Ministry of Production and latterly the Ministry of Supply, had been Sir William Stanier, the distinguished former chief mechanical engineer of the London Midland and Scottish Railway. Stanier, who had come to the LMS from the Swindon works of the Great Western Railway in 1932, was in a direct line of locomotive engineers stretching back to Daniel Gooch, and thus to Isambard Kingdom Brunel and the heroic early days of an industrial Britain and the creation of new forms of high-speed transport. It was Brunel who appointed the twenty-year-old Gooch as Superintendent of Locomotive Engines to the Great Western Railway in 1837, weeks after Queen Victoria ascended to the throne. Gooch's Iron Duke class 4-2-2s, built from 1846 to 1855, were extremely fast for their day. Graced with resonant names like *Lightning* and *Tornado*, they reached speeds of 80 mph and, from as early as 1852, span *The Flying Dutchman* – the world's fastest train for many years – along Brunel's beautifully aligned broad-gauge railway from London to Exeter at an average speed of 53 mph. On 11 May 1848, with driver J. Michael 'Mad Sandy' Almond at the controls, *Great Britain*, the second of Gooch's Iron Dukes, ran *The Flying Dutchman* from Paddington to Didcot in forty-seven minutes at an average speed of 67 mph. For a train of the time, that really was flying.

Gooch went on to lay the first transatlantic telegraph cable – another new form of high-speed communication – with the help of Brunel's steamship SS *Great Eastern* and sat in the House of Commons for twenty years. It was wholly appropriate that such a brilliant engineering dynamo should have been a parliamentarian in that intrepid age of steam, speed, invention and skill. A Northumbrian by birth, he was the son of an ironfounder, thus taking us back to the very crucible of the Industrial Revolution. When the family moved to South Wales, the young Gooch trained under Thomas Ellis senior, chief engineer of the Tredegar Ironworks. His employer was Sam Homfray, who had commissioned Richard Trevithick to build the world's first steam railway locomotive at the Penn-y-darren ironworks in 1804 in the reign of George III. The connections between new forms of power and Pyestock therefore stretch back in a chain of hands and minds to the beginning of the nineteenth century. Significantly, Sir William Stanier had built a steam-turbine express passenger locomotive for the London

Midland and Scottish Railway in the mid-1930s and had hoped to build a fleet of fifty such engines for the West Coast main line. He and Frank Whittle would have had plenty to talk about.

As it is, Pyestock's demise is a sorry reflection of the decline of industrial manufacturing in Britain. Although it is frequently argued today that research into the performance, aerodynamics and durability of jet engines can be carried out by computer programs and assessed on screens in muted air-conditioned offices resembling call centres and with as much character, this does not entirely explain why the French, once our joint partners in the development of Concorde, continue to maintain a considerable research and test infrastructure comparable to Pyestock.

The Pyestock buildings were really quite ghostly when I visited them, inhabited only by those dedicated urban explorers. The world's first successful demonstration of gas turbine jet propulsion had been made, by Whittle, in 1937, just fourteen years before the first government building opened at Pyestock, on the site of the former Bramshot golf course, and seventeen years after Dr J. W. Stern of the Air Ministry Research Laboratories had stated categorically that 'the gas turbine has no foreseeable future'.

Prince Philip opened the last new building on the site, the Anechoic Chamber, in 1971. The Three-Day Week and the Oil Crisis were looming and Concorde had only just taken wing and would not be in service for another five years. At this time, Pyestock employed around 1,600 people. But the clock was running very fast indeed. In 2004, the incomprehensibly and unpronounceably named QinetiQ, a private company formed in 2001 as part of the right-wing New Labour government's sell-off of the British defence industry, and the owner of Pyestock, announced that it was putting the site on the market. True to the spirit of Tony Blair's New Britain, plans were made to demolish all but the very latest buildings, including the valuable Anechoic Chamber, and to turn Pyestock into a business park. The most important new building was to become an improbably large warehouse and distribution depot for Tesco. It was as if someone at government level was laughing in the public's face while plunging the knife into the corpse of half a century of British research and development, manufacturing skill and collaborative brilliance. Here, as one commentator put it, turbines were now to be replaced by stacks of toilet rolls. And the spirit of Concorde and the ghosts of all those brilliant engineers and innovators stretching back in jet slipstreams and clouds of flying steam from Whittle to Brunel and Trevithick were to be chased out by New Britain's witless commitment to non-stop shopping. There was to be some consolation, at least, in the fact that Tesco had its come-uppance in 2014 and was abruptly forced to rein in its aggressive and insensitive ambitions.

The New Labour government nonetheless overrode all objections in 2010, and three years later demolition would begin in earnest. Baron McKenzie of Luton, the then minister for communities and local government, overruled an earlier decision to reject the Pyestock mega-depot; he had been in his job for eleven weeks when he did so. 'In accordance with normal practice,' quoth his Lordship, 'I did not visit the site.' If he had deigned to, perhaps he might have been wafted in from Luton Airport, of which this former accountant had been chairman.

Luton Airport had long been a paradise for those who believed passionately in low-cost flying. Concorde rarely paid a visit, although, when it did, it not only drew crowds but changed lives. 'I was privileged to fly on Concorde on October 29, 1983,' a Mr John Baggott told the BBC, 'having been allocated one of the 100 seats available through the Vauxhall Motors Concorde Cavalier Challenge Competition. Captain Colin Hutchinson was in command, and the highlight was our departure from Bordeaux just before sunset, carrying out a fly-through along the Bordeaux runway following a circuit around Bordeaux, catching up with the sun and watching it set for the second time in half an hour, and finally landing at Luton in the dark and watching all the camera flashlights going off along the perimeter fence as we landed. As a result of that experience, I later took up flying and gained my private pilot's licence in 1990 at the age of fifty-five.'

I happened to be travelling to Venice at the time the government-approved wreckers moved in to Pyestock. I had taken the Eurostar from London to Paris and from there, after a cocktail in the faded yet still appealing Train Bleu brasserie at the Gare de Lyon, boarded a Milan-bound TGV. After a 300-kmh sprint to Lyon, the train writhed far more slowly up into the Alps. The last stop before Italy, a little over four hours from Paris, is Modane. There, I broke my journey to Italy for a short taxi ride up into the magnificent Parc National de la Vanoise, flanked by seemingly countless snow-clad peaks, many rising above 10,000 ft, and home to Alpine chamois and ibex, lynx and wolf and those magnificent high-soaring birds of prey, the bearded vulture and golden eagle.

The park is also home to the magnificent wind-tunnel test station at Avrieux, a mountain outpost of the state-owned ONERA (Office National d'Etudes et de Recherches Aérospatiales).

Established in 1946, and powered by hydro-electricity, this site is where test work has been carried out on the supersonic Dassault Mirage and latest Rafale military jets as well as on the infamous Exocet anti-ship missile, which in Argentine hands sank British ships in the Falklands War, and the wholly benign Airbus 320. It was in this spirited Alpine setting that essential work was carried out in the development of Concorde.

It was heartwarming to see ONERA in full swing at Avrieux, and there was something affirmatory in the conjunction of a supersonic research facility, high mountains, deep snow, a piercing blue sky and circling eagles: it was as if everything around me here spelt high flight. Indeed, if you had to dream up a top-secret research laboratory for Concorde, it would be hard to out-imagine Avrieux. The balcony of the local hotel overlooks ONERA and the L'Arc valley, which stretches as far as the eye can see; French, Swiss and Italian families come here to ski, to trek through the mountains, explore old fortresses and to cross swaying rope bridges over ravines echoing to the roar of deep, plunging waterfalls. It is all a world away from Pyestock, past or present.

Later, while visiting Paris in 2014, I went to the Musée des Arts et Métiers to look at some of the beautiful scale models used in the development of Concorde's airframe. By chance, there was an exhibition of superb new black and white photographs by Antoine Gonin of ONERA. Here, truly, was a fine and stirring marriage of art and industry. It was again somehow heart-warming to see French science, mathematics and engineering being celebrated in the heart of Paris.

The utter prosaicness of the Pyestock site today reflects fundamental changes in the workings of the British economy, the aspirations of British society and our attitude towards flight and civil aviation. These came about, or were intensified, in the years between the deep economic recession of the 1970s and the rise of neo-liberalism from the end of that decade, which led very quickly to a deregulation of financial markets, the privatization of state-owned and other public companies, and an unparalleled boom in consumerism. Such was the collective desire and demand for new consumer goods and services, including flights, that the prices and quality of these at the mass-market level went into a kind of free fall, a steep dive that has only steepened since.

While canny commentators insisted that this was all to the good, representing a democratization of goods, services and travel, anyone with the slightest fondness for aircraft, with the merest inkling of poetry in their winged souls, knew that this all spelt the end of the romance of flight. Of course, it was true that romantic flight – the semi-mythical Golden Age of civil aviation, which stretched from, say, a tiny two-seat Benoist XIV flying boat skedaddling over Florida's Tampa Bay in 1913 to champagne and caviar in a Concorde spearing across the Atlantic a lifetime later – had been the preserve of the truly adventurous, followed by the simply well-off and those in business or on government service, and yet it seemed axiomatic that the democratization of flight spelt banality. While there is no question that the Airbus A320 and Boeing 737 are nothing other than fine, reliable and profitable machines, they will be forever associated with the idea, forced on us by airline management and advertising, that flying is much the same as travelling by coach – or bus or train, of course – and that the destination is what matters most rather than the journey. And if this means being crammed into a cabin innocent of thoughtful, much less inspired, design, then so be it as long as the tickets are as cheap as our package holidays. Once, we flocked by train to Blackpool or Scarborough, Margate or Skegness; now we think nothing of flying hundreds or thousands of miles to find our brief place in the sun.

Concorde made its first regular flight from Heathrow to JFK on 22 November 1977. Two months earlier, Freddie Laker's budget Skytrain had made its debut, flying passengers from London's Gatwick Airport to New York for just £59, a third of what you would normally have expected to pay at the time and much, much less than a ticket for Concorde. Low-cost charter flights, usually involving all-in cheap holidays to destinations such as the Spanish Costas, newly ruined by a rash of cheapskate concrete hotels and other notoriously low-grade development, had been available for some years before Skytrain.

The best-known British operator was Dan-Air, a charter airline that flew from Gatwick for a number of years with a fleet that included more than forty de Havilland Comet 4s, although less than twenty were in service at any one time. They flew until the beginning of the 1980s. As a student, I paid for a package holiday to Crete so I could fly on a Comet – a 4C – for the first, and last, time. All I wanted was the flight. The journey was what mattered to me. I never got as far as the hi-de-hi resort. I hiked to the ruins of Knossos, took a ferry to Athens, visited the Parthenon and other ancient Greek monuments and flew back with a cheap ticket on a scheduled flight to Heathrow. Dan-Air did make it across the Atlantic, though, and in 1969, it first flew a Comet from Gatwick to Trinidad. But what Laker did was something quite different, and so much so that this English pilot-entrepreneur was to change the face of civil aviation.

It took Laker several years of arguing and litigation, but he was finally given the go-ahead to take on British Airways over the Atlantic with his turn-up-and-walk-on Skytrain by James Callaghan's Labour administration in 1977. Although Laker was to become one of Margaret Thatcher's business heroes, it was the same Labour government that knighted him in 1978. Perhaps they saw Laker's cocky venture as a fingers-up salute, a proletarianization as it were, of the Atlantic air routes. If Concorde appeared to fly serenely and so very high above Laker's wide-bodied Douglas DC-10s, with its complement of business tycoons, Hollywood stars and media celebrities, it was partly to be brought down to earth by the triumph of budget airlines, their cut-price ticketing and by the idea – anathema to pioneers of aviation, and to many pilots and enthusiasts alike – that an aircraft was about as special and exciting as a Leyland National bus, an Austin Maxi or the latest Tesco warehouse and distribution depot.

It was not as if Laker had it in for aircraft. He was, after all, a pilot. He served with the Air Transport Auxiliary through much of the Second World War. He converted redundant Handley Page Halifaxes into freighters and took part in the 1948–9 Berlin airlift, helping to save that imperilled city from Soviet aggression. He even produced a new aircraft of his own. This was the ATL-90 Accountant – the name says everything – a twin-engine, twenty-eight-seat turboprop intended to replace the Douglas DC-3s still flown by many small British and European airlines. In the event, only a single prototype ever flew. That was in 1957; it was grounded the following year and scrapped in 1960.

Laker, however, was a businessman above all else, tirelessly looking for new aviation ventures. Expelled from his Canterbury grammar school, he seems to have enjoyed cocking a snook at the establishment and, especially, at the big, established airlines. He certainly never stood still. As managing director of British United Airways, he was the launch customer for BAC's One Eleven short-haul jet airliner. He bought brand-new Vickers VC-10 jets and with these he was able to take over BOAC's loss-making routes to South America. And, in 1979, with the aim of starting a European Skytrain network, he was among the first airline bosses to order the A300, the first of the Airbuses of which, altogether, some 8,000 would be flying in 2015.

Although much hyped at the time, Skytrain went bankrupt in February 1982. There were several reasons for this. The airline had expanded too rapidly. It had borrowed money at too high a rate of interest. It was undercapitalized. The major airlines cut prices ruthlessly to fight it. And yet, although Laker failed, he was a major inspiration not just to Richard Branson and his Virgin Airways, formed in 1984, but to the founders and operators of a large number of budget airlines including easyJet, founded by Stelios Haji-Ioannou, a Greek Cypriot businessman, in 1995 and Ryanair, formed in Dublin ten years earlier. Both these no-frills airlines operate a single type of aircraft. These are, perhaps inevitably, the Boeing 737-800 in Ryanair's case and in easyJet's the Airbus A319/320. Neither of these competent machines has the slightest hint of Concorde's beauty, dynamics and poetry.

This, though, as Michael O'Leary has made clear, is not only not the point, but also far from the point. The forthright, Jesuit-educated CEO of Ryanair advocates passengers standing on short-haul routes and charges for on-board lavatories. He considers seatbelts useless and believes that 'the problem with aviation is that for fifty years it's been populated by people who think it's this wondrous sexual experience; that it's like James Bond and wonderful and we'll all be flying first class when it's really just a bloody bus with wings. Most people just want to get from A to B. You don't want to pay £500 for a flight. You want to spend that money on a nice hotel, apartment or restaurant . . . you don't want to piss it all away at the airport or on the airline.'

In 2001, when Concorde was temporarily grounded after the Paris crash, O'Leary went so far as to tell the *Sunday Times*, 'The other airlines are asking how they can put up fares. We are asking how we could get rid of them.' The idea, punchily expressed as always, is that Ryanair could make the money it needed through hotel bookings, car hire and any number of extras and add-ons, with the result that passengers might indeed be able to fly, nominally, for free. Although he had once said that 'Ryanair will never fly the Atlantic route because one cannot get there in a Boeing 737 unless one has a very strong tail wind or passengers who can swim the last hour of the flight', by 2014, O'Leary was talking of $10 one-way flights to New York and Boston within a few years as budget airlines like Norwegian extended their reach with airliners such as the new Boeing 787 Dreamliner.

Even then, there has been something of a backlash by passengers who feel that they should be treated like humans at the very least and that – an astonishing thought today – perhaps the quality of the journey does matter after all. When the Dallas-based airline Southwest began flying the first of its low-cost flights across the US in 1971, it went over the top in trying to prove that this new form of budget transport could be the 'wondrous sexual experience' derided by O'Leary. Southwest's stewardesses – dancers, cheerleaders and majorettes with Farrah Fawcett legs and smiles – were dressed uniformly in hot pants and go-go boots or the shortest miniskirts. Sexist then as now, it was a clunky attempt to make cheap flying glamorous and fun.

More significantly, Southwest has only operated one type of aircraft, the 737. Today it has a fleet of 630 of these American 'bloody buses with wings'. It also has a safety record almost second to none. Not a single Southwest passenger has died as a result of a crash. The same is true of Ryanair and easyJet, although, as Michael O'Leary has been at pains to point out, 'I don't give a fuck if no one likes me. I am not a cloud bunny. I am not an aerosexual. I don't like aeroplanes. I never wanted to be a pilot like those other platoons of goons who populate the airline industry.'

But the airlines and the design of the aircraft themselves have not been the sole culprits in the full-on retreat from the idea of civil flight being in any way glamorous, romantic or indeed civil. Today, as hundreds of millions of people around the world know all too well, the whole experience of flight – especially international flight – has become a semblance of purgatory, if not quite hell itself. It begins in negotiating crowded roads or surviving crammed public transport to airports and declines precipitously from there. Then there are the improbably long queues to check in; the surliness and bullying experienced when grinding through security; the glare and heat of arcades of dizzying and pointless shops; the grim lavatories; and the people, the noise. And finally, having been herded into boarding lounges, a sardine-tin bus or windowless tube, you reach the aircraft itself, evidently the least important element of the airport world. If you seek the slightest hint of romance in contemporary civil flight, you must look for small airports, small airlines and, yes, higher fares. There may well be no business- or first-class seats on the smaller aircraft operated by the smaller airlines, yet these nearly always offer an infinitely more stylish and more enjoyable experience than that provided to those willing to pay through the nose – or their employer's nose – for a little more leg room and a glass of champagne on a flight with one of the major players.

Something really did change from the early 1970s. Journeys by train began to ape those of airlines, too, and so much so that, no matter how expensive tickets are for trains in Britain in 2015, the experience never rises above that of a no-frills flight from Gatwick to Marbella. Equally, just as the aircraft itself has become a machine that few passengers even look at as they tweet, message and talk, talk, talk their way on board, travellers by train have no locomotive to take an interest in and sit by windows that are usually so small as to discourage even the most determinedly romantic passenger from taking in the view. Increasingly few bother with passing scenery, not least because they are seduced, at all waking hours, by the siren call of their computer screens, mobile phones and other demanding digital devices. Captains of 737s, Airbus A320s and doubtless other aircraft too have almost given up mentioning vivid views of passing cities and mountain ranges to passengers who are glued to screens or else bombarded by commercial announcements.

Significantly perhaps, ocean liners gave up the maritime ghost the very same month Freddie Laker's Skytrain took to the Atlantic airwaves. The Union-Castle's RMS *Windsor Castle* set sail from Southampton to South Africa on 12 August 1977, carrying mail and cargo as well as passengers and crew. When she berthed back at Southampton on 19 September, and her powerful steam turbines were shut down, this really was the end of an era. Designed and built for speed, *Windsor Castle* was a mail ship, a liner that brought diplomats and other high-ranking civil servants, along with settlers, to South Africa. The rising cost of oil and Britain's increasingly ill-starred relationship with South Africa in those long years of apartheid were factors, but *Windsor Castle* – the last ocean liner of all – was mostly undone by the Boeing 747, the mighty airliner that had made its maiden flight within weeks of Concorde. With its large seating capacity – and thus lower fares than before on the air routes to South Africa – and its big holds, the Jumbo Jet was more than a rival for a 36,000-ton ship built by Cammell Laird in Birkenhead and launched as recently as 1959. Meanwhile, today's truly titanic cruise ships, looking for all the seven seas like floating apartment blocks and with all the grace of one of the latest London buses, have little or nothing in common with RMS *Windsor Castle*, a ship whose lineage can be traced back to Brunel's *Great Eastern*.

On the railways, too, overtly luxurious trains were withdrawn from service in Britain and across Europe. They had, of course, largely vanished in the United States with the advent of jet airliners, long before the 1970s. In England, the much-loved

Brighton Belle, a highly distinctive and unusual Art Deco-style electric train, was taken out of service in 1972. It was not to be replaced. Trips by train from London to Brighton are no quicker four decades on, while the trains themselves, aside from being routinely overcrowded, are grim and often rather sordid affairs. Certainly no white-jacketed attendant is likely to offer you champagne, hock or claret, a Havana cigar, Dover sole, kippers or Welsh rarebit.

On the *Midland Pullman*, a handsome blue-and-white, air-conditioned diesel train that, from 1960, revolutionized the quality of business travel from Manchester to London St Pancras, attendants proffered plaice and halibut as well as sole. As the Pullman sped through the industrial Midlands at 90 mph, a choice of fillet or rump steak was on the menu along with lamb cutlets and lobster mayonnaise, followed by pear melba or crème caramel. There were wines from Australia and South Africa as well as from France and a choice of mineral waters – still and fizzy – at a time when mineral water was either unknown to the vast majority of the British public or else thought of as something to do with vegetarians, those with medical conditions and nature-cure cranks.

Even in Italy, one of the great culinary nations, the idea of a luxury train speeding from Milan to Rome in record time while providing excellent food in a superbly realized setting was to have gone by 1984. I feel very lucky to have ridden the Ferrovia Statale's *Settebello* (Beautiful, or Lucky Seven, the top card in the Italian game *scopa*) between Milan and Rome. Designed inside and out by some of Italy's best engineers, architects and artists, this striking electric train, which went into service in 1953, was a high-speed and prestigious symbol of Italy's post-war economic miracle. The first-class-only ETR300 trains were very special, with observation cars, passenger accommodation arranged in a set of club-like compartments, a separate luggage car for all heavy bags, exquisite futuristic décor, highly experienced staff and a fine 90-mph restaurant run by Wagon-Lits.

These three trains – there were others, too, of course – required those travelling on them to pay a supplementary fare. In the case of the *Settebello*, this was quite high compared to standard Italian rail fares, but as these were, and remain, rather cheap compared, for example, with those demanded in Britain, the Beautiful Seven was something of a bargain for international travellers. The supplement for the first-class-only Midland Pullman was modest, while the extra cost of riding either first or second on the *Brighton Belle* was little more than a snip. For the price of a pint of Double Diamond, here was the opportunity to ride in a train unlike any other in the world: one of just three sets of 5BEL electric multiple units picking up current from a third rail just like any slam-door, green suburban train whining out of Victoria, yet decked out in exquisite Art Deco marquetry, plump armchairs and ornate lampshades, and each parlour, or restaurant, car not a number but a name. Although the train was taken out of service in 1972, individual Pullman cars – *Audrey*, *Gwen* and *Vera* – are still very much active and form part of the Orient Express as it glides from London to Dover on the first leg of its opulent journey to Paris and Venice. Meanwhile, the 5BEL Trust is restoring a 5BEL and hopes to run it in service for enthusiasts and connoisseurs of luxury trains.

I mention these ships and trains in the story of Concorde because they help tell the story of how, for the most part, the world has come to look on regular travel as a purely matter-of-fact means of getting from A to B, whether that means Ashford to Bromley or Amsterdam to Bangkok. The cheaper the fare, the better, and never mind much else. Travel is no longer an adventure – and even if you pay for first class, you are these days unlikely to receive a first-class service. This may all be a welcome and admirably democratic development in the greater scheme of things, but it is hard not to feel that something special has been lost along the way.

Meanwhile, the very idea of caring about who designed and built the machine that might carry you safely and reliably halfway around the world is essentially redundant in the second decade of the twenty-first century. By and large, airports are designed so that aircraft are for the most part invisible. They have become just one part of an ideally seamless, if all too often frustrating and uncomfortable, conveyor-belt experience. How can it possibly matter if your aircraft is a Boeing or an Airbus? And as for Concorde, even if a few passengers might look its way today, how many would be prepared to spend a small fortune on a ticket to fly on board this supersonic jet? Actually, quite a few people would, just as they would to ride a contemporary equivalent of the *Brighton Belle*, *Midland Pullman* or *Settebello*. And if there were to be a new generation of smaller, truly first-class ocean liners, perhaps a new generation of business people would take to this more elegant and relaxing form of transport.

I flew once from New York to London by Concorde, a thrilling experience, of course. But my pleasure had been more than doubled by the fact that I had gone out to New York on board the *QE2* when she was still operating as a liner. Both forms of transatlantic travel were special and memorable. And the whole point of the return trip was to experience these particular machines. Sailing to New York on board a giant cruise ship and returning whether by 747 or Airbus A340 could never match the excitement and romance of shouting along corridors of Atlantic air in Concorde, or rebuffing restless waves while visiting the bridge of the Cunard liner, touring the engine rooms and letting time go by in a round of delicious meals, long books, self-consciously modern interiors and the sway of the sea. The ship's engines at the time were a pair of Brown-Pametrada (Parsons and Marine Engineering Turbine Research & Development Association) double-expansion steam turbines developing 110,000 shaft hp. Sadly, they could be troublesome and were thirsty for increasingly costly oil, so were replaced by diesel engines in the mid-1980s. But what a wonderful sound they made: so smooth, so purposeful, so suited to the very last express liner built in Britain. (The much bigger Cunard RMS *Queen Mary 2*, launched in 2003 and decked out in pseudo-historic bling décor, was built at Saint-Nazaire.)

Less than a year after my Atlantic crossings, the *QE2* was ploughing through a decidedly choppy South Atlantic on her way to South Georgia, and thus to the Falklands, with a volunteer crew and 3,000 members of the 5th Infantry Brigade on board. Her speed made her an ideal troopship in time of war. No slow-moving twenty-first-century floating hotel bullying its way through Venice and other historic cities could have kept pace with this lithe, turbine-powered liner, a ship that went into service in 1969, the year of Concorde's maiden flight. The two were photographed together several times, and, yes, having been alerted by the crew, I did see – albeit as no more than white specks in front of pulsing contrails – and certainly heard Concorde aircraft racing backwards and forwards so very high above the decks of the Cunard liner.

There are, of course, pockets of resistance to the trend towards banality in the worlds of everyday public transport. Many smaller airlines flying modern turboprops from small airports keep alive a real sense of flight. Intriguingly, though, the most exciting new high-speed machines are perhaps trains rather than planes. Anyone who has ridden the latest Shinkansen or Bullet trains in Japan will know just how singular an experience regular super-fast transport can provide. I travelled from Tokyo to Akita for the sake of it, as many Japanese rail fans have done, because the new E6 trains operating the Komachi Shinkansen are perhaps the most exciting in the world. It is not simply that these trains run for long distances at 200 mph, with the promise of 225 mph by 2020, but more because they are superbly designed, styled and engineered – veritable Concorde aircraft of the rails. Designed with aerodynamics uppermost in mind, the noses of the seven-car electric trains are no less than 42 ft long, or more than half the length of *Mallard*, Sir Nigel Gresley's record-breaking A4 steam locomotive built in 1938 for the London and North Eastern Railway. Concorde's famous droop snoot measured just 24 ft. The E6's elongated nose allows the train to rush through and out of tunnels with a minimal build-up of air pressure around it; it also cuts down on the noisome tunnel booms – the railway equivalent of Concorde's sonic boom – that have, to date, held up the further acceleration of Shinkansen trains.

Styled by Ken Okuyama, a Japanese car designer best known for his work for the Italian *carrozzeria* Pininfarina and Ferrari, the streamlined crimson-and-white E6 turns heads at every station it stops at on its 325-mile run from Tokyo to Akita. The Komachi service is named after the Akita-born ninth-century poetess Ono no Komachi; in turn, her name means 'beauty' or, yes, 'belle'. So, this is the *Akita Belle*. The interiors are well resolved. Fitted with active suspension, the trains ride as if on air. Lavatories are, of course, clean and, in stark contrast to the experience of travelling on British trains or planes, passengers are asked to comply graciously with the Shinkansen code of manners:

Line up on the platform before boarding.

Don't block the aisle with luggage.

When having a conversation, keep your voice down.

Set your mobile to silent mode. Don't talk on your phone except in the deck area between cars.

Recline your seat with consideration for the person behind you. Return the seat to its original position before exiting the train.

What the trains do not have, because space is at a premium and because they are very fast, is catering to match their sensational looks and performance. Instead, experienced travellers buy *eki-ten* lunch boxes from *bento* counters at stations. These are usually as delicious as they look. How much more civilized, more tasty, less smelly and far more satisfying to toy with sushi wrapped in persimmon leaves or rice dishes with salmon, mackerel, trout, crab or squid, or beef, chicken or pork washed down with green tea than to barge on board with a family-pack-for-one of the biggest, stinkiest and flatulence-inducing sub-American takeaway, which is, mystifyingly, deemed acceptable in Britain's fastest, and ineffably expensive, trains.

A new generation of high-speed trains in Japan, France, Germany, Italy and elsewhere has robbed airlines of a considerable amount of traffic. And though the trains have been showing signs of wear and even abuse, who would think of travelling from Paris to London and vice versa except by Eurostar, the 300-kmh trains that scythe from St Pancras to Gare du Nord in two and a quarter hours? While it must have been an eye-opening experience to see your car loaded aboard a twin-engine Silver City Airways Bristol Superfreighter at Lydd on the Romney Marshes and then to be flown for twenty minutes over the miniature steam expresses of the Romney Hythe and Dymchurch Railway and the busy, boisterous Channel to Le Touquet at an altitude of no more than 1,000 ft, this would have made for a slow, if delightful, way of getting to Paris from London in time for dinner.

It does seem strange. Aircraft are inherently fascinating machines and sustained flight by powered, heavier-than-air machines is still little more than a century old. And yet, for all the poetry of flight and the verses that have been written in celebration of it, for all the skill required to pilot a small aircraft and the wonder of doing so, for all the ever-changing sorcery of skies and cloudscapes, we really have learned to take flight for granted – far too much for granted – and, in the process, have stripped air travel of any sense of adventure or delight. Perhaps, though, one of the reasons that so relatively few passengers take a real interest or delight in aircraft, their design, engineering and performance is that many frequent, novice or nervous flyers prefer not to think about all that spinning machinery, those turncoat airways with their sudden dips and turns, and the sheer distance between their air-conditioned cabins and the ground below.

Even so, the banality of workaday flight today is a sorry episode in humankind's quest to take to the air, to race with the gods, to soar like eagles, to vault across oceans in machines of athletic grace and purposeful beauty of line. For Gene Kranz, the former Korean War jet fighter pilot and NASA flight director, a lot of the excitement and public involvement in advanced and daring aerospace projects dried up after the US Moon landings. When asked in 2000 if NASA was rated in the same way as it was in the 1960s – *the* era of technological optimism – Kranz said, 'No. In many ways we have the young people, we have the talent, we have the imagination, we have the technology. But, I don't believe we have the leadership and the willingness to accept risk, to achieve great goals.'

Kranz hoped humankind would go on to explore the universe, and not just with the aid of telescopes and unmanned probes, yet politicians and business became ever more down to earth from the 1970s onwards, shying away from measures and investments that would allow us, in Captain Kirk's happy split infinitive, 'to boldly go where no man has gone before'. In a December 2014 article for the online magazine *Aeon*, the science journalist Michael Hanlon argued that there truly had been what he describes as a 'Golden Quarter' between approximately 1945 and 1971, when 'just about everything that defines the modern world either came about, or had its seeds sown, during this time. The Pill. Electronics. Computers and the birth of the internet. Nuclear power. Television. Antibiotics. Space travel. Civil rights.' There was, of course, much more, as Hanlon made clear, describing this era as 'a time when innovation appeared to be running on a mix of dragster fuel and dilithium crystals', while 'Today, progress is defined almost entirely by consumer-driven, often banal improvements in information technology . . . look up and the airliners you see are basically updated versions of the ones flying in the 1960s – slightly quieter Tristars with better avionics. In 1971, a regular airliner took eight hours to fly from London to New York; it still does . . . now, Concorde is dead. Our cars are faster, safer and use less fuel than they did in 1971, but there has been no paradigm shift.'

Like Kranz, Hanlon puts this down to risk aversion, along with the decline of public-sector investment in new technology, an aspirational consumer society that is unhappy unless it has a new smartphone at least every year and because today, according to a Credit Suisse report published in October 2014, 1 per cent of humans now owns half the world's assets and likes to spend them on 'super-yachts, fast cars, private jets and other gewgaws of Planet Rich . . . and, though they are no doubt nice to have, these fripperies don't much advance the frontiers of human knowledge. When wealth accumulates so spectacularly by doing nothing, there is less impetus to invest in genuine innovation.'

This fundamental shift in global society's aims and desires – affecting China, run by an authoritarian Communist Party, most strikingly as well as Europe, the United States and the rest of the developed and developing world – has allowed us, and encourages us, to wallow in an ever-growing and wholly unsustainable tide of banal consumption. The idea that humans might be happier, or certainly more content, as producers – as inventors and makers of worthwhile and even precious things – is considered somehow old-fashioned and wrong. The world of contemporary civil aviation exemplifies this spiritless quest for all people to have all things at all times at the lowest possible price and with the least possible thought, and never mind anything else. Customer surveys request us to rate our experience, but how in all honesty can we rate something so dull, so entirely lacking in any spirit of adventure as modern air travel? Concorde was far from perfect, but it hardly stood a chance, beginning commercial operations at the very time when Hanlon's Golden Quarter was drawing to a close.

Concorde was not directly responsible for its own fall, and the considerable research and development that went into the supersonic airliner was to benefit Airbus greatly. As Jean Reich, former Concorde chief engineer at Sud Aviation and Aerospatiale, put it in the late 1990s, 'In some forty years, the civil aircraft industry in Europe has come from a very weak situation (though with occasional successes such as the Viscount and Caravelle) to a much stronger situation today. And if you ask the question, "Has Concorde contributed to that situation?", I think the answer is yes. We are sorry that we could not sell it, but we do not have the impression of having wasted the money of the British and French taxpayers.'

From a technological viewpoint, risk aversion and strictly commercial sense have encouraged the civil aviation industry to progress steadily along a gently sloping upwards curve over the past four decades. Aircraft such as the Airbus have grown bigger, quieter and more fuel-efficient since the A300 entered service with Air France in May 1974. The latest Airbus variant, the A350, flying with Qatar Airways since January 2015, features a fuselage and wings fashioned from lightweight carbon fibre-reinforced polymer. Powered by quiet and powerful Rolls-Royce Trent engines, it has a range of 8,000 miles. A competitor to Boeing's 787 Dreamliner, it is an aircraft with a truly global range that will, in all likelihood, sell and fly profitably for many years to come.

The 787, which is also powered by a version of the Rolls-Royce Trent (GM GEnx engines are an option), is fabricated largely from composites along with titanium and aluminium. Range, as with the Airbus A350, is 8,000 miles and, like all long-distance airliners since the Boeing 707, cruising speed is Mach 0.85. The global nature of the 787 is highlighted by the sourcing of sub-contracted components for the aircraft, among them central wing boxes from Japan, horizontal stabilizers from Italy and South Korea, passenger doors from France, cargo doors from Sweden, software from India and landing gear from Messier-Bugatti-Dowty, an Anglo-French company with operations in Asia, Europe and North America.

Meanwhile, the Boeing 777 – the world's largest twin-engine airliner – is being upgraded, compounding the certainty that the world's major air routes will be the preserve of lookalike European and US jets into the foreseeable future. Aircraft enthusiasts will always be able to tell one make and each variant from another, yet for the travelling public airliners will look identical; for the most part, in 2015, they already do. Changes are incremental rather than radical, and – partly as a consequence of this – faults are increasingly rare, although the Boeing 787 fleet was grounded for three months in 2013 because the aircraft's sophisticated lithium-ion batteries had a tendency to catch fire.

Passenger focus, meanwhile, is increasingly towards screens and other digital diversions rather than on the aesthetics and technological provenance of aircraft themselves, and talk of windowless airliners is not so very unrealistic now that so many passengers, glued to their screens, find little of interest in views, however epic, of skies, stars, clouds, mountain ranges, deserts, rivers and other natural phenomena, outside their steady Mach-0.85 aerial cocoon.

As for the distinctive Boeing 747, the aircraft that spelt an alternative path of progress to that of Concorde from the moment it made its assured maiden flight in 1969, its time, too, has finally come. The lighter and more fuel-efficient new Airbuses and Boeings are directing even the impressive 747-400 to early retirement in desert graveyards.

Concorde, at heart the most poetic of machines, was not destined to fly on into this era of Airbuses and prosaic flight. We might, of course, rediscover the adventure of flight, with new forms of aircraft using harmless and renewable fuels, or future generations that will take us boldly into those dark, star-studded skies, and even towards the same stars witnessed by passengers from the windows of Concorde, as every day these magnificent flying machines, largely bereft of in-flight gewgaws and other distractions, traced the curvature of the Earth.

EPILOGUE

IN December 2012, I drove from London to Bristol at the wheel of a Bristol 411, a bespoke British 140-mph grand tourer built at Filton, where all British Concorde aircraft were assembled. This handsomely crafted, fast and supremely comfortable car was made in 1969, the year Brian Trubshaw lifted Concorde 002 into the air for the first time.

Parked discreetly, I watched a crowd gather along the A38 as Airbus and BAE Systems employees also arrived from their nearby offices. They came not to see the Bristol, although this rare car is a happy by-product of the Bristol Aircraft Company based here for many years, but to look at and to listen to a beautifully rebuilt 1944 Spitfire Mk IX taking off from Filton aerodrome. This aircraft had been remanufactured, from components sourced from around the world, at a cost said to be £2.5m by a team led by John Hart for Martin Phillips, an Exeter businessman, and its flight was a pitch-perfect affair. Up and around it went, then down and low over the Filton site in a happily blue sky, winning the hearts of all who watched it do so.

This, I thought, could only be Britain in the twenty-first century. What I was watching with an enraptured crowd was the maiden flight of the very last aircraft to be built at Filton. Within less than a fortnight, the famous aerodrome, owned by BAE Systems, and its hangars would close and with them a manufacturing history stretching back to shortly before the First World War, and leading forward through the 1960s and 1970s, when Concorde was Filton's star, to 2012 and a solitary Supermarine Spitfire.

In 1909, just sixty years before Concorde 002's maiden flight, the Bristol tramways entrepreneur Sir George White was in Paris to watch demonstration flights by the Wright brothers. The following year, he set up his own aircraft manufacturing business, the British and Colonial Aeroplane Company, in the Bristol Tramways maintenance depot. In 1911, White laid out an airfield taken over and extended during the First World War by the Royal Flying Corps, a branch of the army that would be equipped with the formidable Rolls-Royce Kestrel-powered Bristol Fighter, a fast, manoeuvrable two-seat biplane that later served with air forces as far afield as those of Argentina and Mexico, Afghanistan and New Zealand.

Bristol Blenheims, Beauforts, Beaufighters, Brigands and Buckinghams were built at Filton during the Second World War, alongside re-assembly lines busy preparing US military aircraft shipped across the Atlantic for operations in Europe. Squadrons of Hawker Hurricanes and Supermarine Spitfires scrambled from what was now RAF Filton and protected both the works – attacked on 25 September 1940 by an aerial flotilla of fifty-eight Heinkel He 111 bombers escorted by Messerschmitt Bf 110 twin-engine fighters – and Bristol itself.

The runway at Filton was greatly extended soon after the war to allow the Bristol Brabazon, a brobdingnagian eight-engine airliner, to take off on its conquest, or so it was hoped, of the transatlantic route from London to New York. But the Brabazon was simply too big and just one was built, although not before the village of Charlton, which stood in its way to the skies, was demolished rather as were entire districts of central London in the nineteenth century to allow the mainline railway companies room for their grand new stations.

BOAC serviced its transatlantic Boeing Stratocruisers and Lockheed Constellations here while the elegant Bristol Britannia took shape alongside them. And then came Concorde, along with a number of English Electric Lightning interceptors, spiritual successors to Supermarine's glorious Spitfire. Perhaps it was fitting that a Spitfire should have made the last flight by an aircraft built or rebuilt at Filton; after all, it was those high-speed RAE test flights with Spitfires during the Second World War that had helped to spur on British advancement in supersonic flight. There was, though, something infinitely sad in the fact that a veteran aircraft – the first Spitfire Mk IXs entered service in 1942 – should be the last product of a workshop that had once made Concorde. And something sad, too, in the fact that, although Airbus and BAE Systems retained some offices at Filton, manufacturing had for some while become the province of Toulouse.

For me, though, the saddest sight of all that December day was that of a Spitfire, an aircraft that represented some of the most advanced technology of its era, flying above dismal-looking new executive homes – the airport's future – that would have looked just as dreary and grimly old-fashioned had they been built on the site back in the 1930s. Filton had been flogged off to a London property company, Bridgehouse Capital Ltd, for a reputed £120m. The plan was to build 2,500 of these homes and the inevitable accompanying business park. 'I have a terrible feeling,' said George Ferguson, architect and mayor of Bristol, 'that BAE Systems are taking the short-term economic option rather than thinking long-term. That would be the worst thing, if we lose some of that pioneering industry from Bristol because of the loss of the airfield.'

A fortnight later, mechanical diggers moved in to break up the runway to ensure there would be no chance that a rogue Spitfire or indeed any other aircraft, veteran or ultra-modern, could take off or land here in the future. What a pity. At least Filton aerodrome and its historic hangars might have been developed into some forward-looking design, engineering and manufacturing base that we might all be proud of. While, in 2015 at least, Airbus, BAE Systems and Rolls-Royce continue to have a non-manufacturing, non-flying presence in and around Filton, the love of making things and a love of aircraft in particular seems to have been banished from the site. As far as actual aircraft are concerned, the future here appears to lie with another museum, albeit one for Concorde.

In the December 2011 issue of *History Today* – I looked this up online sitting in the back seat of the Bristol 411, my leather-lined office before I slipped back into the driving seat for the return run to London – the historian Jad Adams noted of the early 1960s:

> In a period of industrial decline, there was a particular need for Britain to prove itself. Aircraft production along with shipping, cars and other manifestations of manufacturing might were dwindling. It was a unifying apprehension in a divided country, something that both Labour and Conservative governments and the

people they represented could agree upon. Duncan Sandys, Harold Macmillan's minister of aviation, said: 'If we are not in the supersonic aircraft business, then it's really only a matter of time before the whole British aircraft industry packs in. It's obviously the thing of the future. It may pay. It may not pay, but we cannot afford to stay out. If we miss this generation of aircraft we shall never catch up. We will end up building executive aircraft.'

Geoffrey Rippon, a young Tory modernizer and parliamentary secretary at the Ministry of Aviation, thought the alternative to Concorde was 'flogging hand-knitted Union Jacks to tourists'. Rippon had been so keen as a rising young Tory politician to see Concorde get the go-ahead that, secretly, he gave a copy of the 1959 STAC report to the French. Of Treasury officials and their fear of the costs that might be – and were – involved, Rippon said, 'They have no concept of the national interest. They judge everything with the narrowest possible perception.'

Rippon was certainly right about the Union Jacks, as flogging them to tourists seems to be more or less all we have learned to do when not shopping or texting, even if these days hand-knitted national flags are more likely to be made in China than Britain. However, when I got back to London that December day, I learned about the possible future of Bristol Cars, scion of the Bristol Aeroplane Company and owned since 2011 by Frazer Nash Research, a Surrey-based technology company owned in turn by Kamkorp, an Anglo-Swiss holding company owned by the Indian-born entrepreneur Kamal Siddiqi. Bristol had gone out of business some years earlier. Its last car was the 200-mph Bristol Fighter. Now, I heard, although details were tentative, it was preparing to launch a petrol-electric hybrid GT promising 200 mph, 100 mpg and great panache. If not at Filton, the new car is to be built in Britain, and perhaps the marque's new owner might, unlike Tony Crook, who owned Bristol Cars from 1973 to 2007, be willing to sell cars to all comers. Crook had been famously selective. Sir Richard Branson, Peter Sellers and King Hussein of Jordan could buy a Bristol. But Michael Winner could not.

As it is, and despite all the time, effort and money spent on it, supersonic air travel seems to be on the back burner, as does British, if not French, involvement in any related project. Perhaps this should come as a relief. Perhaps it is simply inevitable since, as Jad Adams concluded, 'In the end, Concorde was a hopeless hybrid: the aircraft of the future had become the aircraft of past fantasies, a flying symbol of a science fiction world that never came to be.'

I still sigh for Concorde, though. It was much bigger – and much noisier – than Mitchell's elegant creation, and was designed with an entirely different purpose in mind. But, like the Supermarine fighter, it thoroughly deserves a place in the pantheon of aeronautical achievement. Its presence in the air was a source of wonder, just as the sight of a restored Spitfire still is. And Concorde was as much a mechanical and aerodynamic marvel as it was a flawed – and yet magnificent – compromise. In that sense, and in most others, it was a truly Olympian machine, one whose enduring, dazzling presence in our memories will surely continue to haunt both our dreams of the future and that future itself.

ACKNOWLEDGEMENTS

Thanks go to Christopher Orlebar, author and former Concorde pilot with British Airways, for reading my manuscript for accuracy and to the late Sir Freddie Page, Brian Trubshaw and Tony Benn for discussing Concorde with me over the years. Dr Virginia Preston and Dr Michael Kandiah of the Institute of Contemporary History, King's College, London have kindly given me permission to quote from the ICBH Witness Seminar Programme: Concorde, held at the Science Museum in November 1998, when many of those who had been involved with the development, testing, operation and challenging politics of the supersonic airliner on both sides of the English Channel were gathered together in one room. Antoine Gonin's superb black and white photographs of the wind tunnels of ONERA in the Maurienne Valley displayed at the Musée des Arts et Metiers, Paris from September 2014 sent me back again to this inspiring French research institute and its sorry counterpart in Hampshire. Thanks, too, of course, to Angus MacKinnon, my knowledgeable editor, James Nightingale at Atlantic Books and Sarah Chalfant, my high-flying agent.

SELECT BIBLIOGRAPHY

Beniada, Frederic, *Concorde* (Cassell, 2006)

Calvert, Brian, *Flying Concorde: The Full Story* (Airlife Publishing, 1981)

Conway, Eric, *High-Speed Dreams: NASA and the Technopolitics of Supersonic Transportation, 1945–1999* (JHU Press, 2005)

Deregel, Xavier; Jean-Philippe Lemaire, *Concorde Passion* (Editions LBM, 2009)

Ernoult, Alain, *Concorde: La Legende Volante* (Du May 2002)

Falconer, Jonathan, *Concorde: A Photographic History* (J. H. Haynes 2008)

Feldman, Elliot J., *Concorde and Dissent: Exploring High Technology Project Failures in Britain and France* (Cambridge University Press, 1985)

Knight, Geoffrey, *Concorde: The Inside Story* (Weidenfeld & Nicolson, 1976)

Lewis, Rob; Lewis, Edwin, *Supersonic Secrets: the unauthorised biography of Concorde* (Exposé, 2003)

Marc, Yves, *Concorde: Le Magnifique* (Privat, 2008)

Marlow, Tim, *Concorde: The Last Summer* (Thames and Hudson, 2006)

Masse, Xavier, *Avion Concorde* (Nouvelles Editions Latines, 2004)

Orlebar, Christopher, *The Concorde Story* (7th Edition, Osprey Publishing, 2011)

Owen, Kenneth, *Concorde: story of a supersonic pioneer* (Science Museum, 2001)

Schrader, Richard K., *Concorde: The Full Story of the Anglo-French SST* (Pictorial Histories Publishing, 1989)

Simons, Graham M., *Concorde Conspiracy: The Battle for the American Skies 1962–77* (The History Press, 2012)

Skinner, Stephen, *Concorde* (Midland Publishing, 2009)

Sparaco, Pierre, *Concorde: La Veritable Histoire* (Editions Larivière, 2005)

Talbot, Ted, *Concorde: A Designer's Life; the journey to Mach 2* (The History Press, 2013)

Tillmans, Wolfgang, *Concorde* (Walther Konig, 1997)

Trubshaw, Brian with Edmondson, Sally, *Test Pilot* (Sutton Publishing, 1998)

Trubshaw, Brian, *Concorde: The Inside Story* (Sutton Publishing, 2000)

Turcat, André, *Concorde – Essais d'hier, batailles d'aujourd'hui* (Le Cherche Midi, 2000)

Other Sources:

Institute of Contemporary British History, King's College London (Concorde Witness Seminar, Science Museum, November 1998)

www.concordesst.com (the best and most comprehensive Concorde website)

INDEX

5BEL Trust 279
9/11 terrorist attacks 167, 209, 212–13
223 proposal 20
2001: A Space Odyssey (film) 1–2, 238, 242, 243–4

A2, hypersonic airliner 242
Abba 152
Ackeret, Jakob 37
Adams, Jad 294–5, 296
Adams, John 214
Advanced Fighter Project Group 47–8
Advanced Passenger Trains (APT) 251–2
Aeon (online magazine) 285–6
Aerion AS2 252, 254–5
Aerion Corporation 253–5
aerodynamic characteristics, supersonic aircraft 31
Aerodynamic Research Institute, Gottingen 65
aerodynamic testing 58–60
Aeroflot 111, 112
Aerojet Rocketdyne 245
aerospace industry: fuel demands 14; income forecasts 259
Aero Spaceline 377SGT 89–90
Aerospatiale 84, 188
Afghanistan 216
afterburners 37, 77
Airbus 5, 218–19, 224, 259
Airbus A300 45–6, 288
Airbus A319/320 270, 273
Airbus A350 288
Airbus A380 134, 220–1
Airbus Defence and Space 254
Air China 2
air ducts 76–7

air-flow data 69
air flow separation 62–5
Air France 3, 3–4, 84, 131; Concorde cabin design 180–1, 183–5; Concorde fleet grounded 196–7; Concorde flight officers 145; female pilots 154–6; final Concorde flights 224–5; flight training 137; liveries 187–9; losses 161, 197; options to buy 92; Paris to Rio de Janeiro service 137, 141, 146–7; profitability 164; resumes New York flights 214–17; retirement announcement 217–18; retirement cost 221
air-intake geometry 76–7, 87
airliners, demand for 259–61
airline traffic, volume 260
Airplane! (film) 190
Airport (film) 189–90
airport design 280
Alcock, John 165–6
Alco Hydro-Aeroplane Company 244
Aldrin, Buzz 1, 60
Al Khalifa, Sheikh Isa bin Salman 146
All Nippon Airways 246
al-Qaeda 209, 216
Alsbury, Michael 249
American Airlines 92
American Institution of Aeronautics and Astronautics 100
Amery, Julian 3, 25, 26, 27, 85, 108, 122
Anderson, Gerry 103, 240
Andrews Field, Washington DC 216
Anglo-American Aeronautical Conference, 1961 66
Anglo-American relations 25

Anglo-French collaborations 43
Anglo-French relations 24, 25
Anglo-French treaty 3, 25, 75, 122
Angola 136–7
Anti-Concorde Project 126–8
Apollo 11 128
Apt, Milburn 49
Armstrong, Neil 1, 60, 69, 109
Armstrong Whitworth 10; AWP.13 54; AWP.171 54–5; design proposals 54–5
around-the-world air speed record 42
Ashampstead, Berkshire 145
Atkins, Darren 195
ATL-90 Accountant 272–3
Atlantic Monthly 26, 132, 135, 142
Attlee, Clement 46–7, 264
Auriol, Jacqueline 155–6
Auriol, Vincent 155–6
Auschwitz 65–6
Australia 140
Auty, Godfrey 71, 72–3
Aviation, Ministry of 7, 13–14; Concorde division 82
Aviation Safety Network 200–1
Avrieux, wind-tunnel test station 268–9
A. V. Roe 10
Avro 504K 69
Avro Lancaster heavy bomber 13, 34, 217
Avro Vulcan strategic bomber 13, 23–4, 76, 217, 229
AWP.13 54
AWP.171 54–5
Ayers, Ron 255
Ayling, Robert 'Bob' 186

299

BAC 221 43, 70–1
BAC TSR-2 74–5
BAC Type 198 78
BAC Type 223 78, 79
Bacher, Steven 197
Backchivandzhi, Grigori 45
Bader, Douglas 69
BAE Systems 291, 294
Baggott, John 268
Bahrain 146
Bain, Neville 215
Baldwin, Sir Peter 75
balloons, first flight 193
Bannister, Mike 4, 205, 208, 215–16, 217, 225–7, 230
Barbados 149, 201
barrel-rolls 148
Bassett, Jackie 159
Bass, Robert Muse 253–4
Bastin, Ricky 77
Baxter, Raymond 93, 116
BBC 116; Great British Design Quest 171–6
BEA (Bureau d'Enquêtes et d'Analyses pour la sécurité de l'aviation civile) 20, 197, 198
Beckham, David 154
Beck, Harry 172–3
Bedford, RAF 69
Bell, Charles 107
Bell Aircraft Corporation 32, 34–5
Bell X-1 rocket plane 31–2, 35–7, 39
Bell X-2 rocket plane 14, 49
Benderov, V. N. 111
Benn, Anthony Wedgwood 85–6, 118–19, 122–3, 124, 133, 136
Bereznyak, Alexander 45–6
Berman, Caroline 128, 130
Bertoni, Flaminio 180
BI – Blizhnii strebitel (close-range fighter) 45
bin Laden, Osama 216
Biscay, Bay of 123–4, 200
Bishop, Patrick 195
Blair Force One 216
Blair, Tony 216, 234–5, 267
Blohm & Voss 56
BMC Mini 175–6
B model 233–4

BOAC 8, 20, 25, 92, 273, 293
Boeing 367-800 53
Boeing 377 Stratocruiser 14, 90
Boeing 707 3, 8, 53, 66, 87, 132–3, 179
Boeing 707 Whisky Echo, engine failure 202–3
Boeing 737 94, 270, 275
Boeing 737-800 273
Boeing 747 1, 2–3, 5, 134, 277, 288
Boeing 747-8 Intercontinental 2
Boeing 747-400 221
Boeing 777 288
Boeing 787 Dreamliner 274, 288
Boeing 2707 68, 102–5, 106–7, 125
Boeing B-52 221
Boeing KC-135 tanker 50
Boeing, supersonic airliner design 101
Boeing X-51 247–8
Bond, Alan 242, 243
Boothman, John 157
Bordeaux 268
Born, Max 60, 62
Boston, Logan Airport 3–4
Boyle, Danny 151
brakes 88–9, 201
Brandt, Irene 35
Braniff International Airways 159–60
Branson, Richard 219, 248–50, 252, 273
Brasilia 91, 92
Braun, Werner von 34, 37, 60, 235
Brazil 92
Brazilian Air Force 91
Breakfast with Frost (TV programme) 203–4
Brezhnev, Leonid 99
Bridgehouse Capital Ltd 293–4
Brighton Belle (train) 278, 279
Bristol (city) 81
Bristol 188 72–3, 74
Bristol Aircraft Company 10, 60; 223 291; contract 22; design proposals 20, 54
Bristol Brabazon 81, 88, 292–3

Bristol Britannia 179, 293
Bristol Cars 295–6
Bristol Fighter 292
Bristol Hercules engine 23
Bristol Post 108
Bristol Siddeley 79
Bristol Siddeley Olympus 22R 23–4, 74–5, 76, 76–7
Bristol Siddeley Viper turbojet 69
British Aerospace 48
British Aircraft Corporation 70
British Airports Authority 129
British Airways 3, 89; call sign 165; Concorde cabin design 180–1, 182–3; Concorde flight officers 144–5; Concorde policy 162–4; defence of Concorde 197–8; female pilots 154; flight training 137; handover of the last Concorde to 48; liveries 185–7; London to Bahrain service 137, 139–46; losses 161; maintenance costs 220–1; privatization 163; profitability 197; resumes New York flights 214–17; retirement announcement 217–18; retirement cost 221; tail-fin logos 186, 186–7
British and Colonial Aeroplane Company 292
British Caledonian 161
British Interplanetary Society 243
British Rail, Advanced Passenger Trains (APT) 251–2
British Railways 121
Britton, John 205
Brize Norton, RAF 207–8
Brodie, Les 228
Bronowski, Jacob 65–6
Brooklands Museum, Surrey 229–30
Brown, Arthur 'Teddie' 165–6
Brown, Captain Eric 'Winkle' 37–8

Brunel, Isambard Kingdom 264
Buckingham Palace, flypast, 2002 149, 217
budget airlines 5, 151, 160, 208, 271–5
budget cuts, post-war 36
bullets, flight of 35–6
Buonanno, Michael 257–8
Burj Khalifa, the, Dubai 211
Burning Man Festival 256
Busemann, Alfred 60–2
Busemann's Biplane 61
Bush, George W. 216
Butler, Richard 'RAB' 26–7
Byron, Robert 254–5

cabins 180–1, 182–5, 206
Calder, Alexander 159–60
Calder Hall nuclear power station 16
Callaghan, James 135, 272
Calvert, Brian 143–4, 145, 147
Calvert, Margaret 173–4
Camm, Sidney 48
cancellation threats 74–5, 86, 121–3, 133, 163–4
Cape Verde islands 124
captains 144–5
Carrington, Lord 125
cars 12
Carter, Jimmy 152
Cavelle, Marcel 146
celebrity pilots 125–6
Central Policy Review Staff 133
Central Programme Office 88
certificate of airworthiness 87, 137; withdrawn 197, 222
chairman 81–2
Chalons-Vatry Airport 208
champagne 227
Chanoine, Pierre 141
Chapman, Colin 169
Charles de Gaulle Airport 194, 230–1
Charles, Jacques 193
charter airlines 271
charter flights 156–9, 225
Chatelain, Jean-Louis 225
Che Guevara 94
Cheshire, Leonard 139–40
Chillaud, Edgar 208, 216
China 94; internal aviation market 259–60; railways 260; skyscrapers 211–12

China Southern Airlines 260
Chirac, Jacques 195
Christmas Eve flight, 1985 164–5
Christmas flights 159
Churchill, Winston 40
Citizens' League Against the Sonic Boom 128
Citroën DS 180
Civil and Scientific Research and Development, Cabinet Committee on 26–7
civil aviation, 1950s 14–15
Civilian Space eXploration [sic] Team 256
Clarke, Arthur C. 243–4
Clark, F. G. 85; Concorde 116
Clifton Suspension Bridge 228
Clinton, Bill 234–5
Cochran, Jacqueline 155–6
cockpit 145, 167
Coelho, Paulo 179
Coen, Peter 258
Colby, C. B. 30
Cold War, the 43–7
Coleman, Herb 142, 143
Coleman, William 132
collaborators, search for 20–2
Collard, Dudley 233–4
Collins, Michael 60
colour schemes 185–9
concept testing 57–60
Concorde: achievement 6, 296–7; age 221; appeal 153; beauty 57, 169, 170–1, 176, 179–80, 191; Central Policy Review Staff judgement on 133; excitement of 166–7; final flights 4; final wing configuration 71; first reference to name 25–6; genesis 3; innovations 87; low speed flight 52; loyalty to 203–4; perceived obsolescence 223–4; poetry 289; precursors 78; range 4; service history 227; singularity 4–6; status 163, 217, 223; threat to America 95–6; ticket prices 5
Concorde 001: assembly 92–3; career 116; first flight 1; first goes supersonic 119; maiden flight 41, 115–17; presented 85–6;

preservation 42; retired 116; rolled out for first time 93; Turcat's opinion of 116–17
Concorde 002 92–3; first goes supersonic 119; high-altitude performance trials 136–7; maiden flight 73, 117–19
Concorde 01 125, 137
Concorde 02 137
Concorde 201 137
Concorde F-BTSC: crash 189, 194–7
Concorde F-BTSD 42, 188, 214–17, 224, 229
Concorde F-BVFA 141, 146–7, 221
Concorde F-BVFB 206–7, 208, 225
Concorde F-BVFF 230–1
Concorde F-WTSA 3–4
Concorde F-WTSB 188–9
Concorde, G-BBDG 230
Concorde G-BOAA 139, 171–2
Concorde G-BOAB 228
Concorde G-BOAD:
Buckingham Palace flypast, 2002 149, 217; fastest transatlantic crossing 165, 166; flying hours 221; paint schemes 187
Concorde G-BOAE 214–17
Concorde G-BOAF 207, 227–8
Concorde G-BOAG 4,107, 225–7
Concorde . . . Airport '79, The (film) 189–90
Concorde B 233–4
Concorde Fan Club 159
Concorde flight simulator 230
Concorde Management Board 82
Concorde Symposium, Institute of Contemporary History 122
Conran, Sir Terence 182–3, 209
Conran and Partners 182–3
conservation 14, 125
construction material 71–5
construction techniques 92–3
Continental Airlines 92, 199–200
Convair B-58 Hustler 49–50

Coolidge, Calvin 209
Cormery, Gilbert 81
Cornet-Templet, Joelle 225
correspondence 90–1
cosmic rays, effects of 90
cost-benefit analyses 22
costs 25, 87, 89, 91–2, 121,
    132–3, 163–4, 218
Courcel, Geoffroy de 3, 25
Cripps, Stafford 47
Crook, Tony 296
Cuban Missile Crisis 97
Culham Science Centre,
    Oxfordshire 242
Curtis, Colin 175
Curtiss Wright 102

Daily Mail Trans-Atlantic Air
    Race, 1969 55
Daily Telegraph 121, 195, 259
Dakar 146
Dallas-Fort Worth 159–60,
    160
damages 129
Dan-Air 271
Dan Dare: Pilot of the Future
    (comic strip) 236–7
Dar Al-Handasah architects
    212
Dassault Mirage III 13, 42–3
Dassault Mirage IIIA 23
Dassault Mirage 2000 91
Dassault Mystère IV 155–6
Davies, John 125
Debouck, Frank 200
Defence: Outline of Future
    Policy (White Paper) 17–18
Defer, Gilbert 118
de Gaulle, Charles 24, 25, 85,
    94, 121–2
de Havilland 10
de Havilland, Geoffrey, Jr 40
de Havilland Comet 8, 14,
    21, 179, 271
de Havilland DH.108
    Swallow 39–40
de Havilland DH.110 Sea
    Vixen 40
Delon, Alain 189
democratization 270
departure lounges 154, 209
de Quetteville, Harry 195
Derry, John 39–40
Desert Island Discs (radio
    series) 118, 179
design and development:
    agreement 24; B model
    233–4; compromises
    234–5; construction

material 71–5; discussions
    88; drawings 81; engines
    74–5, 76–7; language
    barrier 80; redesigns 75;
    test airframes 74; Tupolev
    Tu-144 108–9; wings
    19–20, 37, 38, 52, 57–60,
    62–8, 71
design, artistry in 169–76
design features, supersonic
    aircraft 35, 37
design proposals 19–20;
    Armstrong Whitworth
    54–5; Bristol (aircraft
    manufacturer) 54; Handley
    Page 55–7; Hawker
    Siddeley 54; swing-wing
    67
DFS 346 45–6
Diana, Princess of Wales 205
digital gizmos 223–4
Dittmar, Heini 33, 50
Donaldson, Edward 'Teddy'
    141–2
doors 234–5
Douglas DC-3 178–9
Douglas DC-7 15
Douglas DC-8 8, 221
Douglas DC-10 272
Douglas, Paul 228
Doyle, James 108
drawings 81
droop snoot 70–1
Dubai, Burj Khalifa, the
    211
Dudal, Pierre 141, 148
Duggan, Donald, archbishop
    of Canterbury 126
Duke, Neville 40
duplication, manufacturing
    89
Durrant, A. A. M. 175
Dutch rolls 69

Eagle, The (comic) 235–7
easyJet 273, 275
Ecart studio 184
economic recession, 1970s
    270
Eddington, Rod 198, 214,
    218, 224
Eden, Anthony 17
Edwards, Sir George 82, 83,
    85, 109, 119, 139
Eisenhower, Dwight D. 96
elevons 201
Elizabeth II, Queen 126,
    149–50, 151, 217;
    Coronation 15

Elizabeth, the Queen Mother
    150
Ellis, Thomas 265
Elvington, RAF 83
e-mail 215
Emergency Coalition to Stop
    the SST 128, 131
emergency landings 201
Emerson, Lake & Palmer
    150–1
Empire State Building, New
    York 211
engines: air-intake 76–7, 87,
    234–5; Boeing 2707 103;
    choice 23–4; design and
    development 74–5, 76–7;
    failures 201, 202–3; first
    test 77; hypersonic flight
    238–9; modifications
    resulting from 207; testing
    264; thermal efficiency 76;
    thrust 77; Tupolev Tu-144
    110; variable-geometry
    nozzles 77
English Electric Canberra 23
English Electric P.1 Lightning
    47–8, 55, 127, 293
Enterprise, VSS 249
environmental concerns 4,
    14, 105–6, 125, 126, 129,
    217
espionage 108–9
Ettedgui, Isabel 185
Ettedgui, Joseph 185
European Commission 122
European Common Market
    25
European Organization for
    Nuclear Research 36
European Space Agency,
    LAPCAT (Long-Term
    Advanced Propulsion
    Concepts and
    Technologies) programme
    241–2
Eurostar 284
exclusivity 260
Exmouth (HMS) 76

F-86 Sabre 155–6
F-100 Super Sabre 47
Fage, Etienne 81
Fairey Delta 2 13–14, 43,
    47, 70
Fairford, RAF 73, 117–18,
    119–20
Falklands War 281
fare prices 274, 280
farewell tour 225–7

Farnborough Air Show: 1952 40; 1962 69
faults 200–4
feasibility report, 1954 52–3
Federal Aviation Administration (FAA) 258
Federal Aviation Agency 95–6, 100; Office of Supersonic Transport Development 104
Ferguson, George 294
Fiat ETR 450 252
Fiat Ferroviaria 252
Field, Sir Malcolm 201–2
film appearances 189–91
Filton 24, 88; closure 291–4; Concorde 002 maiden flight 117–19; final flight to 227–8; history 292–3; redevelopment 293–4; runway 117; test rigs 89
final flight 227–8
final flights 225–8
Fireflash 240, 242
firemen, national strike, 1977 151–2
first officers 144–5
Fleet Air Arm Museum, Yeovilton 70, 119
flight deck 145
flight engineers 145
flight officers 144–5
flight, romance of 270; loss of glamour 275–7
flight-test programme 119–20, 124
flight times, New York to London 15
flight training 137
fly-by-wire 87
flying hours 227
Fontenay Abbey, Montbard 184–5
food 146–7
Ford, Stanley 199–200
Forgeard, Noel 218–19
Foster, Norman 248
France, partnership with 20–2
France, Pierre Mendes 40–1
France, SS 146
Franchi, Jean 148
Franklin, Benjamin 193, 214
Frantzen, Claude 199–200
Frazer Nash Research 295–6
Free French Air Force 41
French Aerospace Museum, Le Bourget 42, 116
Frost, David 153

fuel consumption 52, 134, 141, 147
fuel demands, aerospace industry 14
fuel, new sources 256–7
fuel tanks 183, 188, 199; Kevlar liners 205, 206
fuselage, heat build-up 20
Futurist Manifesto 177–8
Fyodorov, Ivan 46

Gagarin, Yuri 96–8
galleys 88
Gardner, Charles 85, 130
Gaska, Jonathan L. 131
Gaskell, Eric 65
Gatwick Airport 188
Gautier-Delaye, Pierre 184
General Dynamics F-111 68
genesis 3, 9–11
German Space Agency 240–1
Germany 53
G-Force Engineering 255
Gillman, Peter 26, 131–3, 135–6, 142
Girard, Alexander 160
Giuliani, Rudolph 214
Goddard, Robert H. 34
Golden Quarter, the 285–6
Gonesse 193
Gonesse crash, 25 July 2000: air crew 194; cause 194, 201–2; certificate of airworthiness withdrawn 197; Concorde fleet grounded 196–7; criminal case 199–200; fire 194–5; flights resume after 208; ghosts of 231; ground casualties 196; investigation 197–8, 199; memorial service 205; modifications resulting from 205–8; passengers 194; take off 194, 202; tyre damage 194; witnesses 195–6
Gonin, Antoine 269
Gooch, Daniel 264–5
Goodmanson, Lloyd 130
Goodwood Travel 158
Gottingen 60, 62, 65
Goussainville 111
Gower Peninsula, declared Area of Outstanding Natural Beauty 14
Graf Zeppelin 181
Graves, Peter 190
Gray, W. E. 57–60

Great British Design Quest 171–6
Great Eastern, SS 265
Greater London Council 129
Great Flood, the 210
Green, Andy 254–5
Greig, Air Commodore D'Arcy 158
Gresley, Sir Nigel 169, 282
Groot, Fritz August Breuhaus de 181
Grove, Valerie 215
Guardian 226
Guignard, Jacques 41
Gulf War, First 216–17
Guttridge, Peter 189–90
Gyron Junior jets 72

Hailey, Arthur 189–90
Haji-Ioannou, Stelios 273
Halaby, Najeeb 95–6, 100, 105
Hale, Mike 48
Hall, Sir Arnold 23, 24
Hamilton, Sir James 82–3, 119
Hampson, Frank 236–7
Hampton, Virginia 61
Handley Page 10; design proposals 55–7; HP.115 68–70, 71
Handley Page Hampden 56
Handley Page Victor V-bomber 56
handling qualities 124, 145, 148
Hanlon, Michael 285–6
Hare, Sid 195
Harley, Don 236
Harmer, Barbara 154, 171–2
Harrison, Barbara Jane 203
Hart, John 291
Harvard Crimson 128
Hastings, Max 140
Hawker Hunter 40
Hawker Siddeley 22, 54
Hawker Siddeley Harrier jump jet 55
Heath, Edward 133, 134–5
Heathrow 129
Heathrow Airport 129: Boeing 707 Whisky Echo engine failure 203; Concorde model 229; departure lounges 209; final flight from 227–8; London Underground extension 152; Terminal Five 229

heat tests 74
Henderson, Jack 69
Heritage Concorde 229
high-altitude performance
  trials 136–7
High Speed Flight Unit 38
high-speed railway network
  120–1
Hiller Aviation Museum, San
  Carlos, California 107
Hindenburg 181–2
History Today 294–5
Holliday, Roger 205
homages 222–3
Hooker, Sir Stanley 139, 157
Horror at 37,000 Feet, The
  (television shocker) 190
Hossein, Samir 196
Hôtelissimo Les Relais Bleus
  196
HOTOL (Horizontal Take Off
  and Landing) 242–3
Houston, Lady Lucy 158
HP.115 68–70, 71
Hufton, Philip 132
Hughes, Howard 183
Hunting Aircraft 70
Hutchinson, Colin 268
Hutchinson, John 202–4
hypersonic flight 234, 235,
  237; airliner projects
  67, 239–48; engines
  238–9; passengers 240;
  temperatures 237–8;
  windows 238

ICBM (Intercontinental
  Ballistic Missile) 21
Iceland 137
India 136, 140
industrial manufacturing,
  decline of 266
in-flight control systems 224
in-flight entertainment 147
information technology,
  impact of 215
innovations 87
Institute of Contemporary
  History, Concorde
  Symposium 122
Inter-City 125 High Speed
  Train 180
interior design 180–1,
  182–5, 206
international tour, 1972 126
IRA 152
Iran, Shah of 125–6
Iraq, invasion of 216–17
Isaev, Alesksei 45

Ishikawa, Takashi 250–1
Issigonis, Alec 175–6
Istre-Le Tube air base,
  Marseilles 206–7
Italian Job, The (film) 176
Italy 251–2, 278–9

Jack Tinker and Partners
  160
Japan 282–4
Japan Aerospace Exploration
  Agency (JAXA) 250–1
Japan Air Lines 5
Jardinaud, Gilles 194
Jefferson, Thomas 213–14
Jenkins, Roy 121–2
jet airliners, first 8
John Paul II, Pope 189
Johnson, Boris 175
Johnson, Clarence 'Kelly'
  244–5
Johnson, Lyndon B. 100
Jones, Robert 57
Joseph, Ernest 7
Junkers Jumo 004.B.2
  engine 41
Justin, John 31

Kachoria, Vik 252–3
Kai Tak, RAF, Hong Kong 39
Kauba, Otto 35
Kaufman, Gerald 132, 135
Kennedy, John F. 95–6,
  96–7, 100
Kent, Duke of 139
KGB 108
Khrushchev, Nikita 99, 100
Kincheloe, Captain Iven C.
  14
King, Sir John 162–3
Kinneir, Jock 173–4
Korolev, Sergey 44
Kozhov, Mikhail 110–11
Kracht, Felix 45–6
Kranz, Gene 99, 285
Kubitscheck, Juscelino 92,
  115
Küchemann, Dietrich 60, 62,
  62–5, 78, 132

La-176 46–7
Lachmann, Gustav 56
Laker, Freddie 151, 271–3
Laker Airways 5, 151
Lancaster House, London 25
landing 52, 71
Landor Associates 186
land speed record 255–6
language barrier 80

LAPCAT (Long-Term
  Advanced Propulsion
  Concepts and
  Technologies) programme,
  European Space Agency
  241–2
Lapland 159
lavatories 183
Lawley, Sue 179
Lawrence, Harding 160
Lawrence, T. E. (of Arabia)
  158–9
Lean, David 31
leases 160
Le Bourget: Air and Space
  Museum 42, 116, 229
Le Bourget aerodrome
  195–6
Lecky-Thompson, Tom 55
Lee, Godfrey 56
Lefèbvre, André 180
Le Figaro 176–7
Levine, Beth 160
Lewis, Rob 220–1
Leynaert, Jacky 77
Libeskind, Daniel 213
Lickley, Robert 43
Lidiard, John 145
Lindbergh, Charles 195–6
Lippisch, Alexander 33
Lisbon/LIS for Paris/CDG 224
liveries 185–9
Lockheed A-12 101
Lockheed CL-823 102
Lockheed F-104 Starfighter
  214, 44
Lockheed L-1011 TriStar
  108, 246
Lockheed L-2000 190
Lockheed L-2000-7A 102
Lockheed P-80 Shooting Star
  244
Lockheed SR-71 101, 244–5
Lockheed SR-72 237, 245
Lockheed Super
  Constellation 15, 179
Lockheed Martin F-16XL
  254
Lockheed Martin N+2
  supersonic airliner 257–8
Lockspeiser, Sir Ben 36
Loewy, Raymond 183–4
London: Lancaster House
  25; Olympic Games, 2012
  151; Science Museum
  58; Shell-Mex House 7,
  8–9; St Giles Court 9–11;
  Whitechapel Gallery
  15–16

London Midland and
  Scottish Railway 264
London Passenger Transport
  Board 175
London to Bahrain service
  137, 139–46
London to New York service
  149, 152–4
London Underground,
  Heathrow extension 152
London Underground map
  172–3
losses 161, 162, 197
Loughead, Allan 244
Loughead, Malcolm 244
low-boom supersonic aircraft
  258–9
Lowe, Jock 150, 163, 164,
  234–5
low speed flight, supersonic
  airliners 52, 71
low-speed handling
  characteristics 123–4
Luftwaffe, the 32–4
Lundberg, Bo, *Speed and
  Safety in Civil Aviation* 126
Luton Airport 267–8
luxury travel, decline of
  277–80

McCartney, Paul 147
McDonald, Bob 107
MacDonald, Ramsay 158
McDonnell Douglas DC-10
  5
MacGregor, Sue 118–19
Mach, Ernst 29
Macmillan, Harold 17, 24,
  43
maiden flight: Concorde 001
  41, 115–17; Concorde 002
  73, 117–19
maintenance costs 218,
  220–1, 221
Malaysia 136, 140, 141
Mallard (train) 282
Mallory, George 136
managing director 81–2
Manchester United 154
Mannix, Patrick 153
manufacturing 88–90
Marine Aircraft Experimental
  Establishment,
  Helensburgh 82
Marinetti, Filippo Tommaso
  177–8
Marlow, Peter, *Concorde: the
  Last Summer* 222
Marshall, Lord Colin 224

Martindale, Squadron Leader
  Anthony 38
Marty, Alain 205
Marty, Christian 194–5,
  195–6, 202
Massachusetts Institute of
  Technology 105
Maxwell, Jewell C. 104
Me 163 Komet 32–3, 38, 50
Me 262 33–4, 41
meals 88
measurements, problems
  81
Mecca Royal Hotel Clock
  Tower 212
Mentzer, William 'Bill' 88
menus 146–7
Messiaen, Olivier 16
Michaelson, Ky 256
Michelin 207
Middle East Airlines 92
Midland Pullman (train)
  278, 279
Mikoyan MiG-15 47
Mikoyan MiG-19 47
Mile High Club 225
Miles Aircraft 32–3, 35–7
miles flown 227
Miles M.52 35–7
miniskirt, the 174–5, 175
Mironenko, Aleksandr 113
Missile Gap crisis, the 96–7
Mitchell, Reginald 157,
  169–70, 172
Mitterrand, Jacques 146
Model 76 Voyager 250
modifications, resulting from
  Gonesse crash, 25 July
  2000 205–8
Moffett Field, California 245
Molchanov, Valery 110–11
More, Kenneth 69
Morgan, Morien:
Morgan, Morien Bedford:
  on air flow separation
  64; background and
  character 18–19; feasibility
  report, 1954 52–3; and
  partnership with French
  21–2; power-operated
  stabilators tests 38; Shell-
  Mex House meeting 8–9;
  STAC chairmanship 9–11;
  STAC report 132
Moscow, Vostok Tower 212
Moss, Geoffrey 203
motorways 12
motorway signs 173–4
Mott, Sir Nevill 127

Musée des Arts et Métiers,
  Paris 269
Museum of Flight, Seattle
  107, 227
Musgrave, Sir Cyril 7, 8
music 16–17, 150–1, 152

Nader, Ralph 220
name: first reference to
  25–6; origin 84–5; spelling
  84–6
NASA 56–7, 60, 244, 254,
  285; Airborne Science
  Program 245; High Speed
  Project 258; High-Speed
  Research Programme
  246–7
Nasser, Gamel Abdel 17
National Aero-Space Plane
  247
National Gas Turbine
  Establishment, Pyestock
  263–4, 266–7, 268, 269–
  70; Anechoic Chamber
  266–7
national pride 92, 99
National Supersonic
  Transport Program, United
  States of America 95–6
National Transportation
  Safety Board (NTSB) 198
National Union of
  Mineworkers, work-to-rule,
  1974 134–5
Nazi Germany 32–4, 44,
  60–1
Neil A. Armstrong Flight
  Research Center, Palmdale,
  California 245
neo-liberalism 270
Newell and Sorrell 186
New Labour 168, 266–7
New York 125, 130–1, 132,
  137, 147–9, 153; Empire
  State Building 211; final
  Concorde flights 225;
  flights resume 7 November
  2001 214–17; Freedom
  Tower 213; One World
  Trade Center 211
New York Stock Exchange 216
New York Times 131
Nicholson, David 162
Nielsen, Leslie 190
Niemeyer, Oscar 91, 92
nitrous oxide 105
Nixon, Richard 105
noise 23–4, 61, 90–2, 126,
  129–30, 147–8, 150, 254,

257; low-boom supersonic aircraft 258–9
Nord 1500 Griffon 41–2
Nord Gerfault 1A 40
Nord Gerfault II 40–1
North American P-51 Mustang 254
North American X-15 49, 69, 94, 102
North American XB-70 Valkyrie 21, 102
nose, droop snoot 70–1
nps 212
nuclear weapons 127–8

OAPEC (Organization of Arab Petroleum Exporting Countries) 134
Observer, the 126
ocean liners 277
Oil Crisis 133–4, 137
oil prices 134
OKB-293 45–6
Oklahoma City 105
Okuyama, Ken 283
O'Leary, Michael 208, 274, 275
Olympic Games, London, 2012 151
Olympus 593 group 229
one millionth scheduled transatlantic passenger 153
ONERA (Office National d'Etudes et de Recherches Aérospatiales) 62, 268–9
OPEC 133–4
Operation Paperclip 33, 34, 57
opposition 126–7, 129–33
Opron, Robert 180
optimism, 1967 93–4
options to buy 92, 130
Orient Express 158
Orlebar, Augustus Henry 'Orly' 157, 158–9
Orlebar, Christopher 144–5, 156–8, 171–2, 227–8
Orlebar, Nicola 156–8
O'Sullivan, Jim 205
Ouille, Aurelie 146
ozone layer 105

Page, Freddie 48
Page, Hervé 205
paint schemes 185–9
Pakistan Air Force 42
Panair do Brasil 92
Pan Am 3, 92, 95, 101, 130

Pan Am Space Clipper 1–2, 238, 243–4
Panavia Tornado 68, 83
Papon, Maurice 84
Parc National de la Vanoise, Italy 268–9
Parent Trap, The (film) 190–1
Paris 79–80, 81, 193; the Madeleine 205; Musée des Arts et Métiers 269; Pompidou Centre 125
Paris Air Show: 1961 78; 1965 109; 1973 98, 109–11
Paris International Air Show, 1969 119
Paris Orly 3–4
Paris to New York service 149, 152–4; final Concorde flights 224
Paris to Rio de Janeiro service 137, 141, 146–7
parts, shipping 89–90
passenger experience: budget airlines 274–5; diversions 288; loss of glamour 275–80, 284–5
passenger loads 52–3, 102
passengers 152–4, 227; hypersonic flight 240
Pathé News 40, 94
Patrick, Nigel 31
patriotism 187
payload 66
Payne, William 49–50
Pepsi-Cola 188
Perceived Noise Decibels (PNdb) 23–4
Perrier, Henri 124, 199–200
Perry, Alan 59
Pevsner, Donald L. 219–21, 224
Philip, Prince 125, 149
Phillips, Martin 291
Piano, Renzo 125
pilots: female 154–6; qualities 144
piston-engine airliners 14–15
Polan, Brenda 174
Pompidou, Georges 125
Pople, Brian 197
Popular Science 30
Port Authority of New York and New Jersey 23–4
Poukhov, Aleksei 99–100
Power Jets Limited 264
power-operated stabilators 37–8

Powers, Gary 245
Powles, Flight Lieutenant Ted 39
Prague 35
Prandtl, Ludwig 60
precursors 78
preservation 42, 228–31
price 25–7
Prickett, Sir Thomas 120
production lines 88
production run 135
profitability 22, 27, 161, 162, 164, 197
Project Daedalus 243
prototypes, construction 92–3
Proxmire, William 106
publicity material 85
public opinion: opposition 126–7, 129–33; support 128–9
Public Records Office 78
Pucci, Emilio 160
Puget, André 82, 83–4, 85
Putman, Andrée 184–5
Pyestock 265–6, 269–70; National Gas Turbine Establishment 263–4, 266–7

QE2, RMS 280–2
QinetiQ 266–7
Quant, Mary 174, 175, 183
Queen Mary, RMS 94
Queen Mary 2, RMS 281
Quill, Jeffrey 39

railways 11–12, 120–1, 251–2, 260, 264–5; decline of luxury 277–9; high speed trains 282–4
Raisbeck Aviation High School 227
ramjets 35, 41–2
range 2, 4, 1472
Rastel, Daniel 41
Rattigan, Terence 31
Ravetz, Jerry 127
Reach for the Sky (film) 69
Reaction Engines 242
Reagan, Ronald 246–7, 247
reheat jet pipes 37
Reich, Jean 287
Resch, Jean 81
researchers, pressure on 99–100
research programme, outline 20

responsibility: division of 81–2; manufacturing 88–9
restoration plans 229
retirement cost 221
retirement date 164
retirement decision: announcement 217–19, 221; backward step 224; conspiracy theories 220–1; reactions to 219–20
Reunion, The (radio series) 119, 122–3
Richardson, Ralph 31
Rich, David Lowell 189, 190
ride 142
Rio de Janeiro 124, 146
Rippon, Geoffrey 295
risk aversion 286–8
Robert, Anne-Jean 193
Robert, Nicolas-Louis 193
rocket planes 49
Roddenberry, Gene 103
Rogers, Richard 125
Rolls-Royce 10, 23–4
Rolls-Royce Avon engine 21, 48
Rolls-Royce Nene turbojet, Soviet version 46–7
Rolls-Royce/Snecma Olympus 593 74
Rome, Treaty of 121
Rose, David 201–2
Rossing, Hans 45–6
Roswell Incident 249
Rothschild, Lord 133
Routemaster buses 12–13, 175
routes, restrictions on 130–1, 136
Rovaniemi 159
Roxburgh, Gordon 230
Royal Aircraft Establishment (RAE), Farnborough 9, 19, 62, 71, 73, 243; Advanced Fighter Project Group 47–8; High Speed Flight Unit 38; Turbine Division 264
Royal Air Force 13
rudders 201
runways 52, 117
Russell, Sir Archibald 24, 66, 78, 80, 81, 90
Rutan, Burt 248
Rutan, Dick 250
Ryanair 208, 273–4, 275

Saatchi & Saatchi 163
Saddam Hussein 216–17
safety record 128, 144, 196–7, 198–9, 200, 203, 249

St Giles Court, London 9–11
Salisbury Cathedral 211
Sandys, Duncan 17–18, 20–1, 72, 295
Sanger, Eugen 34–5
Sarah, Duchess of York 153
Satre, Pierre 24, 81
Saturn V rocket 94
Save Concorde Group 229
Sayer, Malcolm 176
Sazmolyot (aircraft) 346 46
Scaled Composite White Knight Two 248
Schneider Trophy, fiftieth anniversary of Britain winning 156–8
Schwegger Associated Architects 212
science-fiction 14
Science Museum, London 58
Scotland 85–6
Scott, Douglas 175
Scott, Sheila 118
scramjets 238–9, 247–8
seating configuration, Boeing 747 2
Seattle 107, 227
Second World War 7, 32–5, 178
senior engineers 81
Servan-Schreiber, Jean-Jacques 122
Servanty, Lucien 24, 41, 81
service 167–8
Settebello (train) 278–9
Sex Pistols 150–1
Shanghai 211–12
Shanghai Maglev, the 260
Shanghai Tower 212
Shatner, William 190
Shell-Mex House, London 7, 8–9
Shepard, Alan 96, 97–8, 99
Shinar 210
Shinkansen bullet trains 282–4
shockwaves 37–8
Shore, Peter 139
Short Brothers 10
Shurcliff, William 127–8
Shuttleworth Collection 69
Siebel Flugzeugwerke 46
Silbervogel (Silver Bird) rocket bomber 35
silverware 184
Singapore 140–1
Singapore Airlines 140
Sippel, Martin 240
Sissons, Peter 203–4

Skoda-Kauba Sk P.14 ramjet 35
skyscrapers 209–10
Skytrain 5, 151, 271–3
slew-wing designs 55–7
Smith, Group Captain Leonard 158
smoking 118
Snecma 23, 79
SO.6000 Triton 41
SO.9000 Trident 41
social change, 1950s 15–17
Sokolov, Oleg 46, 47
sonic booms 61, 90–2, 105–6, 106, 136, 250, 257–8
sound barrier: breaking silently 61; British finally break 39–40; broken on land 255–6; challenge of 29–31, 39; first broken 31–2; first woman to break 155–6; France breaks 40–2; Soviets break 43–7; Spitfires approach 37–9; Tupolev Tu-144 breaks 107–8
Sound Barrier, The (film) 31, 40, 50
sound, speed of 29–30
South American market 161
Southampton University Air Squadron (RAF) 144
South Atlantic 124
Southwest 275
Spaceliner 240–1
space programmes 1–2, 14, 96–8
Space Shot 2004 'Go Fast' 256
speed, beauty of 177
speed records 13, 33, 42, 94, 142, 157, 165–6, 239, 244, 255–6
Spike Aerospace 252–3
Spike Aerospace S-512 252–3
Spinetta, Jean-Cyril 214, 218, 220–1
Sputnik 96
SST Aviation Exhibit Center, Kissimmee, Florida 107
SST: Death Flight (film) 190
Stainforth, George 157
Stalin, Joseph 44
Stanier, Sir William 264, 265–6
Star Trek (TV series) 103, 249, 285–6
Stern, Dr J. W. 266

Stockhausen, Karlheinz 16
Storms, Harrison 102
Strang, Dr William 24, 81
Street, Mike 197
subsonic flights 159–61
Sud Aviation 21, 24, 60, 80, 83
Sud Aviation Caravelle 21, 43
Sud Aviation Super Caravelle 22, 77–8, 79
Sud-Ouest 41
Suez Crisis, 1956 17
Sullivan, James V. 244
Sumeria 210
Sunday Times 274
Supermarine S.6B 169
Supermarine Spitfire 18, 37–8, 169–70, 172, 217, 291, 293, 296
Supermarine Swift 31
Supermarine Type 224 169
Supermarine Walrus 169
supersonic airliners 7; challenge of 51–2; low speed flight 52, 71
supersonic research aircraft 13
supersonic tourists 221
Supersonic Transport Aircraft Committee (STAC) 3, 9–11, 19–20; report 22, 53–4, 78, 132
Supply, Ministry of 7
Swallow swing-wing airliner 67
Swedish Aeronautical Research Institute 126
swing-wing designs 66–8, 101
Sycamore slew-wing airliner 55–7
Sydney 130
symbolic value 214–15, 217

tail-fin logos 186, 186–7
take off 52, 53, 62–3, 71
Talbot, Ted 73, 74, 79
TAT-1, transatlantic telephone cable 15
Taylor, Cliff 203
Taylor, John 199–200
technical support withdrawn 222, 224
TEE (Trans-Europe Express) trains 121
temperatures, hypersonic flight 237–8
tenth anniversary 164–5

test aircraft: BAC 221 70–1; HP.115 68–70, 71
test airframes 74
test facilities 120
test-flight circuits 123–4
test flights 119, 127, 136–7, 148, 207–8, 209
testing 20, 87, 264
test models 58–60
test rigs 89
TGV 120–1
Thatcher, Margaret 139, 168, 186–7, 272
Thesiger, Ernest 260
'This is Tomorrow' exhibition, Whitechapel Gallery, London 15–16
Thorne, Doug 81
Thorneycroft, Peter 21
Thorpe, D. R. 17
Thrust SSC 255–6
Thunderbirds (TV series) 103, 240, 242
ticket prices 5, 215
Tillmans, Wolfgang, *Concorde* 222–3
Time magazine 184
Tobin, Squadron Leader J. R. 38
Todd, Ann 31
Todd, Norman 139, 140, 143, 146, 147, 149
Tomorrow's World (TV series) 93
Torrey Canyon disaster 94
Toulouse 71, 74; Concorde 001 maiden flight 115–17; Concorde 001 rolled out for first time 93; production line 88; runway 117; test facilities 120; test rigs 89
Tovey, Alan 259
trade unions, support for Concorde 124
transatlantic commerce 214–15
transatlantic demonstration flight 3–4
transatlantic flight 165–7; budget 272; final 225–6; pleasure in experience of 280–1
transatlantic telegraph cable 265
transatlantic telephone cable 15
transport alternatives, 1950s 11–13
transporters, *Star Trek*-style 235

travel, pleasure in experience of 280–1
Treasury, the 26
Tredre, Roger 174
Tressy, Sister Mary Lou 131
Trevithick, Richard 265
trial and error 59
Trubshaw, Brian 19, 69, 84, 119, 139; background 51; *Brian Trubshaw: Test Pilot* 120; Concorde 002 maiden flight 117–19; Convair B-58 Hustler flight 49; high-altitude performance trials 136–7; on the Tupolev Tu-144 113; on union support for Concorde 124
TSR-2 48, 83
Tupolev, Aleksei 109, 111
Tupolev Tu-135 112–13
Tupolev Tu-144 98–100, 113–14, 137, 179; breaks the sound barrier 107–8; cancelled 112; career 111–12; engines 110; espionage suspicions 108–9; freighters 112; improvements 109–10; interior 112; maiden flight 110; Military versions 113; NASA Supersonic Research Programme 246–7; Paris Air Show crash, 1973 110–11; sales 111; test flights 109, 111
Tupolev Tu-160 'Blackjack' 112–13
Turcat, André 1; Concorde 001 maiden flight 115–17; Concorde maiden flight 41; Nord 1500 Griffon test pilot 41–2; Nord Gerfault II test pilot 40–1; opinion of Concorde 001 116–17
Turnill, Reginald 82
Turunmaa (Finnish corvette) 76
Turvey, Peter 58–60
Tuttle, Sir Geoffrey 120
TWA 3, 92, 130
twentieth anniversary 188–9
Twiss, Peter 13–14
Typhoon Eurofighter 48
tyres 205, 207; failure 198–9, 201

U-2 spy plane 101–2, 245
Ulm Cathedral 211

undercarriage, 205-6 206
United States of America:
Air Deregulation Act
160; ban on commercial
supersonic flights 130-1;
environmental lobby
105-6; German scientists
resettled in 33, 34, 57, 60;
Joint Sub-Committee on
Economy in Government
106-7; Mach-3 agenda
21; Missile Gap crisis
96-7; National Supersonic
Transport Program 95-6,
100-7; Port Authority of
New York and New Jersey
23-4; space program 96,
97-8; SST development
budget 100; SST funding
cancelled 106-7; threat of
Concorde to 95-6
upgrades 164
US Declaration of
Independence 213-14
US National Advisory
Committee for Aeronautics
61
USSR: Britain shares
information with 46-7;
collapse of 112; Council of
Ministers 98; espionage
108-9; German scientists
resettled in 44; OKB-
293 45-6; space program
96-8; Stalin's purges
44; supersonic aircraft
development 43-7;
supersonic airliner program
98-100, 107-14; threat of
43-4; war booty 44, 45-6

V-2 34, 235
variable-geometry wings 104
variable thrust reheat system
48
Varley, Eric 139
Vaughan Williams, Ralph 16
Vauxhall Motors Concorde
Cavalier Challenge
Competition 268
vertical takeoff and landing
proposal 54-5
Vialle, Beatrice 154-5, 225
Vickers 581 68

Vickers Armstrong 10, 67,
83
Vickers Valiant V-bomber
83
Vickers VC-10 83, 108, 179,
273
Vickers Vimy 165-6
Vickery, Doug 81
Vignon, Pierre-Alexand 205
Virgin Airways 219, 273
Virgin Galactic 248-50
Virgin Rail 252
Vogt, Richard 56-7
Voisin, Gabriel 180
vortices, uplifting 62-3, 115
Vostok Tower, Moscow 212
VTOL flying wing 54-5
VTOL (Vertical Take-Off and
Landing) 54-5, 252-3
Vulcan to the Sky Trust 229

Waddell, Jack 1
Wallis, Barnes 67-8
Wall, Sir Robert 108
Walpole, Brian 148, 149,
150, 163, 165-6
Walther liquid-propellant
rocket engine 45-6
war on terror 216
Washington Dulles
International 130, 147,
159-60, 160
washrooms 183
Watson, Deryn 19
Weber, Johanna 65
Wedgwood Benn, Michael 86
Wedgwood Benn, William 86
weight 66, 75, 88, 102, 147,
183, 206
Wells, Mary 160
Westland Aircraft 70
Whicker, Alan 171-2
Whitechapel Gallery, London
15-16
White, Roger 49
White, Sir George 292
Whittle, Frank 37, 264,
265-6
Widdifield, Noel F. 244
Wiggs, Richard 126-7, 128,
131
Wilde, Mick 81
Williams, John 'Shon' Ffowcs
18

Wilson, Andrew 126,
129-30
Wilson, Harold 25, 74-5,
108, 121, 122-3, 133, 135
windows 167; hypersonic
flight 238
Windsor Castle RMS 277
wind tunnels, supersonic
60-1
wines offered 147
wings: air flow 62-5; cracks
201; delta 54, 59-60;
design 19-20, 57-60, 62-
8, 71; final configuration
71; functional beauty
169-70; leading edges
37; low speed flight 52;
manufacturing 88; paint
schemes 188; passive
laminar-flow 254; shape
37, 38, 62; swept 36, 39,
48, 61; swing-wing 66-8;
testing 68-70; variable-
geometry 104
Winter of Discontent, 1974
134-5
Wood, the Reverend J. G.
69-70
World Cup, 1998 154
World Trade Center, 9/11
terrorist attacks 209,
212-13
Wright, Frank Lloyd 211
Wuhan–Guangzhou High
Speed Railway 260

X-43 247
X-43A 239, 248
Xenakis, Iannis 16

Yeager, Charles 'Chuck' 31-2
Yeager, Jeana 250
Yeger, Sergei 112-13
Yeovilton, Fleet Air Arm
Museum 70, 119
Yom Kippur War 133-4
Young, Pierre 79
Youngren, Jim 107

Zeise, Wolfgang 46

Ziegler, Henri 84

A NOTE ABOUT
THE AUTHOR

Jonathan Glancey is well known as the former architecture and design correspondent of the *Guardian* and *Independent* newspapers. He is also a steam locomotive enthusiast and pilot. A contributor to the *Daily Telegraph* and a broadcaster, his books include *Harrier*, *Giants of Steam*, the bestselling *Spitfire: The Biography*, *Nagaland: A Journey to India's Forgotten Frontier*, *Tornado: 21st Century Steam*, *The Story of Architecture*, *Lost Buildings*.